W9-DAF-107

HENRY JAMES

CRITICAL ISSUES SERIES

General Editors: John Peck and Martin Coyle

Published:

Virginia Woolf	*Linden Peach*
Henry James	*Jeremy Tambling*

In preparation:

Jane Austen	*Robert Clark*
William Shakespeare	*Richard Dutton*
Geoffrey Chaucer	*Ruth Evans*
George Eliot	*Pauline Nestor*
Charles Dickens	*Lyn Pykett*
James Joyce	*Kiernan Ryan*
D. H. Lawrence	*Rick Rylance*
William Wordsworth	*John Williams*

Critical Issues

Henry James

Jeremy Tambling

St. Martin's Press
New York

St. Martin's Press, Scholarly and Reference Division, 175 Fifth Avenue, New York, N.Y. 10010

First published in the United States of America in 2000

This book is printed on paper suitable for recycling and made from fully managed and sustained forest sources.

Printed in Hong Kong

ISBN 0–312–22886–4 clothbound
ISBN 0–312–22887–2 paperback

Library of Congress Cataloging-in-Publication Data
Tambling, Jeremy.
Henry James / Jeremy Tambling.
p.   cm. — (Critical issues)
Includes bibliographical references and index.
ISBN 0–312–22886–4 (cloth) — ISBN 0–312–22887–2 (pbk.)
1. James, Henry, 1843–1916—Criticism and interpretation.   I. Title.

PS2124 .T26   2000
813'.4 21—dc21   99–043514

Contents

Acknowledgements

I am grateful indeed to Martin Coyle and John Peck for commissioning this book and for their scrupulous and insightful comments on the manuscript. Thanks also to my friends, Chris Barlow for reading the draft, and especially to Graham Martin, who read it all, sometimes more than once, has corresponded with me about James and talked about him, and has also been very encouraging about what I have written. I am much in debt to the Hong Kong UGC for a grant which aided much in research for the book, as well as financing a research assistant, Adrian Smith. Coming when it did, not only has the grant meant that I have travelled over much of the States in pursuit of James and the sites of *The American Scene*, but it has also meant that this book will lead, I hope, to another on James and cities. In the United States I have been helped by Millicent Bell of Boston University and by Robert Kiely at Harvard. I remember Kitty Clarke's hospitality and her driving me to Lake Chocorua and our discussion of Boston marriages. In Rome I gave an early version of the chapter on *The Aspern Papers* at a conference of the Hawthorne Society, and had the pleasure of meetings with Jamesians or Hawthornians such as Robert Martin, Peter Walker, Susan Griffin, Priscilla Walton, Leonardo Buonomo and Ruth Golin. In London I am grateful to Tim Armstrong for the invitation to give a paper – the draft chapter of *The Golden Bowl* – to the University of London research seminar on US studies. In Hong Kong I am grateful to Eleanor Heginbotham for generous comments on two chapters, to Douglas Kerr for comments on another, to Priscilla Roberts for the loan of books and to Ackbar Abbas for a continual flow of intellectual stimulation.

Parts of Chapter 4 originally appeared in the *Henry James Review* and I am grateful to the editors for permission to reproduce this material here.

Writing this book involved traumas, but it has been very pleasurable. My children, Kirsten and Felix, now think they know as much about James as me, and Pauline has as usual done everything to enable the book's existence, while running her own life as well. I dedicate the book to these three.

A Note on Editions

Writers on James often use the New York edition for page references, but this is difficult to follow as it is practically unavailable outside university libraries. Though preferring the readings of the New York edition where these are published in modern paperback editions, I have usually given references to the most easily available text. I indicate the edition and abbreviations used in the text in the list below. In citations, I have tried to be as full as possible with part, chapter and page references, to facilitate readers following my references with whatever edition they possess.

Editions of James

The Ambassadors	*The Ambassadors*, ed. Christopher Butler (Oxford: World's Classics, 1985).
The American	*The American*, ed. William Spengemann (Harmondsworth: Penguin, 1985).
The American Scene	*The American Scene*, ed. John Sears (Harmondsworth: Penguin, 1994).
AN	*The Art of the Novel*, Introduction by R. P. Blackmur (New York: Charles Scribner's Sons, 1962).
The Aspern Papers	*The Aspern Papers*, edited and introduced by Anthony Curtis (Harmondsworth: Penguin, 1984).
Autobiography	*Autobiography*, ed. Frederick W. Dupee, 3 vols (Princeton, N.J.: Princeton University

Press, 1983)
    vol. I: *A Small Boy and Others*
    vol. II: *Notes of a Son and Brother*
    vol. III: *The Middle Years*

The Awkward Age	*The Awkward Age* (Harmondsworth: Penguin, 1966).
The Beast in the Jungle	in *Tales of Henry James*, ed. Christof Wegelin (New York: Norton, 1984).
The Bostonians	*The Bostonians* (Harmondsworth: Penguin, 1966).
Daisy Miller	in *Selected Short Stories*, ed. Michael Swan (Harmondsworth: Penguin, 1963).
The Golden Bowl	*The Golden Bowl*, edited and introduced by Virginia Llewellyn Smith (Oxford: World's Classics, Oxford University Press, 1983).
Hawthorne	*Hawthorne*, Introduction and notes by Tony Tanner (London: Macmillan, 1967).
The Jolly Corner	in *Tales of Henry James*, ed. Christof Wegelin (New York: Norton, 1984).
The Last of the Valerii	in *Selected Short Stories*, ed. Michael Swan (Harmondsworth: Penguin, 1963).
LC I	*Henry James: Literary Criticism: French Writers, Other European Writers, The Prefaces to the New York Edition*, vol. 1 (New York: Library of America, 1984).
LC II	*Henry James: Literary Criticism: Essays in Literature, American Writers, English Writers*, vol. II (New York: Library of America, 1984).
Letters	*Letters of Henry James*, ed. Leon Edel, 4 vols (Cambridge, Mass.: Belknap Press, 1984) (referred to by volume and page number).

vol. I: *1843–1875*
vol. II: *1875–1883*
vol. III: *1883–1895*
vol. IV: *1895–1916*

Notebooks	*The Complete Notebooks of Henry James*, ed. Leon Edel and Lyall H. Powers (New York: Oxford University Press, 1987).
The Portrait of a Lady	*The Portrait of a Lady*, ed. R. D. Bamberg (New York: Norton, 1995, 2nd edition).
The Pupil	in *Tales of Henry James*, ed. Christof Wegelin (New York: Norton, 1984).
The Sacred Fount	*The Sacred Fount*, ed. John Lyon (Harmondsworth: Penguin, 1994).
The Turn of the Screw	*The Turn of the Screw*, edited and introduced by Anthony Curtis (Harmondsworth: Penguin, 1984).
Washington Square	*Washington Square* (Harmondsworth: Penguin, 1963).
What Maisie Knew	*What Maisie Knew*, ed. Paul Theroux (Harmondsworth: Penguin, 1985).
Story	*William Wetmore Story and His Friends*, in *Letters, Diaries and Recollections*, 2 vols (London: Blackwood, 1903) (referred to by volume and page number).
The Wings of the Dove	*The Wings of the Dove*, ed. Peter Brooks (Oxford: World's Classics, 1984).

Other works

Edel	followed by volume number and page vol. I: *Henry James: The Untried Years: 1843–1870* (London: Rupert Hart-Davis, 1953) vol. II: *Henry James: The Conquest of London: 1870–1883* (London: Rupert Hart-Davis, 1962)

vol. III: *Henry James: The Middle Years: 1884–1894* (London: Rupert Hart-Davis, 1963)

vol. IV: *Henry James: The Treacherous Years: 1895–1901* (London: Rupert Hart-Davis, 1969)

vol. V: *Henry James: The Master* (London: Rupert Hart-Davis, 1972)

Gard   *Henry James: The Critical Muse: Selected Literary Criticism*, ed. Roger Gard (Harmondsworth: Penguin, 1987).

HJR   *Henry James Review.*

Kaplan   Fred Kaplan, *Henry James: The Imagination of Genius: A Biography* (London: Hodder & Stoughton, 1992).

Tales   Nathaniel Hawthorne, *Selected Tales and Sketches*, edited by Michael J. Colacurcio (Harmondsworth: Penguin, 1987).

1

Introduction: Reading
The American Scene

Henry James once declined an offer of $1000 from Macmillan Press to write a book on Dickens. His stated reason was want of time (the literary 'portrait' he was then working on was *The Portrait of a Lady*), but considering the critical attention he gave George Eliot, Balzac, as well as the biographies of the Americans Hawthorne and William Wetmore Story,[1] we may wonder at his motives. Yet all of James is that unwritten book, for Dickens appears more and more to be *the* English writer of the nineteenth century that any American writer would have to compare himself with. Dickens's texts are multi-layered, accessible and popular, as though everything within public life favoured their composition, and James recognised this, though significantly he also wanted to qualify the sense of Dickens's inventive freedom. In 1865, when he was twenty-two, James found *Bleak House* 'forced', *Little Dorrit* 'laboured', and *Our Mutual Friend* (which he was reviewing at the time) 'dug out as with a spade and pick-axe'. This was not his preferred way of taking Dickens. His autobiographical *Notes of a Son and Brother*, written in his seventies, records meeting Dickens when twenty-four, and he says that 'no more modern instance that I might try to muster would give, I think, the least measure of' what it was like to meet the author of Pickwick or Copperfield (James gives the names of characters, not the names of books), adding that 'there has been since his extinction no corresponding case' (*Autobiography*, II, 8, 388). James shows the predicament he feels of the impossibility of a modern American being like, or writing like Dickens.

James's output of novels, tales, plays, travel-writings, reviews, criticism, letters (many still unpublished), auto-criticism in his Prefaces and autobiography, ceased only with his death in 1916 (he left two unfinished novels behind). In comparison with Dickens the writing becomes technically very difficult. Everything in James is markedly more self-conscious, and the novels very deliberated, with all the difficulties associated with Modernism, just as James's own existence seemed more and more withdrawn from public life. While Dickens's letters and Prefaces to his novels suggest little that is self-consciously articulated about his sense of a novel, James's criticism and Prefaces feed directly into narrative theory. It is not surprising that James found Dickens hard to follow, or to write about, and perhaps needed to be adversarial towards him. I have always read Dickens with pleasure, but for a long time I read James with more resistance, aware that Jamesian standards of the novel – his comments on earlier nineteenth-century novels as 'loose baggy monsters' (AN, 5, 84), for instance – worked against Dickens. An Introduction asks that the writer state his or her interests: I begin with the point that I wrote on James in order to discover how I could read his texts, and I have found writing on James to be at least as interesting as writing on Dickens.

The first American that I told I was working on Henry James replied, 'You can't do that! You're not an American.' I liked her dismay, since my interest is in James as American, and American late nineteenth-century and Modernist texts seem, at the end of the American century, to require much more engagement with than equivalent English texts. Much recent criticism, some of it negative, some tinged with nationalist appropriations, has focused on James as an American, and raised questions about his engagements with race and colour.[2] Earlier criticism took a different direction. In 1882, after the appearance of The Portrait of a Lady, the American novelist William Dean Howells credited James with a 'new art of fiction' (a locution James was to use), writing 'the international novel'.[3] But if James is a cultural comparativist, moving between America and Britain, with France and Italy two other important sites and contexts, there is the question of his centre of gravity, and from where his judgements appear. Are they American, or English and European? American criticism in the 1920s and 1930s was cool towards James, on the grounds of his expatriation and eventual taking of British citizenship during the First World War. Van Wyck Brooks in The

Pilgrimage of Henry James (1925) saw James's move away from America as the cause of a decline from the early novels, written before his virtually final severance from the United States in 1883 (he only returned there in 1904). For Brooks, James lost touch with his roots; he was the American writer who was not American. Yet Constance Rourke in *American Humor* (1931), discussing *The American*, suggests that James, writing out of a popular culture such as that associated with Barnum's American Museum, created the American character in a way analogous to Dickens in relation to Britain:

> an entire gallery of characters is created to which Americans may well turn for knowledge and social experience and enlargement, or even for a sense of renewal. They are more than types: they are a whole society of typical individuals: they appear with narrow aggressions and an insular nobility, a careless honesty, a large and delicate purpose.[4]

Rourke saw James's preoccupation with America as keeping him in sympathy with romance so that 'he kept a familiar touch of the fabulous in his narratives' (p. 154). This would make James the popular artist of America, its Dickens; but it also raises the question of what happened to that writer, who had been influenced by American popular culture.

James's critical reinstatement in America occurred during the Second World War. Articles written in 1943, the centenary of his birth, were succeeded by F. O. Matthiessen's book *Henry James: The Major Phase* (1944), concentrating on the three last completed novels, *The Ambassadors*, *The Wings of the Dove* and *The Golden Bowl*. After Matthiessen, to put James back into American literature required accepting 'the major phase' as that. In *The Political Unconscious*, Fredric Jameson notes that James became 'the greatest American novelist of the 1950s'[5] – the novelist America could value in its McCarthyite and Cold War period – who would seem to offer to critics the opportunity to appreciate fine style and complexity, to be examined with the tools of New Criticism, hardly referring beyond the text. The Rourke-type Americanness of James was hardly taken up in English criticism. F. R. Leavis's study *The Great Tradition: George Eliot, Henry James, Joseph Conrad* (1948) argued for the importance of James's early fiction, from *Roderick Hudson* to *The Bostonians*, but he also gave special attention to two later texts,

What Maisie Knew and *The Awkward Age*. Leavis was negative about Matthiessen's 'major phase', and disliked the last three completed novels. In contrast to Brooks and Rourke, he contended that America could give James little in comparison to what Europe could give, but lack of critical esteem meant, according to Leavis, that James

> suffered from being too much a professional novelist: being a novelist came to be too large a part of his living; that is, he did not live enough. His failure in this respect suggests, no doubt, some initial deficiency in him. Nevertheless, the peculiarities in terms of which it demands to be discussed are far from appearing as simple weakness.... [w]e find him developing into something like a paradoxical kind of recluse, a recluse living socially in the midst of society.[6]

Leavis's English criticism has been highly influential, though it has not been the only voice of English criticism of James. D. W. Jefferson, Tony Tanner and John Goode have been other influential voices, none negative about 'the major phase'. However, negativity towards an American literature not committed to European traditions prompts Leavis's stress on the conservative, nineteenth-century aspects of James, aligning him with George Eliot and Jane Austen. Leavis's own comparative and complex reaction to modernism (his modern novelist was D. H. Lawrence) meant that it was unlikely that he would be interested in the early twentieth-century fiction of James.

I JAMES AND AMERICA

Leavis's downplaying of America, and American criticism's historic conservative appropriation of James, foreclosed on questions now being asked about James's relationship to America. James was capable of arguing for an American nationalism, as when he writes in 1867 from Cambridge, Massachusetts, to Thomas Sargent Perry:

> We are Americans born – *il faut en prendre son parti*. I look upon it as a great blessing; and I think that to be an American is an excellent preparation for culture. We have exquisite qualities as a race, and it seems to me that we are ahead of the European races in the fact that more than either of them we can deal freely with forms of civilization

not our own, can pick and choose and assimilate and in short (aesthetically etc.) claim our property wherever we find it. To have no national stamp has hitherto been a defect and a drawback, but I think it not unlikely that American writers may yet indicate that a vast intellectual fusion and synthesis of the various National tendencies of the world is the condition of more important achievements than any we have seen. We must of course have something of our own – something distinctive and homogeneous – and I take it that we shall find it in our moral consciousness, our unprecedented spiritual lightness and vigour. In this at least we shall have a national *cachet*.
(*Letters*, I, 75–6)

James's life itself was divided between the American Civil War and the First World War, with the first as the caesura. He wrote about Hawthorne, who died in 1864, before it ended:

One may say that the Civil War marks an era in the history of the American mind. It introduced into the national consciousness a certain sense of proportion and relation, of the world being a more complicated place than it had hitherto seemed, the future more treacherous, success more difficult. At the rate at which things are going, it is obvious that good Americans will be more numerous than ever; but the good American, in days to come, will be a more critical person than his complacent and confident grandfather. He has eaten of the tree of knowledge. (*Hawthorne*, 5, 135)

One of James's critical terms – 'relation' – emerges within a context implying that the American has had to learn connectedness, even in the middle of internal fighting, and that connectedness, which defies belief in absoluteness, implies narration, so that the American has now had to learn to tell stories, to write history. In his 1903 biography of William Wetmore Story (1819–95), the Boston-born American sculptor who lived and worked in Rome, James considers 'the American who started on his *Wanderjahre* after the Civil War quite as one of the moderns divided by a chasm from his progenitors and elder brothers' (*Story*, I, 10). Just as Dickens, for James, was divided from him by his status as a 'modern', so too were Hawthorne and William Wetmore Story.

Henry Adams wrote to James about the biography of Story that 'you have written not Story's life, but your own and mine – pure autobiography'.[7] Story's de-centredness provides an image for the New Englander Adams, and for James, and so does his expatriate

status. In *William Wetmore Story and his Friends*, James spoke of the
'feeling... that a man always pays, in one way or another, for expatriation, for detachment from his plain primary heritage', and adds
that 'this tax is levied in an amazing diversity of ways' (I, 333). That
same year (1903), he 'admonished' Edith Wharton:

> in favour of the *American subject*. Don't pass it by – the immediate, the
> real, the ours, the yours, the novelist's that it waits for. Take hold of it
> and keep hold, and let it pull you where it will. It will pull harder than
> things of more *tarabiscotage*, which is a merit in itself. What I would
> say in a word is: Profit, be warned, by my awful example of exile
> and ignorance. You will say that *je parle à mon aise* – but I shall have
> paid for my ease, and I don't want you to pay [as much] for yours. But
> these are impertinent importunities – from the moment they are not
> developed. All the same, *Do New York*! (*Letters*, IV, 235–6)

There could not be a stronger suggestion that James's interest was in
the very seat of modernity – America, New York, the world capital
city. But he hardly 'did' New York, though he had already written
Washington Square, a title full of New York and of revolutionary
history, and was to write about it in *The American Scene*, in his
autobiography, and to give to the collected edition of his novels and
tales the title 'the New York edition'. His works, in this sense, are
marked by an absent centre. He told Hamlin Garland, the Chicagoan
novelist, that he would be an American if he could, that 'the mixture
of Europe and America which you see in me has... made of me a
man who is neither American nor European. I have lost touch with
my own people.'[8] Taking account of this implies that the absent
centre in James's writing is America. He says of Story, 'we are not
able to say what a lifetime of Boston would have made in him, or
would have marred', showing his interest in 'alternative visions in
respect to the American absentee' (*Story*, II, 223). Story should have
worked in Boston. The topic of the alternative life that could have
been lived is a theme of *The Jolly Corner*, where the ghost illustrates
an alternative, maimed existence, which solicits attention, for as
James says, 'we must let no ghost pass who turns to us the least
kind of a queer face, and cultivating, as I have said, a vanished
society [the society of expatriate artists in Rome]; we must, if only
for whimsical pity, for proper tenderness of memory, allow even the
more vague of the wandering shades as much of the poor freedom of
it as the more vivid' (*Story*, I, 75–6).

In *A Small Boy and Others*, James's first volume of autobiography, memories of people are inseparable from memories of books, and a 'mild apparitionism' disturbs everything: which is real, the person in the memory or the text which they evoke and which has evoked them? 'To look back at all is to meet the apparitional, and to find in its ghostly face the silent stare of an appeal. When I fix it, the hovering shade, whether of person or place, it fixes me back and seems the less lost – not to my consciousness, for that is nothing, but to its own – by my stopping however idly for it' (*Autobiography*, I, 8, 54). The ghost returns the gaze, and gains in reality, but there is no equivalent gain in James's consciousness. The tales and novels suggest that the encounter with the ghostly is not always a matter of the ghost registering its inadequacy. In the first quotation, the queer faces of ghosts evoke the word 'queer'. The word is defined in *Notes of a Son and Brother* in relation to William James's science at Harvard, 'his interest in the queer, or the incalculable effects of things' (*Autobiography*, II, 5, 308), but the incalculability extends to current 'queer theory', which, in James's case, by giving a strong and perhaps ahistorical reading to the word 'queer',[9] has done much to appropriate his texts. Ghosts themselves, by their afterlife, are demonstrations of the effects of things, but they are already queer, already out of place, without needing the additional 'queer', so that the pleonasm resonates by evoking an absence of articulated signification which demands further looking at, while it also implies that looking, which involves reading a history, a narrative, confirms ghostliness. Story the American absentee, and the absence in Rome, by 1902, of Story's American community, 'a vanished society' (*Story*, I, 11) – these things fit with James's own subjects for writing.

In *The Sacred Fount* (1901) the setting, the English country house, is not described, nor the occasion, nor the narrator, nor, barely, the other characters. Everything has gone into conversation, which is difficult, evasive, indirect, controlled by what it does not say, and also aware of differences, which are often minute, which it highlights, but which may actually not be there at all. The conversation in this novel questions the centre from which James wrote. At the beginning of *The Sacred Fount*, the narrator and Mrs Brissenden in the train on the way to a country-house weekend party discuss a putative relationship between Lady John and Gilbert Long, two other house-guests also on the train. Mrs Brissenden says that Gilbert

Long seems to be getting a little more clever, and the source of this must be Lady John:

> 'I don't mean to say, of course', she replied, 'that he looks fluttered if you mention her, that he doesn't in fact look as blank as a pickpocket. But that proves nothing – or rather, as they're known to be always together, and she from morning till night as pointed as a hat-pin, it proves just what one sees. One simply takes it in.'
> I turned the picture round. 'They're scarcely together when she's alone with Brissenden.'
> 'Ah, that's only once in a way. It's a thing that from time to time such people – don't you know – make a particular point of: they cultivate, to cover their game, the appearance of other little friendships. It puts outsiders off the scent, and the real thing meanwhile goes on. Besides, you yourself acknowledge the effect. If she hasn't made him clever, what has she made him? She has given him, steadily, more and more intellect.'   (*The Sacred Fount*, 1, 8)

At the end, the narrator and Mrs Brissenden argue. Mrs Brissenden affirms again that Gilbert Long and Lady John are having an affair. The narrator says to Mrs Brissenden that she had described the 'purpose' of Brissenden's coming to the weekend party to be 'a screening of the pair':

> 'I described to you the purpose of it as nothing of the sort. I didn't describe to you the purpose of it,' said Mrs Briss, 'at all. I described to you,' she triumphantly set forth, 'the *effect* of it – which is a very different thing.'   (14, 182)

Mrs Brissenden is a clever woman, and perhaps she and Gilbert Long are having an affair, and she has been diverting the narrator from perceiving that, by feeding him with the alternative idea that if anyone is having an affair with Gilbert Long it is Lady John. But I do not want to get involved in the plot of *The Sacred Fount* and the relativity of the points of view of what is happening, especially since Mrs Briss calls the narrator mad. Rather, I want to look at how nothing gets said, in spite of the appearance of everything being very clear. 'It proves just what one sees,' says Mrs Briss, in the first quotation given. 'One simply takes it in.' Never could a statement be less clear or prove less. There is no clarity at all about what 'one' sees; empirical vision is unreliable; or rather, the visual field is capable of reversals, as the statement 'I turned the picture round' goes on to suggest. Two people being seen together may imply that they are together sexually, or it may be that they are screening another relationship, and this screening may be intentional (with a 'purpose') or unintentional, though it produces an 'effect'. What is seen may be what there is to see, or it may not.

Mrs Briss's triumphant speech at the end tries to establish differences – hence her triumphant distinction between purpose and effect – but these are based on the absence of anything primary to make difference meaningful. It is not clear that Mrs Briss's retrieval of her word 'effect' as she used it in the first extract is the same as her use of it in the second, even though she says it is. Nor is it clear that the first dialogue describes anything substantial, anything real at all. Difference is built up on a trick of language, inseparable from the temporal disjuncture of the two statements: the words may be the same but that is all.

This building up of difference from absence, writing from an absent event, is at the heart of much of James, and H. G. Wells, to give one famous example, represented it negatively in James's lifetime. The first paragraph below, from Wells's essay on James, could be on *The Sacred Fount*:

> The only human motives left in the novels of Henry James are a certain human avidity and an entirely superficial curiosity. Even when relations are irregular or when sins are hinted at, you feel that these are merely attitudes taken up, gambits before the game of attainment and over-perception begins.... His people nose out suspicions, hint by hint, link by link. Have you ever known living human beings do that? The thing his novel is *about* is always there. It is like a church lit but without a congregation to distract you, with every light and line focused on the high altar. And on the altar, very reverently placed, intensely there, is a dead kitten, an egg-shell, a bit of string.... Like his 'Altar of the Dead' [1894], with nothing to the dead at all.... For if there was they couldn't be all candles and the effect would vanish.... And the elaborate, copious emptiness of the whole Henry James exploit is only redeemed and made endurable by the elaborate, copious wit. Upon the desert his selection has made, Henry James erects palatial metaphors.... The chief fun, the only exercise, in reading Henry James is this clambering over vast metaphors...
>
> Having first made sure that he has scarcely anything left to express, he then sets to work to express it, with an industry, a wealth of intellectual stuff that dwarfs Newton. He spares no resource in the telling of his dead inventions. He brings up every device of language

to state and define. Bare verbs he rarely tolerates. He splits his infinitives and fills them up with adverbial stuffing. He presses the passing colloquialism into his service. His paragraphs sweat and struggle...[10]

Wells's comments are easy and journalistic; he is sure that a centre could be described, an event and its representation, its mimesis. I am more interested in the idea that James's texts start with a non-event, permitting only endless representation, as in conversation, or as in a 'picture' to be turned round as though it were a rebus; there is nothing but representation, which is not representation *of* something. Mrs Briss rejects the word 'purpose' for the word 'effect' – so she turns away from causes, or from the past altogether, towards present appearances. This disavowal that there may be anything there represents part of the 'ambiguity in Henry James', the title and theme of an essay of 1934 by Edmund Wilson, who suggested that James himself did not know what he thought in certain of his later texts. Ambiguity – radical undecidability of meaning – has become a key to a particular deconstruction-inspired reading of James, and especially of *The Turn of the Screw*, the text Wilson begins by analysing. *The Turn of the Screw* has been given the most attention of any James tale; I examine it in Chapter 5. It is central to the question whether there is anything in the scene which is behind representation, whether it is possible to 'go behind' (*AN*, 11, 201).

II ABSENCE

If one part of James, in texts like *The Sacred Fount* and *The Turn of the Screw* set in solid English country houses, which should have their own reality, implies that there is nothing behind representation, then could there be something in America to fill up that empty space? Hawthorne, in the Preface to *The Marble Faun* (1859), shows how difficult writing was for the American contemporary of Dickens, and James refers to these difficulties, saying that 'even to the present day [1879] it is a considerable discomfort in the United States not to be "in business." The young man who attempts to launch himself in a career that does not belong to the so-called practical order; the young man who has not...an office in the business-quarter of the town, with his name painted on the door, has but a limited place in the social system, finds no particular bough to perch upon' (*Hawthorne*, 2, 45).

James returns to the disadvantage of this business-bound America for a writer who is not in business, in *The American Scene*, published in 1907, after he had visited America in 1904–5. It focuses on the unease of the 'restless analyst'. 'It takes an endless amount of history to make even a little tradition, and an endless amount of tradition to make even a little taste, and an endless amount of taste, by the same token, to make even a little tranquillity' (*The American Scene*, 4, 2, 127). Tranquillity, missing for James in the club-atmosphere of New York, is one of the 'flowers of tradition'. In chapter 2, I refer to James's ambiguity towards 'tradition', and to the necessity of betraying it, but the point here is the absence of anything to nurture it. The American male's dedication to business creates an absence which operates in gender-terms, wittily illustrated in James's *An International Episode* (1878), when Mr J. L. Westgate, the American businessman, spends the whole of the hot summer in his ten-storey office block in New York and never turns up at Newport, where the rest of the family are hospitable to his English contacts whom he, not they, has met in New York. In *Notes of a Son and Brother*, James recalls the embarrassment of a father outside 'the American ideal' (*Autobiography*, II, 4, 278) – not in business of any kind. Discussing Washington in *The American Scene*, the one place where 'nobody was in "business"', he returns to the American businessman everywhere else in the United States, whose preoccupations mean that he has vacated the social sphere, which 'lies there waiting, pleading from all its pores to be occupied – the lonely waste, the boundless gaping void of "society"; which is but a rough name for all the *other* so numerous relations with the world he lives in' (11, 2, 254). The sexual imagery of this void is significant; and if we recall the sexual politics of *The Bostonians*, it fits that the 'void' must be filled, if at all, by the woman. She, however, epitomises the situation of being outside America's dominant ideology, and this displacement and the question of gender it prompts, is as evident as sky-writing:

> The phenomenon may easily become, for a spectator, the sentence written largest in the American sky: when he is in search of the characteristic, what else so plays the part? The woman is two-thirds of the apparent life – which means that she is absolutely all of the social; and as this is nowhere else the case, the occasion is unique for

seeing what such a situation may make of her.... The woman produced by a women-made society alone has obviously quite a new
story... (11, 3, 255–6)

The American Scene has attracted much commentary over the past
twenty years, since gender, race, colour and nationhood are prominent within it, prompting in the light of critical theory new specula-
tions about James's own position in reading difference within
America. In one assessment, Mark Seltzer argues that his 'analysis
of the American scene reveals precisely an underlying unity and
continuity between art and power'.[11] Seltzer's analysis is Foucault-
inspired in that he sees textual production as a form of power, not a
resistance to it, and here he argues against John Carlos Rowe, whose
deconstructive readings of James argue for the complexity of the
literary to undo discourses of power.[12] James appears to endorse a
freedom which seems to require the subject's independence from law
and power, but Seltzer claims that 'the law is already inscribed in
James's novelistic practice' (Seltzer, p. 18). Seltzer's position, however, relates to older and other arguments: which James aestheticises.[13] The elitist author who is corralled off from mass culture is
also secretly in love with the commodity and marked by commodity
culture; there is no oppositional politics in James.

Resistance to Seltzer is not to restore an author-centred criticism,
where the argument is what James personally could or could not
think, or what he intended to do; nor would it be to save James for
'literature'. Yet an argument which sees James's texts as complicit
with structures of power must also consider James's own lack of
utility as far as that bourgeois power is concerned. Writing as he
did separated James from his own modernity and made him a
prisoner to it. If the writing reproduces power, it also produces its
own resistances to it, which make the single author, the object of this
study, not a single author, and the texts profoundly double, marked
by the dominant discourse, and by their own response to that.

There seems to be a move towards redefining politics when James
comments on the 'void', absence in relationships, in *The American
Scene*. Discussing the old State House, or Capitol, in Richmond,
leads to his consideration of Washington, which

bristles, for the considering eye, with national affirmations – big
builded forms of confidence and energy; but when you have embraced

them all, with the implication of all the others still to come, you will find yourself wondering what it is you so oddly miss. Numberless things are represented, and one interest after the other counts itself in... but something is absent more even than these masses are present – till at last it occurs to you that the existence of a religious faith on the part of the people is not even remotely suggested. Not a Federal dome, not a spire nor a cornice pretends to any such symbolism, and though your attention is thus concerned with a mere negative, the negative presently becomes its sharp obsession. You reach out, perhaps in vain for something to which you may familiarly compare your unsatisfied sense. You liken it, perhaps, not so much to a meal made savourless by the failure of some usual, some central dish, as to a picture, nominally finished, say, where the canvas shows, in the very middle, with all originality, a fine blank space. (12, 3, 280)

James continues with the image of the picture with 'the white oval of the face... innocent of the brush'. (An emphasis on whiteness never seems far away.) It is not that American life has no place for the Church, but rather that a blankness prevails in terms of the representation of this reality. What is to be seen is not what there is to see. The observer of 'the American scene' – the title focuses on the representable – 'has early to perceive... that there will be little for him in the American scene unless he be ready, anywhere, to read "into" it as much as he reads out' (9, 3, 215). The visual field, however much the picture is 'turned round', is inadequate; reading must be of what is not there, symptomatic; a reading for symptoms, for the trace. As James puts it earlier, 'I draw courage from the remembrance that history is never, in any rich sense, the immediate crudity of what "happens," but the much finer complexity of what we read into it and think of in connection with it' (4, 4, 136–7).

There are implications in this for James's re-reading of his texts to write the Prefaces, and in writing his own and American history in the *Autobiography*. His intention from the period of his American visit in 1904 onwards was to re-read his history, so that the 'immediate crudity of what happens' is not what can be taken away from an examination of James's autobiography, for instance. None the less, this is not my point: I am more interested in America as an absent centre, which relates to gender and race questions alike. The 'big builded forms of confidence and energy' are masculine in meaning, and the woman is missing; the best example of America's architecture being, for James, the hotel.

In *The American Scene* James writes about the then Waldorf-Astoria hotel (1898, Fifth Avenue and 34th Street, demolished 1929) as the form of refuge that New York gives from the relentlessness of its gridded streets, where 'the electric cars, with their double track, are everywhere almost as tight a fit in the narrow channel of the roadway as the projectile in the bore of a gun' (2, 3, 78). The machinic and military implications of this are strong. Christine Boyer discusses the French Renaissance-style building, designed by Henry J. Hardenbergh, as the first skyscraper hotel.[14] The Waldorf-Astoria, symbol of the Astors' wealth, built by two segments of the Astor family, including Caroline Schermerhorn who founded the list of the New York's elite, the 'Four hundred', epitomises the hotel in its essence in New York, that for which 'the American spirit has found so unprecedented a use and a value[,] leading it on to express so a social, indeed positively an aesthetic ideal, and making it so, at this supreme pitch, a synonym for civilization . . . that one is very tempted to ask if the hotel spirit may not just *be* the American spirit most seeking and most finding itself' (2, 3, 78–9). The hotel symbolises a 'gregarious' (2, 3, 80) spirit that thinks in terms not of privacy, which would suggest the feminine, but of building large for 'publicity'.

James returns to the hotel spirit when discussing Charleston, contrasting it with Europe. There, 'there are endless things . . . to your vision, behind and beyond the hotel, a multitudinous, complicated life; in the States . . . you see the hotel as itself that life, as constituting for vast numbers of people the richest form of existence' (13, 2, 299). There could be no better suggestion of a certain form of postmodernism. Uncoincidentally, Fredric Jameson chooses the John Portman-designed Westin Bonaventure Hotel in Los Angeles to illustrate 'a new total space' whose glass skin 'repels the city outside', a 'postmodern hyperspace' whose architecture 'transcend[s] the capacities of the individual human body to locate itself, to organize its immediate surroundings perceptually, and cognitively to map its position in a mappable external world'.[15] The hotel cocoons the subject from the world outside, reducing the importance of what is outside in an implosion of meaning, where the hotel does not give to the outside, but subtracts meaning from that outside. In so far as the hotel spirit may be regarded as a metaphor for America, the state to which America aspires, it may be thought of as the attempt to suspend meaning in its embrace, so that it discourages the search for anything 'behind and beyond', thus making the 'scene' non-indicative of what is there to be read.

James continues this theme by another symbolism, comparing the hotel to the Pullman railway sleeping cars. 'The Pullmans ... are like rushing hotels and the hotels ... are like stationary Pullmans' (13, 2, 300). The Pullman was the inspiration of George Pullman (1831–97), whose Palace Car Company and Chicagoan model town named after him and built for his workers made him the emblem of American business, forging the American nation in his own image.[16] Pullman influenced the World's Columbian Exposition of 1893 at Chicago; and the first Baedekers, making America (and Pullman) a tourist venue, were produced for it. The Pullman thus embodies everything of this capitalised and hegemonic America, 'exhaling modernity at every pore' (14, 7, 339). James stresses the idea of what can be seen outside the Pullman being like a theatre 'scene' – hence he refers to 'the great moving proscenium of the Pullman' (14, 2, 319). The Pullman frames what can be seen; it allows only so much in and dispatches it fast, while the spectator on the inside, in this great moving hotel (a sleeper train), 'cushioned and kitchened' (13, 1, 293), looks out as from a hotel window, separated, alien, but with external reality reduced. Going to America under these circumstances is a tourist experience, the tourist seeing nothing unless he or she becomes 'the restless analyst' – a phrase which contains the danger of obsessiveness, madness – and unless 'impressions' become critical readings. The connection between the railway and the hotel could go further. Many hotels in Florida, including those at St Augustine, which James visited, were opened by the Standard Oil millionaire Henry Flagler (1830–1913) who created East Coast railways to attract winter visitors to Florida. The railways produced the hotels and the hotels the railways.

The emptiness in America also relates to race. James's actual journey to America involved dotting round from place to place and with several returns to different cities, especially New York. It took him as far as Chicago and San Francisco, but *The American Scene* is crafted as an account of arriving at New York and then moving into New England and so down the East Coast to Florida. James moved south, into territory he had previously not visited. Richmond, the Confederate capital, James wrote, 'looked to me simply blank and void' (12, 2, 272). That said, James mentions the 'great modern hotel, superfluously vast'. The snow on the ground, which covers up and also indicates whiteness, assists in the sense of a place with no 'references' (12, 2, 273). The whole is a concealment of what is known otherwise, that 'the negro had always been.... "on the nerves" of the South' (12, 2, 277), and this insistence had required the evasiveness and social enclosure of 'a general and permanent quarantine;... the eternal bowdlerization of books and journals ...all literature and all art on an expurgatory index' (12, 2, 275).[17] So, James suggests, racial exclusion, itself generated by erotic fears, produces an exclusion of the erotic; the removal of the sexual from American history contributing to the blankness that drives the American out of America and, guiltily, back to Europe.

In Charleston, where the war started, James returns to 'vacancy': 'How can everything so have gone that the only "Southern" book of any distinction published for many a year is *The Souls of Black Folk*, by that most accomplished of members of the negro race, Mr W. E. B. Du Bois? Had the *only* focus of life then been Slavery? ...To say "yes" seems the only way to account for the degree of the vacancy' (13, 3, 307–8).[18] A white South which had become 'monomaniacal' in defending slavery, could now say nothing; what could be said must come from the black writer. In this vacancy, all that is left is the empty houses of the Southern planters of the ante-bellum period. Du Bois, whose second sentence in *The Souls of Black Folk* says that 'the problem of the Twentieth Century is the problem of the color-line', characteristically speaks of the black as being 'within the veil' – invisible to the gaze of the white, who is outside it.[19] These pages, which James knew, confirm what appears in his text, that the to-be-seen is not what can be seen, especially from the Pullman.

The account of the South is succeeded by a chapter on Florida. Returning from St Augustine by Pullman from which he sees nothing but the desecration of landscape – not even a road – James thinks from the standpoint of the absent native American, addressing the Pullman, which epitomises 'the general conquest of nature and space' (14, 7, 340): 'If I were one of the painted savages you have dispossessed, or even some tough reactionary trying to emulate him... I should owe you my grudge for every disfigurement and every violence, for every wound with which you have caused the face of the land to bleed.' But he adds another indictment, 'you touch the great lonely land...only to plant upon it some ugliness about which... you then proceed to brag with a cynicism all your own. You convert the large and noble sanities that I see around me...to crudities, to invalidities, hideous and unashamed; and so you leave them to add to the number of myriad aspects you simply spoil' (14, 7, 341). 'Spoil' and 'dispossessed' are Jamesian words: their use will appear in later chapters. And there James leaves it, with a signal to the reader of a further 'impression' to follow, of the Mississippi, as though affirming that he is part of the hegemonic world inside the Pullman.

III

William James commented that *The American Scene* gave 'the illusion of a solid object' being made 'wholly out of impalpable materials, air, and the prismatic interferences of light, ingeniously focussed by mirrors upon empty space'. Inside this image may be seen the idea of America as empty space. He says that James's 'account of America is largely one of its omissions, silences, vacancies. You work them up like solids, for those readers who already germinally perceive them.... I said to myself over and again in reading, "How much greater the triumph, instead of dwelling only upon America's vacuities, he could make positive suggestion of what in 'Europe' or Asia may exist to fill them." '[20] Absences worked up like solids describe the space of disappearance that James renders; the Jamesian text, like architecture, both creates a space and emphasises its artificiality. The positivism of William James's demand of his brother which makes him speak for the 'intolerance' of James's readers – ' "Say it *out* for God's sake," they cry, "and have done with it" ' – must, however, be answered by a negation. It is no longer a question of being a cultural comparativist, posing Europe against America. The early chapters of *The American Scene*, dealing with the European immigrations into America, show how the opposition between Europe and America has become unsustainable. It is true that James did not respond adequately to the otherness which was coming into New York's East Side, and that his writings show nostalgia for the old New York. Nor is it difficult to detect racism in what he says about the black. But these are signs of entrapment; and James is aware at the end that he is shut in in the Pullman. Prison images – as when he is 'caged' in the hotel (14, 3, 325) – characterise the book. 'One excrescence on [the] large smooth surface' (9, 4, 221) of Philadelphia architecture is the prison, which Dickens had discussed in *American Notes*, and to which James alludes (9, 4, 221). James is confined to the world vision that George Pullman and hegemonic values intend for him and for America; homogenising, rendering the other invisible. Perhaps he should, as it were, have got off the train. But there is an opposition to it and the framing that the Pullman has achieved has become so powerful that it sucks up Europe too, and threatens to turn everything into negative space, into disappearance.

Perhaps what is left of that otherness is uncanny. Accompanied by F. P. Sargent, the Commissioner of Immigration, James visited Ellis Island, the point of entry for new arrivals to the United States (in 1904 one million immigrants passed through it):

> I think indeed that the simplest account of the action of Ellis Island on the spirit of any sensitive citizen who may have happened to 'look in' is that he comes back from his visit not at all the same person that he went. He has eaten of the tree of knowledge, and the taste will be forever in his mouth. He had thought he knew before, thought he had the sense of the degree in which it is his American fate to share the sanctity of his American consciousness, the intimacy of his American patriotism, with the inconceivable alien; but the truth had never come home to him with any such force. In the lurid light projected upon it by those courts of dismay it shakes him – or I like to imagine it shakes him – to the depths of his being; I like to think of him, I positively *have* to think of him, as going about ever afterwards with a new look, for those who can see it, in his face, the outward sign of the new chill in his heart. So is stamped, for detection, the questionably privileged person who has had an apparition, seen a ghost in his supposedly safe old house. Let not the unwary, therefore, visit Ellis Island.   (2, 1, 66)

The passage reverts to the image used in *Hawthorne*. The Civil War had been the bite of the fruit of the tree of knowledge. Mass immigration is now the second bite, whose effect on the three-times repeated 'American' in the third sentence makes the point that the definition of 'American' cannot – in contrast to Europe – ever be realised. James's complacency about being American had come after the end of the war; but the issue of immigration displaces that struggle and the character it had produced. He returns to the image of the ghost (for all James's narratives contain the possibility of the ghostly). The ghost is that which is not in the picture and yet which fills the picture, *punctum* to any *studium*, as Barthes uses these terms in *Camera Lucida*[21] – the *punctum* piercing the certainties usually held. The American citizen need not visit Ellis Island, a separate space specially designated for the purpose of receiving the immigrant, and need not be aware of the unsettling power of the other, and the grid nature of New York may mean that there will be no awareness of the other once they are in the city, but the point remains that there has been a shift, a dis-location, and the 'American scene' is not what it was. Though *The American Scene* came late in James's writing, after he had seen what he did he went on to re-read and revise his texts for the New York edition, so that all those texts – including the ones not collected there – belong under the sign of that new experience, and have it informing their unconscious, ghosting it. Ghosting, existing through a feminine, 'queer' existence, would be James's opposition to the dominant ideology.

The following chapters show how the unsettling and ghostly operates in James's pages, disturbing their realism – which would have its analogue in the view from the Pullman – and making them not a record of the known and the observable, but evocative, beneath the vacancy, of the ghostly as the buried, erotic, disturbing history. In selecting James's texts, my gravitation has been towards the architecture of the later works, and towards the New York edition, but I have picked out those whose theme is James's writing the history of the nineteenth century, especially that of America. In the following chapter, I refer to James's criticism, situating him in relation to realism and the attempt to find something else in Hawthornian 'romance' and allegory. This leads into a study of two paradigmatic texts: the early tale *The Last of the Valerii*, and *The Ambassadors*. The latter has been often read autobiographically, making James as disabled by modernity and by the sexual demands of the modern. In reading *The Ambassadors*, I focus on an erotic tableau and a trope which seems to run through so much of James, and which I come back to later, in *The Portrait of a Lady* and *The Turn of the Screw*, and in *The Golden Bowl* (Chapter 9).

After Chapter 2, the book works chronologically, and asks to be read culminatively, for a developing argument. The third chapter, on *The Portrait of a Lady* and *The Bostonians*, looks at James on women, morbidity and hysteria. The fourth chapter continues this in relation to the history of buried lives in *The Aspern Papers*, while the fifth does the same through *The Turn of the Screw*. The sixth chapter, on nineteenth-century modernity, reads *Washington Square*, *The Bostonians*, *What Maisie Knew* and *The Awkward Age*. Later chapters focus on late James – Chapter 7 on *The Wings of the Dove*, and James's relationship to Dickens and Thackeray, and their narrative freedom in contrast to his own. Chapters 8 and 9 examine damaged lives, and an either damaged or symmetrical narration, through *The Beast in the Jungle* and *The Golden Bowl*. The last chapter, on *The Jolly Corner*, returns to issues fusing with *The American Scene*. The subject suffers a *dérèglement de tous les sens* in relation to his own certainties, and with regard to his house – symbol, in James, of otherness and familiarity together, the site of history and hysteria, of the ghost and of the impossibility of linkage between rooms, or of single narrative space.

2

'The Interest behind the Interest': *The Last of the Valerii* and *The Ambassadors*

[Strether] continually knocked at [Maria Gostrey's] door to let her have it afresh that Chad's case – whatever else of minor interest it might yield – was first and foremost a miracle almost monstrous. It was an alteration of the entire man, and was so signal an instance that nothing else, for the intelligent observer, could – could it? – signify. 'It's a plot,' he declared, 'there's more in it than meets the eye.' He gave the reign to his fancy. 'It's a plant!'

His fancy seemed to please her. 'Whose then?'

'Well, the party responsible is, I suppose, the fate that waits for one, the dark doom that rides. What I mean is that with such elements one can't count. I've but my poor individual, my modest human means. It isn't playing the game to turn on the uncanny. All one's energy goes to facing it, to tracking it. One wants, confound it, don't you see?' he confessed with a queer face – 'one wants to enjoy anything so rare. Call it then life' – he puzzled it out – 'call it poor dear old life simply that springs the surprise. Nothing alters the fact that the surprise is paralysing, or at any rate engrossing – all, practically, hang it, that one sees, that one can see.'

(*The Ambassadors*, 4, 2, 118–19)

Lambert Strether in *The Ambassadors* is excited by the change in Chad Newsome. Expecting to find him corrupted by a wicked woman in Paris, the signs make him wonder. Something 'more than meets the eye' is at work. Perhaps Strether is being tricked by a plot, a 'plant' – a clue to set the detective in the wrong direction. Perhaps there is no plot. Perhaps the enchantment is real, or Strether's 'fancy' is making the romance. Perhaps Chad has not changed, perhaps he has.

James's plots repeat the 'plots' that Lambert Strether thinks Life may be engineering, as ways of eliciting, or allowing for, the 'uncanny' or the 'queer'. The uncanny and the queer will have gender-implications. Perhaps the uncanny implies a hesitation between gender-positions. As in Freud, it is sexual.[1] Again, James's plots have the power of paralysing (like Medusa) or of surprising, engrossing vision, producing distinctions between what 'one sees' and what 'one *can* see'. These terms, questioning vision, making problematic the real, and what can be seen through a mode of writing committed to realism, can also be approached through a comment James made in 1905 about Hawthorne, that 'he saw the quaintness or weirdness, the interest *behind* the interest, of things, as continuous with the very life we are leading' (*LC* II, 471). This fascination of Hawthorne's – whose force James acknowledges in a late tribute to an American predecessor after being relatively cool about him in *Hawthorne* (1879) – is also a fascination in James. In this chapter, I look at the 'interest behind the interest' through James's novel criticism, and also through an early tale, *The Last of the Valerii* (1874), and the late work, *The Ambassadors* (1903) – which James called 'frankly, quite the best, "all round", of my productions' (*AN*, 17, 309).

I   JAMES, ELIOT AND ZOLA

James travelled alone in Europe first in 1869, taking in Italy, for the first of fourteen visits. 'At last – for the first time – I live,' he wrote to William James. In Italy, 'one is conscious . . . of the aesthetic presence of the past'.[2] An obsession appears: history, the past. In the *Nation* in 1865, the year he began publishing, James had referred to 'the so-called principle of realism' in France, preferring this to American and British fiction, and in Europe he made first-hand contact with realism in 1875 with Turgenev in Paris, and, in 1876, Flaubert, Zola, Daudet, Maupassant and Edmond de Goncourt at an exhibition of the Impressionists. But in December 1876, James settled in London, while deciding whether to be an American in America, or an expatriate; and if the latter, in which capital. French novelists, Balzac especially, were crucial to him.[3] Three conscious influences intersect and conflict in James: Hawthorne; Balzac and Zola; and George Eliot, on whom James wrote ten essays in all,[4] as a tribute to her effect upon his work, and whom he first met in 1869.[5]

The conflict shows when James takes a sentence of George Eliot's of 1859, quoted in J. W. Cross's biography of her, which James reviewed: 'We [Eliot and G. H. Lewes] have just finished reading aloud *Père Goriot*, a hateful book.' James thought this novel 'a masterpiece'. The difference between Balzac and Eliot is focused when James says that, for George Eliot, the novel 'was not primarily a picture of life' – not realism – 'capable of deriving a high value from its form, but a moralized fable, the last word of a philosophy endeavouring to teach by example'. The Balzac critique

> testifies to that side of George Eliot's nature which was weakest – the absence of free aesthetic life. I venture this remark in the face of a passage quoted from one of her letters...: 'My function is that of the *aesthetic*, not the doctrinal teacher; the rousing of the nobler emotions, which make mankind desire the social right...'. [I]t is a good example of the manner in which George Eliot may be said to have acted on her generation.... We feel in her, always, that she proceeds from the abstract to the concrete; that her figures and situations are evolved, as the phrase is, from her moral consciousness, and are only indirectly the products of observation. They are deeply studied and massively supported, but they are not *seen* in the irresponsible plastic way. (Gard, pp. 207–8)

James has to periodise Eliot, referring to 'her generation' and saying *Middlemarch* 'sets a limit... to the development of the old-fashioned English novel' (Gard, p. 81). In 'The Art of Fiction' (1884), discussing 'the importance of exactness – of truth of detail' (Gard, p. 195), 'the only reason for the existence of a novel is that it does attempt to represent life' (Gard, p. 188).[6] 'The analogy between the art of the painter and the art of the novelist is, so far as I am able to see, complete... as the picture is reality, so the novel is history.'

But the history, which is a history of the present, is not simply objective, as an essay on Daudet (1883) argues:

> The success of a work of art, to my mind, may be measured by the degree to which it produces a certain illusion; that illusion makes it

appear to us for the time we have lived another life – that we have had a miraculous enlargement of experience.... I am perfectly aware that to say the object of a novel is to represent life does not bring the question to a point so fine as to be uncomfortable for any one.... For after all, may not people differ infinitely as to what constitutes life – what constitutes representation?   (*LC* I, 242)

In James, it is always 'another life' – the other – that fascinates.

In contrast, he writes, 'there are certain things [Daudet] does not conceive – certain forms that never appear to him. Imaginative writers of the first order always give us an impression that they have a kind of philosophy' (*LC* I, 248). This contrasts with George Eliot, whose determination to be 'real' in *Middlemarch* (Gard, p. 81) James praised, even though her native tendency was 'idealist', working from ideas to 'life'. But *Middlemarch*'s 'diffusiveness' leads to the aphorism 'If we write novels so, how shall we write History?' (Gard, p. 81). James writes that 'history' – of the present, of the buried past, a history of sexuality and of America – through realism and through allegory.

'The Art of Fiction' accuses English and American novelists of 'moral timidity,' in contrast to the French, especially in relation to sexuality. Since 'a novel is...a personal, a direct impression of life' (Gard, pp. 191–2), the impression of life is sensory, and it glances at the ghostly and the unknown, the 'uncanny', as Strether calls it:

> The power to guess the unseen from the seen, to trace the implication of things, to judge the whole piece by the pattern, the condition of feeling life in general so completely that you are well on your way to knowing any particular corner of it – this cluster of gifts may almost be said to constitute experience.... If experience consists of impressions, it may be said that impressions *are* experience, just as (have we not seen it?) they are the very air we breathe. Therefore, if I should certainly say to a novice, 'Write from experience and experience only,' I should feel that this was rather a tantalizing monition if I were not immediately to add, 'Try to be one of the people upon whom nothing is lost!' (Gard, pp. 194–5)

As Eliot-like stresses on 'ideas' are confronted by James's stress on 'impressions', so 'experience' – Eliot's empiricism – becomes the demand to 'guess the unseen from the seen'. In the light of George Eliot's hatred of *Père Goriot* (1835), presumably on account of its sexuality, the drift becomes apparent: the unseen is also the obscene.

Britain's Obscene Publications Act (1857), passed two years before Eliot's comments, received this interpretation by Justice Cockburn (1868): 'the test of obscenity is this, whether the tendency of the matter charged as obscenity is to deprave and corrupt those whose minds are open to such immoral influences, and into whose hands a publication of this sort may fall'.[7] The test is the response of a readership defined in terms of vulnerability and openness to 'immoral infuences.' Eliot's dislike of Balzac makes her writing proceed from the abstract to the concrete, unable to start with the primacy of the senses, because that means the primacy of the sexual.

That James thinks this, is evident from his discussion in 1888 of the senses in Guy de Maupassant's fiction. He concludes:

> the other sense, the sense *par excellence*, the sense which we scarcely mention in English fiction, and which I am not very sure I shall be allowed to mention in an English periodical, M. de Maupassant speaks for that, and of it, with extraordinary distinctness and authority. To say that it occupies the first place in his picture is to say too little; it covers in truth the whole canvas, and his work is little else but a report of its innumerable manifestations. These manifestations are not, for him, so many incidents of life; they are life itself, they represent the standing answer to any question that we may ask about it. He describes them in detail, with a familiarity and a frankness which leave nothing to be added.... M. de Maupassant would doubtless affirm that where the empire of the sexual sense is concerned, no exaggeration is possible. (*LC* I, 528)

James, writing on impressions, on senses, and the real, circles round sexuality. If George Eliot does not see her characters in an 'irresponsible plastic way', this is her repression. According to 'The Art of Fiction', the English novel is addressed 'in a large degree to "young people" and that this is itself constitutes a presumption that it will be rather shy. There are certain things which it is generally agreed not to discuss, not even to mention, before young people' (Gard, p. 205). James invests in realism because the deep meaning of realism is sexuality, the discovery of sexual difference. The drive in James is to know what else is in the articulated fully described scene: what other representation haunts it, with power to cancel out the represented visible scene.

If representation is bound up with the sexual, this throws the art of fiction into crisis. The intuition of the sexual refuses narrative, representation and realism itself, because it is the discovery of difference, of the split subject. How single representation and empirical realism is baffled, James could have learned from Zola's *Nana*, which he reviewed in 1880. Its influence on James is certain: perhaps in *The Bostonians*,[8] certainly in *The Awkward Age*. *Nana* involves a strip-tease, the revelation of the eighteen-year-old Parisian prostitute's 'sex' – her body and her sexual parts[9] – and James knows it could not be written in England. Nor in 'the United States, where the storyteller's art is almost exclusively feminine', and

> is mainly in the hands of timid (even when very accomplished) women, whose acquaintance with life is severely restricted, and who are not conspicuous for general views. The novel, moreover, among ourselves, is almost always addressed to young unmarried ladies, or at least always assumes them to be a large part of the novelist's public. This fact, to a French storyteller, appears, of course, a damnable restriction, and M. Zola would probably decline to take *au sérieux* any work produced under such unnatural conditions. Half of life is a sealed book to young unmarried ladies, and how can a novel be worth anything that deals with half of life?   (*LC* II, 825–7)

James's scepticism about such women-writers appears in reviewing Elizabeth Rundle Charles, where he refers to French realism as a contrast, and as a model.[10] In the *Nana* review, he says that 'among ourselves' the novel is addressed to unmarried women, or assumes them to be a large part of the reading-public. The 'ourselves' are English novelists, since when he gives instances of novelists working with the system he cites Thackeray, Dickens and George Eliot. But what are the implications of the reference to unmarried ladies? What is the half of life that they are assumed – whether by James or by a French 'Naturalist' writer like Zola – to be ignorant of? Marriage or sex? And what of the unmarried, possibly virginal Henry James? His most absorbing plot is the woman who enters marriage only to discover that her husband or best friend is adulterous or unfaithful: *The Portrait of a Lady*; *The Wings of the Dove*, *The Golden Bowl*. Daisy Miller, Isabel Archer, Hyacinth Robinson, Maisie, and Milly Theale are all innocents betrayed. In *The Ambassadors*, a woman and a man play on the innocence of the middle-aged American, Lambert Strether, a virginal widower. James's suggestion of an incompleteness or limitation in the woman reader, eliding non-marriage with virginity, unconsciously applies to him, questioning the basis of his own knowledge. What unmarried women know becomes the subject, as with Daisy, or Maisie, or the governess in *The Turn of the Screw* or Kate Croy. James draws back from *Nana*, but the review makes the state of not-knowing unacceptable, so that in 'The Art of Fiction' he urges upon novelists the need to know, to intuit the whole, the unseen. It is at the heart of his belief in realism, allowing him to value Zola, to keep away from the values of the young innocent unmarried lady whose existence he presupposes.

Zola plays with the innocence of young unmarried ladies when Nana herself discusses with four men a novel that was causing a sensation in Paris. 'It was the story of a prostitute, and Nana inveighed against it, declaring that it was all untrue, and expressing an indignant revulsion against the sort of filthy literature which claimed to show life as it was – as if a writer could possibly describe everything and as if novels weren't supposed to be written just to pass away the time. On the subject of books and plays Nana had very decided opinions: she liked tender, high-minded works which would set her dreaming and uplift her soul.'[11] Nana says attempts to show everything must fail. In her debut in the operetta *The Blonde Venus*, she comes close to showing everything, 'naked, flaunting her naked-ness with a cool audacity, sure of the sovereign power of her flesh'. But the nakedness is not absolute, any more than the text can be absolute in telling everything. In the next sentence, 'she was wearing nothing but a veil of gauze; and...her whole body...could be divined, indeed clearly discerned, in all its foamy whiteness beneath the filmy fabric.... [T]he woman stood revealed...with all the impulsive madness of her sex (*son sexe*), opening the gates of the unknown world of desire' (1, 44–5). Is Nana naked? Has the text shown everything, or is it veiled? If veiled, then the representation contains a fetishising detail. When Nana stands before the mirror, her 'body was covered with fine hair, reddish down which turned her skin into velvet, while there was something of the Beast about her equine crupper and flanks, about the fleshy curves and deep hollows of her body, which veiled her sex (*son sexe*) in the suggestive mystery of their shadows' (8, 223). Nakedness is never total: the veil defers a full showing. Her bed is 'a throne wide enough for Nana to stretch out the glory of her naked limbs, an altar of Byzantine luxury, worthy of the omnipotence of her sex, which at that moment lay openly displayed in the religious immodesty of an awe-inspiring idol' (12, 444). Bodily representation is still through textual veils, which represents her body as a fetish. The veil of the text, which purports to take everything away, to reveal things as they are, also divides and creates a split. The woman's body as a fetish gives her a sense of wholeness, but the desire to see texts in terms of complete realism is also fetishistic. *Nana*, apparently revealing all, has an illusory appearance of completeness because the text is a veil, distancing the reader. The fetish disallows completeness, divides the text within itself. In the last reference to Nana's body, 'her sex rose in a halo of glory and blazed down on her prostrate victims like a rising sun shining down on a field of carnage' (13, 452–3), the body, far from being shown, is divided from the reader through the veil of heavily metaphorical representation (giving to James his metaphor of 'the empire of the sexual sense'). Realism approaches completeness, but still withdraws. Representation implies division: it shows, but it also shows that it is a veil. The point holds for representation in James's novels, which become more and more opaque, challenging in every way, both through the plot and through the textuality of the text, an unambiguous sense of what is happening.

This opacity, in texts which would like to be as aware of the sexual as Zola, intersects with the strategic in countries when realism can only be relative – relative because the condition of young unmarried women in England or America requires the text to be fetish-like. When James in his review of Zola adds that 'under these unnatural conditions and insufferable restrictions' 'a variety of admirable works have been produced; Thackeray, Dickens, George Eliot, have all had an eye to the innocent classes', the issue is problematic: he seems to suggest that their representations cannot be adequate. While it is clear that for James these writers have an old-fashioned quality, yet he seems to stick with their point of view, suggesting that 'English readers' will note in Zola 'the extraordinary absence of humour, the dryness, the solemnity, the air of tension and effort' (*LC* I, 808–9). This defensiveness is inadequate: the superior tone underestimates how far English opposition to Zola went. In 1888–9, the publisher Henry Vizetelly was imprisoned for translating and distributing Zola. If even George Eliot found Balzac 'hateful', that would not augur well for Zola's reputation in Britain. But finding James inadequate at this point does not take away from his realisation that realism is a matter of national ideology, of what that will allow you to say, and that it breaks down at the crucial dividing ground of gender, where the seen and the unseen meet.

II JAMES AND HAWTHORNE

The logic of James's reading and the attachment of importance to the erotic in Balzac, de Maupassant or Zola, separates him from George Eliot, though in the next chapter I want to show how her version of the uncanny within sexuality counts within James's texts. Similarly, as *The Last of the Valerii* shows, he is involved in a complex engagement with Hawthorne on whom, in 1879, he published a book. Hawthorne's writing on both America and the history of sexuality entails differentiating between the realist novel and romance, and writing allegory. The Preface to *The House of the Seven Gables: A Romance* (1851) gives the first difference:

> When a writer calls his work a Romance, it need hardly be observed that he wishes to claim a certain latitude, both as to its fashion and material, which he would not have felt himself entitled to assume had he professed to be writing a Novel. The latter form of composition is presumed to aim at a very minute fidelity, not merely to the possible, but to the probable and ordinary course of man's experience. The former – while, as a work of art, it must rigidly subject itself to laws, and while it sins unpardonably so far as it may swerve aside from the truth of the human heart – has fairly a right to present that truth under cirumstances, to a great extent, of the writer's own choosing or creation. If he think fit, also, he may so manage his atmospherical medium as to bring out or mellow the lights and deepen and enrich the shadows of the picture.[12]

The distinction between the novel and the romance[13] appears in the context of Hawthorne's interest in American history. The Preface to *The House of the Seven Gables* continues by saying that 'the point of view in which this tale comes under the Romantic definition lies in the attempt to connect a bygone time with the very present that is flitting away from us'. The present is disappearing, the present is the state of ruin. The past in contrast to the present seems secure, for in the next paragraph, announcing his 'moral purpose' in writing, Hawthone says that 'the wrongdoing of one generation lives into the successive ones'. So Marx said that 'the weight of the dead generations lies like a nightmare on the minds of the living.'[14] History crushing the present is Hawthorne's theme as it is James's subject in *The Last of the Valerii*. In America, place of the present, the sculptor Kenyon tells Donatello, in *The Marble Faun*, that 'each generation has only its own sins and sorrows to bear'. In Italy 'it seems as if all the weary and dreary Past were piled upon the back of the Present.'[15]

The logic of this should make the novel, as the form of writing which views the present as absolute, actual and inescapable, the dominant mode in nineteenth-century America. Romance, the form which is not so much the voice of the dominant culture, but rather the voice of the defeated,[16] would be a critique of the dominant and the present, allowing for the perception of modernity as an epoch having energies in it, which, as Walter Benjamin puts it with reference to Baudelaire, 'bring it close to antiquity'.[17] Hawthorne sides with romance and with allegory. In 'Rappaccini's Daughter', in *Mosses from an Old Manse* (1846), he parodies in a frame-narrative his own

> inveterate love of allegory, which is apt to invest his plots and characters with the aspect of scenery and people in the clouds and to steal away the human warmth out of his conceptions. His fictions are sometimes historical, sometimes of the present day, and sometimes, so far as can be discovered, have little or no reference either to time or space. (*Tales*, p. 386)

James comments on this use of allegory – 'a story told as if it were another and a very different story' (*Hawthorne*, 3, 70) – and dislikes it. He judges that 'Hawthorne ... was not in the least a realist – he was not to my mind enough of one' (*Hawthorne* 3, 73). More especially, James finds *The Scarlet Letter* deficient in history: 'little elaboration of detail, of the modern realism of research' (*Hawthorne*, 5, 110). With *The House of the Seven Gables*, the people 'are all figures rather than characters – they are all pictures rather than persons' (5, 119). He begins by wondering whether Hawthorne had ever heard of Realism (*Hawthorne*, 1, 24), which involves him in a comparison with Balzac and Zola.

But allegory, 'speaking other', a form of speech which recognises that utterance in the realist text is already internally divided, that representation veils access to the real, is at the heart of James as much as of Hawthorne. Hawthorne's Preface to *The Marble Faun, Or, The Romance of Monte Beni* (1860), describes Italy as

> chiefly valuable to him [the author] as affording a sort of poetic or fairy precinct, where actualities would not be so terribly insisted upon as they are, and must needs be, in America. No author, without a trial, can conceive of the difficulty of writing a romance about a country

> where there is no shadow, no antiquity, no mystery, no picturesque and
> gloomy wrong, nor anything but a commonplace prosperity, in broad
> and simple daylight, as is happily the case with my dear native land. It
> will be very long, I trust, before romance-writers may find congenial
> and easily handled themes, either in the annals of our stalwart repub-
> lic, or in any characteristic and probable events of our individual lives.
> Romance and poetry, ivy, lichens and wallflowers need ruin to make
> them grow.   (Preface, pp. 4–5)

A world with no shadow, no chiaroscuro, is a midday one, completely lucid, with no ghosts (here 'shadows'), no veil, nothing not
represented. It is a white, middle-class America, of course: it is a
question how far James gets beyond its confinements, either in his
novels or in *The American Scene*. When *Hawthorne* quotes this
Preface, James concurs, saying that the America to be read from
Hawthorne's diaries is 'characterized by an extraordinary blankness
– a curious paleness of colour and paucity of detail' (*Hawthorne*, 2,
54). Blankness, whiteness, absence – this is an important triangula-
tion for James's thinking. This is the section where James sums up the
texture of American life in terms 'almost ludicrous', he says, of its lack:

> No State, in the European sense of the word, and indeed barely a
> specific national name. No sovereign, no court, no personal loyalty,
> no aristocracy, no church, no clergy, no army, no diplomatic service, no
> country-gentlemen, no palaces, no castles, no manors, not old country-
> houses, not parsonages, not thatched cottages, nor ivied ruins; no
> cathedrals, nor abbeys, nor little Norman churches; no great Univer-
> sities nor public schools – no Oxford, nor Eton, nor Harrow; no
> literature, no novels, no museums, no pictures, no political society,
> no sporting class – no Epsom nor Ascot!   (*Hawthorne*, 2, 55)

Hawthorne begins by drawing the 'moral' that 'the flower of art
blooms only when the soil is deep [another quotation from Hawthorne's Preface], that it takes a great deal of history to produce a
little literature, that it needs a complex social machinery to set a
writer in motion' (1, 23).

III   *THE LAST OF THE VALERII*

The state of being modern and the alternative, of being held by
history, is the subject of *The Last of the Valerii* (1874). It is narrated

by an American painter, endowed with money from 'trade' (p. 21), who tells how he gives his god-daughter to marry the Roman Conte Valerio, whose mentality is destabilized when a marble fragmented Juno is dug up in the grounds of his villa, which his wife is modernizing. The statue must be eliminated from his life, and the Americans see to it that it is, and that the Count is brought back to a sanitised and depleted normality, where the statue has no further claim on his emotions.

Near the beginning, Valerio warns his wife about digging up old statues: 'I can't bear to look the statues in the face. I seem to see other strange eyes in the empty sockets, and I hardly know what they say to me. I call the poor old statues ghosts' (p. 21).[18] It is one of James's first references to ghosts. Eyeless figures imply castration, the unmanning of the male subject that looks at them, and ghosts – shadows that do not appear in America – always imply, therefore, feminised figures (the point will return with reference to *The Turn of the Screw*). The modern subject – Valerio – exists only by means of repression, and hardly exists in any completeness, for the narrator says of him (before the unearthing of this particular statue) that he seems absent-minded, not given to lively thought, almost stupid. In the tense he uses to his wife, it is evident that the statue of Juno holds no surprises for him – he has seen it before, has it with him constantly, has dreamed of its discovery. Under its influence, he lapses into a pagan state where he becomes, so the American thinks;

> a dark efflorescence of the evil germs which history had implanted in his line. No wonder he was foredoomed to be cruel. Was not cruelty a tradition in his race, and crime an example? The unholy passions of his forefathers revived, incurably, in his untaught nature and clamoured dumbly for an issue. What a heavy heritage it seemed to me, as I reckoned it up in my melancholy musings, the Count's interminable ancestry! Back to the profligate revival of arts and vices – back to the bloody medley of medieval wars – back through the long, fitfully glaring dusk of the early ages to its ponderous origin in the solid Roman state – back through all the darkness of history it stretched itself, losing every claim on my sympathies as it went. (p. 23)

Possessed by the ruined marble image, 'the modern man is shut out in the darkness' (p. 38), rendered ghostly. The ghostly historical becomes real.

Reading *The Last of the Valerii* as though Hawthorne had written it would suggest the need to live in the present, like the couple in his tale 'The May-Pole of Merry Mount' (1837), who under the influence of the Puritan John Endicott, forswear the superstitions and pleasures of the pagan fertility rites that have been brought almost accidentally to seventeenth-century America along with the Puritanism. The present is contracted, however, as the end of the tale suggests: 'They went heavenward, supporting each other along the difficult path which it was their lot to tread, and never wasted one regretful thought on the vanities of Merry Mount' (*Tales*, p. 184). The process of learning to live in this present is brought about by Endicott's violence with regards to the old pagan worship, speaking as it does of England and the old Europe. The achievement of Hawthorne's text is to have found something of the European spirit in the past of America, to have found a 'shadow'.

Hawthorne's Preface to *The Marble Faun* links ruins – fragmentary signs – via romance implicitly to allegory. Two forms of allegory play through Hawthorne's novel *The Scarlet Letter* (1850), which become one. Hester is condemned to wear the letter A, which makes her a character distinguished by an allegorical naming; an adulteress. 'Giving up her individuality, [Hester] would become the general symbol at which the preacher and moralist might point, and in which they might vivify and embody their images of woman's frailty and sinful passion. Thus the young and pure would be taught to look at her. . . as the figure, the body, the reality of sin.'[19] But this attempt to fix signification turns unstable under the gaze of those who would so fix the sign. *The Scarlet Letter*, chapter 13, 'Another View of Hester', affirms the impossibility of single interpretation, and the scarlet letter becomes a way of affirming Hester's being. Allegory unfixes, undoes systems of thought. With the half-awareness of the lability of images, Endicott cutting down the May-pole in 'The May-Pole of Merry Mount' suggests the desire to eliminate allegory and everything of the sign-nature of reality, to bring about a world of pure fixed meanings.

Hawthorne's tales play with fragmentation, and the use that his writings make of American history is to distort it, while apparently conforming to it and becoming inward with it; to fracture it, creating within it an other space, making it less commanding; folding a space for a shadow inside its lucidity. According to the preamble to 'The May-Pole of Merry Mount':

> There is an admirable foundation for a philosophical romance, in the
> curious history of the early settlement of Mount Wollaston, or Merry
> Mount. In the slight sketch here attempted, the facts, recorded on the
> grave pages of our New England annalists, have wrought themselves,
> almost spontaneously into a sort of allegory. (p. 172)

Hawthorne's doubleness about history, which as a text can only
become allegory, aligned with the feminine form of romance, means
that if he had written *The Last of the Valerii*, it would, recalling 'The
May-Pole of Merry Mount' and *The Marble Faun*, be an equivocal
summing up of the costs of America's modernness, indicating that,
despite the sense of America as shadowless, it is actually ghost-
ridden, the scene of ruins, demanding a romance form to understand
it. To claim America as without shadow is, by the time Hawthorne
has finished with its history, ironic. To read *The Last of the Valerii* as
not by James implies even more the importance of the past and the
unrepresentable. Rather than seeing Europe as 'ruins' in a negative
sense, Europe is the important other consciousness to America,
which has a double unconsciousness: in its own past, as brought to
light by Hawthorne, and in the past of Europe.

Hillis Miller reads *The Last of the Valerii* in two ways. Martha,
Valerio's wife (the name has 'practical' implications) and the father-
figure end by saving the Conte Valerio, but also (anticipating *The
Golden Bowl*) they '"see to it" that this handsome pagan Italian is
made the prisoner of their own values, in an unscrupulous violence of
expropriation and spiritual coercion that mimes the political and
commercial imperialism of the United States over Europe. The only
good European is a dead European. Martha and the narrator see to it
that Camillo the pagan dies for good, that he becomes the survivor of
his own death, the last of the Valerii.'[20] The American modern
banishes the uncanny, tries to efface unassimilable experience. The
Conte Valerio is, as the haunting premonitions from the statues
suggest, a figure of loss, ghostly (hence his absent-mindedness). He
represents that in Europe which ghosts America. Perhaps America
succeeds in exorcising it. A world made safe, protected, is also
diminished: it is an idea lurking at the heart of *The Turn of the
Screw*. The repression of the unseen, the smoothing out of history
connects sexuality with history. James writes this Hawthornian tale
to suggest the power of the unseen. The European realism of which
James was so aware will not do if it means the denial of doubleness, a

belief that everything can be fully stated and that it is possible to show everything. Writing History, if we recall James on Eliot, requires allegory and sexuality, sexuality as allegorical.

IV *THE AMBASSADORS*

In *The Ambassadors*, Lambert Strether has been sent to Paris by Chad Newsome's mother in Massachusetts, to check on Chad's sexual relationships, and bring him home. Strether is not a success at this, being temperamentally unfitted, and likely to be seduced by Paris, as appears in his words to the American art-student Little Bilham, 'Live all you can; it's a mistake not to' (5, 2, 153). Little Bilham, Chad's ambassador – his 'intimate and deputy' (3, 1, 79) – assures him that Chad has a 'virtuous attachment' (4, 2, 128). Strether does not discover from Bilham who the attachment is to, telling his friend Maria Gostrey, 'I found it a kind of refreshment not to feel obliged to follow up' (4, 2, 132). The two possible candidates for the attachment are revealed at the sculptor Gloriani's party (5, 2) – Madame de Vionnet and her daughter Jeanne. While others, including the Pococks (more Newsome family members sent as auxiliary ambassadors), assume that the relation is sexual, Strether deliberately does not, so getting away from New England morality.

Seeing 'the interest behind the interest' is paradigmatic for *The Ambassadors*, and Strether feels inadequate about what 'one *can* see'. In Paris, you can almost see things that have disappeared. Strether in 1900[21] has newly arrived in Paris, empire of the sexual sense, as Massachusetts interprets it. Crossing Paris on foot, he lingers in the garden of the Tuileries palace, destroyed by the Commune in 1871. He would have seen the palace the time that he and his young wife, newly married, had come to Paris immediately after the Civil War. With the palace gone, 'he filled out spaces with dim symbols of scenes; he caught the gleam of white statues' (2, 2, 55–6).

The gap, the absence, indicative of what a French Royalist might figure as analogous to a national castration, is both there and not there, supplemented by symbols produced through subjective vision as much as through the architectural supplements of statues, which give another sense of history, not history as psychic trauma but history as tradition. A related condition of absence appears later when Strether visits Chad's apartments when he is not there. Instead, objects, metonymies of Chad, provide him with 'strange suggestions, persuasions, recognitions'. Something has been added to vision: the uncanny is evoked in ghostly terms:

> The night was hot and heavy and the single lamp sufficient; the great flare of the lighted city, rising high, spending itself afar, played up from the Boulevard and, through the vague vista of the successive rooms, brought objects into view and added to their dignity. Strether found himself in possession as he never yet had been; he had been there alone; had turned over books and prints, had invoked, in Chad's absence, the spirit of the place, but never at the witching hour and never with a relish quite so like a pang.　(11, 1, 353–4)

The passage implicitly asks how the field of vision is set up, and suggests, as Lacan's psychoanalysis does, that it is constructed through desire which is premised on lack, the sense that something is missing, absent, in what is given to be seen. Strether is 'in possession' – possessed, held by something outside him, like Count Valerio, or in a position of domination. Perhaps these two things are the same: Strether is ghosting Chad, which means he has become other from what he was, or he is possessed by Chad and Chad's Paris. Whatever the case, there is something else in the room realist description cannot account for, quite, and if that is so, then the careful build-up of realist detail can never be adequate, save in so far as realism is also a desire for a totality which must disavow absence and fill out gaps. Things unseeable may appear in momentary clarity. The field of vision can always produce something else, vision can never be saturated. Putting these two extracts of Strether in Paris together, we might argue that looking contains within it a structure enabling things not to be seen, or things not seen are replaced by symbols which disavow the presence of loss. Objective looking becomes impossible. Strether's look combines satisfaction with a sense of absence: relish and a pang together.

There is something of fear in this, as when Strether at Gloriani's party feels that 'there was something in the great world covertly tigerish, which came to him across the lawn and in the charming air, as a waft from the jungle' (5, 2, 154). This is also erotic, since of the two people seen, 'it made him admire most of the two, made him envy, the glossy male tiger, magnificently marked'. None the less, the crisis – both 'charming' and terrifying which springs on him like a beast from the jungle – occurs when Strether, sure that there is nothing between Chad and Madame de Vionnet, is in the country, hoping to locate the setting of a picture, 'a certain small Lambinet' (11, 3, 380), which he has seen in Boston. He has felt himself, immersed in the country, to be 'in the picture' (11, 3, 385), not 'overstepp[ing] the oblong gilt frame'. He finds himself overlooking the river, and he sees[22]

> exactly the right thing – a boat advancing round the bend and contain-ing a man who held the paddles and a lady, at the stern, with a pink parasol. It was suddenly as if these figures, or something like them, had been wanted in the picture, had been wanted more or less all day, and had now drifted into sight, with the slow current, on purpose to fill up the measure. . . . For two very happy persons he found himself straight-way taking them – a young man in shirt-sleeves, a young woman easy and fair. . . . The air quite thickened at their approach, with further intimations; the intimation that they were expert, familiar, frequent – that this wouldn't at all events be the first time. They knew how to do it, he vaguely felt – and it made them but the more idyllic, though at the very moment of the impression, as happened, their boat seemed to have begun to drift wide, the oarsman letting it go. It had by this time none the less come much nearer – near enough for Strether to dream the lady in the stern had for some reason taken account of his being there to watch them. She had remarked on it sharply, yet her compan-ion hadn't turned round; it was in fact almost as if our friend had felt her bid him keep still. She had taken in something as a result of which their course had wavered, and it continued to waver while they just stood off. This little effect was sudden and rapid, so rapid that Strether's sense of it was separate only for an instant from a sharp start of his own. He too had within the minute taken in something, taken in that he knew the lady whose parasol, shifting as if to hide her face, made so fine a pink point in the shining scene. It was too prodigious, a chance in a million, but, if he knew the lady, the gentle-man who still presented his back and kept off, the gentleman, the coatless hero of the idyll, who had responded to her start, was, to match the marvel, none other than Chad.
>
> Chad and Madame de Vionnet were then like himself taking a day in the country – though it was as queer as fiction, as farce, that their country could happen to be exactly his; and she had been the first at recognition, the first to feel, across the water, the shock – for it appeared to come to that – of their wonderful accident. Strether became aware, with this, of what was taking place – that her recogni-tion had been even stranger for the pair in the boat, that her immediate impulse had been to control it, and that she was quickly and intensely

debating with Chad the risk of betrayal. He saw they would show nothing if they could be sure he hadn't made them out; so that he had before him for a few seconds his own hesitation. It was a sharp fantastic crisis that had popped up as if in a dream, and it had only to last the few seconds to make him feel it as quite horrible. They were thus, on either side, *trying* the other side, and all for some reason that broke the stillness like some unprovoked harsh note. It seemed to him again, within the limit, as if he had but one thing to do – to settle their common question by some sign of surprise and joy. He hereupon gave large play to these things, agitating his hat and his stick and loudly calling out. . . . The boat, in midstream, still went a little wild – which seemed natural, however, while Chad turned round, half springing up; and his good friend, after blankness and wonder, began gaily to wave her parasol. Chad dropped afresh to his paddles and the boat headed round, amazement and pleasantry filling the air meanwhile, and relief, as Strether continued to fancy, superseding mere violence. Our friend went down to the water under this odd impression as of violence averted – the violence of their having 'cut' him, out there in the eye of nature, on the assumption that he wouldn't know it.

(11, 4, 388–90)

Strether wanted to be reminded of the Lambinet picture, to use it as a mirror for himself (Lambert/Lambinet), and to be inside it, inside the imaginary 'oblong gilt frame' (11, 3, 381). In the country, he is 'freely walking about in it.' The frame 'had drawn itself out for him' (11, 3, 385). He wants to see a particular scene as a framed picture, as he also thinks of a Maupassant story (11, 3, 382), for his thinking is literary, framed by references that link him to his past. Yet he steps across the frame, outside and inside at once, to see 'exactly the right thing'.

'The right thing' implies 'the thing that fills up the picture: makes it right' – a boat coming along this river to increase the sense of pastoral tranquillity – and 'the thing that makes all the difference: the thing that constitutes an event'. If the second, it could be like the *punctum* of Roland Barthes in *Camera Lucida*, wounding and piercing the photograph's carefully composed *studium*. David McWhirter suggests that the fallacy in Strether's reveries in the countryside is that he is trying to put himself outside time: 'The very thing that completes the picture is also the thing that rips the picture from its frame and restores it to time; the filling in of the void in the picture eliminates that space where desire and imagination have lived.'[23] Punctual to Strether's imagination, which, as constructed by painting, has made the picture, is that which supplements it, but cancels it out.

It is as though he *conjures up* the boat,[24] needing it because the picture he is in is incomplete, and he is unconsciously aware of this. The unconscious intersects with the solicitations of art. Richard Hathaway compares the way the Lambinet picture takes over everything with Wallace Stevens's poem 'Anecdote of the Jar'. 'I placed a jar in Tennessee', this begins, but soon, as an emblem of art, the jar is organising everything around it ('It made the slovenly wilderness / Surround that hill') and soon, 'It took dominion everywhere.'[25] It becomes impossible to see outside the frame of reference imposed by art. Chad and Mme Vionnet are turned into appearance only, into Lambinet-like, or Impressionist art, one of hundreds of pictures of lovers in boats. And perhaps nothing else than appearance is to be known about anything: for, as Little Bilham says, 'What more than a vain appearance does the wisest of us know? I commend you . . . the vain appearance' (5, 1, 142). So when the lovers appear, that does not mean that a picture has been replaced by truth; rather, one representation replaces another. The picture was built up on a model of realism, but the realist imagination is impelled by the demand to know what else lurks in or haunts the picture, and so the lovers appear. The passive construction of the second sentence in the passage evades the question of Strether's responsibility for evoking them – 'it was as if these figures . . . had been wanted in the picture, had been wanted more or less all day'. 'Had been wanted' means 'had been wished for' – an unconsciously transgressive desire in Strether – or else 'had been lacking' – that which made the representation (the picture) inadequate. The appearance of the boat is a slight change of a detail which changes the representation, and the dislocation that has changed the representation is called a 'shock'. The German cultural critic Walter Benjamin makes shock definitional for understanding modernity, with its 'collisions' and 'dangerous crossings' (Benjamin, p. 132), as, for Barthes (*Camera Lucida*, p. 32), the *punctum* in the photograph is also a form of shock.

When the lovers appear, the air has 'thickened' so that the earlier clarity is replaced by an otherness, or haunting. Further 'intimations' follow, this repeated word including in it 'intimate' as well as meaning 'intuition'. 'They knew how to do it' has a sexual intimation; Strether feels so 'vaguely', the thought being conscious and unconscious, in and out of the picture. He locates the thought, recognising what has been given to him from his unconsciousness ('recognition', which is a 'shock', is repeated). He has to see that the thought is produced from what is happening in the middle of the picture and from his unconscious. But these are the same; the picture, giving way to these two in the boat, comes from an unconscious formed through art.

'Recognition', in Aristotle's *Poetics*, describes a key event in tragedy, when events understood one way have to be seen in another.[26] Recognition (*anagnoris*) succeeds the reversal (*peripeteia*) that Aristotle also discusses, and both happen here: *The Ambassadors* is Jamesian tragi-comedy (to be 'sighed ... at last all comically, all tragically away' [12, 5, 438]). But there is no final knowledge, no going outside representation into reality; Strether is still held by a picture which may still be inadequate to describe what is happening. We cannot assume that this is a concluding final discovery of the truth. The important word is not recognition but 'betrayal', which shows that things have not been as they were thought to be, but different.

Strether's shock so decentres him that it puts him in the position of the other: he can see what the occupants of the boat are thinking. What is 'strange' for him is more so for Mme de Vionnet; it is uncanny, and this betrays. The narration does not pick her out for special identification; while identifying Chad, it puts the two names together, as though there was no other woman it could be. The gap makes her the centre, the object of an emotional cathexis; a burden placed on her, as the woman out-of-place yet in the right place. She must react by control, otherwise she will be betrayed. (She may be betrayed by Chad at the end, or may not: we do not know whether he will leave her or not.) Strether may feel himself betrayed, and has been, but in the distribution of emotions, the betrayers – specifically the woman – fear betrayal by their own behaviour and feelings, and the betrayed person has to enable them to keep the sense of not being found out, so must allow them to go on betraying him.

V BETRAYAL AND *THE AMBASSADORS*

Betrayal is a key trope for James. In his self-re-readings over the last ten years of his life (re-writing his novels for the New York edition; writing Prefaces and *The American Scene* and his autobiography),

Strether was part of a self-identification. Sending a friend a copy of the book, he wrote, 'if you are able, successfully, to struggle with it try to like the poor old hero, in whom you will perhaps find a vague resemblance (though not facial!) to yours always HENRY JAMES'.[27] In this re-reading, he could see his whole life as betrayed, just as, when the First World War broke out, he wrote to Howard Sturgis:

> The plunge of civilization into this abyss of blood and darkness . . . it is a thing that so gives away the whole long age which we had gradually supposed the world to be, with whatever abatement, gradually better-ing, that to have to take it all now for what the treacherous years were really making for and *meaning* is too tragic for any words.[28]

'Civilization' has been misread, and the two uses of the word 'gradu-ally' focus the point. 'We had gradually supposed' suggests that there has been a slow acceptance of the illusions of civilization, coming to terms with its ideology and way of representing things. 'Gradually bettering' implies that this slow acceptance has been a systematic misreading, *not* seeing that things were getting worse. He has not been practised on; he has tricked himself (trickery and treachery are etymologically the same), betrayed himself. So has Strether, in the 1903 text, betrayed himself, misreading the signs, while the pair in the boat are anxious that they, who have tricked others, should not now become traitors to themselves (betrayal and traitor are also linked etymologically, as are betrayal and tradition), giving them-selves away.

But perhaps the traditional must be betrayed, else it is itself a form of betrayal. Writing to Hugh Walpole, in February 1915 James com-ments on his own form of representation, as tradition betrayed:

> The subject-matter of one's effort has become *itself* utterly treacherous and false – its relation to reality utterly given away and smashed. Reality is a world that was to be capable of *this* – and how represent that horrific capability, *historically* latent, historically ahead of it? How on the other hand *not* represent it either – without putting into play mere fiddlesticks?[29]

James, aged 72, reads his writing negatively, as though the war has shown up his work as false, like the cancellation of Strether's picture. His 'representation' of reality has failed to read it, unable to do justice to horrific latencies (the latent is uncanny). He has failed to do justice to what Strether thought of as the 'covertly tigerish', the unrepresentable.[30]

It is as though, for James not have felt betrayed by his plots, they would have had to have built into them *more* betrayal. *The Ambassadors* writes this deconstructive necessity into itself. In Book 2, chapter 2, reflecting in the Luxembourg Gardens, Strether thinks of the Paris fiction then available, and is reminded by its characteristic lemon-coloured covers of novels he had taken back with him to America in the 1860s, and perhaps never read. 'On this evidence... of the way they [the books in the shops] actually affected him he glared at the lemon-coloured covers in confession of the subconsciousness that, all the same, in the great desert of the years, he must have had of them' (2, 2, 61–2). He took books to America which, if he had read them, would have given him a different kind of education from that in Massachusetts, where he has been editing a journal – with green covers, like the *North American Review* – containing no literature, but economics, politics and ethics, fitting New England's secular puritanism. Back in Paris, widowed, his child also dead (2, 2, 59) – both unnamed, neither having had more than the ghost of an existence – he is widowed metaphorically, deprived of the missed education, and thinking of Massachusetts as like 'the great desert' – like James's 'treacherous years', but with the implication also of emptiness, and an empty history.

Strether's books would have included Balzac. Strether is familiar with some Balzac because his first names are 'Lewis Lambert'. Maria Gostrey says *Louis Lambert* (1832) is the name of an 'awfully bad' novel by Balzac (1, 1, 9).[31] 'Awfully bad' by realist criteria, Balzac's tale is of the boyhood and youth of a genius who believes that 'in each of us there are two distinct beings' – like Strether's 'double consciousness' (1, 1, 2) – and that the aim must be to become like Swedenborg's angel, 'in whom the inner being conquers the external being'.[32] Life is constructed by a belief in the power of the will over the body, and the New Gospel is not *Et Verbum caro factum est* (And the Word was made flesh) but its converse, disincarnation: 'The Flesh shall be made the Word and become the Utterance of God' (p. 276). Such idealism makes Louis Lambert unfit for life in the world, and the night before his wedding he is 'preparing to perform on himself the operation to which Origen believed he owed his talents' – castration (p. 264). He has gone mad, cataleptic, beginning from the moment when his view shifted from 'pure idealism to the most intense sensualism' (p. 262), from which he violently reacts. The Balzacian name implies something impotent about Strether's relationship to the world and to women, but also the destructive power of naming. Strether is *not* that which European tradition would make him. The passage describing Strether's reflections in the Luxembourg Gardens parallels Book 11. It constructs Strether's life as one that may have failed to respond to other possibilities, the life implied in French fiction. In doing so, it points up Strether's own culpability in not reading the situation adequately, bringing about embarrassment and compromise. Everyone must tacitly agree to lie about the situation: Chad and Madame de Vionnet cannot say they were planning to spend the night together at the inn.

The key is the word 'subconsciously' (2, 2, 61), which articulates with Strether's 'double consciousness'. Though Strether has been aware of the books being 'somewhere' at home, in another sense, he has known what they stood for, and the message of sexuality they encoded. Chad and Mme de Vionnet are Balzacian characters whose appearance on the river, which I come back to, suggests that they haunt Strether like the books he has taken to heart only unconsciously. The unconscious rises with these figures on the river, who cancel out earlier acceptable – conscious – representations. The unconscious betrays, subverting the controlled and organized way the conscious mind works, revealing what was always known – that this is a 'typical tale of Paris' (12, 1, 398) – revealing the uncanny, since the uncanny is the familiar which is also, on account of repression, unfamiliar. As Strether's picture which is cancelled out, betrayed by the approach of the lovers, is the production of repression, a fetishistic landscape warding off the sexual, so the lovers are in danger of betrayal by their unconscious: they are no more free than Strether is, their boating idyll as much a product of painting, as though they were putting themselves into an Impressionist landscape. In this 'sharp fantastic crisis that had popped up as if in a dream' the antagonists are, 'on either side, *trying* the other side'. Strether, for a moment, is acting outside his idyll, and becoming the adulterous couple. They have been startled out of *their* idyll into a perception of different possibilities. Should they ignore Strether, in a process of 'violence' and a 'cut' – the word implying castration? If they carried on, would not this be attempting to keep in their enclosed world, where the parasol enacts an approach to reality which evades it? (It also acts like those 'sails' and 'veils' that, according to Derrida writing on Nietzsche, characterise feminine styles, warding off the will to truth. Mme de Vionnet certainly has not, like some masculine philosopher of truth, 'forgotten her umbrella'.[33]) Or, instead of working 'on the assumption that he wouldn't know it,' should the lovers acknowledge his presence? The scene on the river bank is full of other possibilities, and works by suggesting a problematic contingency whatever happens whenever. It suggests there is no single deep 'truth' to a situation, which the end discovers, even though Strether goes through a form of despair in thinking about 'the deep, deep truth of the intimacy revealed', in a reiteration which attributes a value to sexuality, as though this was the truth of the situation:

> That was what, in his vain vigil, he oftenest reverted to: intimacy, at such a point, was *like* that – and what in the world else would one have wished it to be like? It was all very well for him to feel the pity of its being so much like lying; he almost blushed in the dark, for the way in which he had dressed the possibility in vagueness, as a little girl might have dressed her doll. (11, 4, 396)

He has known all along what it was like, but disavowed it: this is virtually Freud's definition of the uncanny, and the uncanny has betrayed him by re-entering his field of vision. But there is an index to the construction of character in Strether's rhetoric of shame, including the image of the girl dressing the doll (hiding its sexual parts, where the dress already conceals their absence). No less interesting than this half-awareness of the doll and the dress of the doll as two forms of the fetish is Strether's siding with the girl's part.[34]

He virtually blushes in the dark, blushing in this context being hysterical, a mark of betrayal, since it is an involuntary movement of the body, resisting the mind's control. But blushing parallels Mme de Vionnet's turning her *pink* parasol as though hiding her face. Going for a belief in depth is the consequence of trying to evade appearances. Strether imagines Maria Gostrey saying to him reproachfully, '"What on earth – that's what I want to know now – had you then supposed?"' His embarrassment is that 'he had really been trying all along to suppose nothing' (11, 4, 396). The adulterous affair of Mme de Vionnet and Chad has been obvious to everyone – out there on the surface: plain, for instance to the unimaginative American Waymarsh as soon as he learned that there was a nice smell (or scent) in Chad's

flat: where there is a scent, there must be a woman (3, 1, 73). Sarah
Pocock, Chad's sister, has no illusions, telling Strether that Mme de
Vionnet is not 'even an apology for a decent woman' (10, 3, 349).
The appearance has been absolutely right. Hence, we can go back to
the quotation given of the meeting on the river and say that what
Strether saw *was* 'the right thing', conforming absolutely to appearances. In believing in the relation as a virtuous attachment, Strether
wants to evade the appearance of things as they are. But what is seen
on the surface, or what is known through textuality, *is* the palpable
reality. There is no fetish, since there is no hidden reality. Strether,
recognising this in conversation with Maria Gostrey, says that the
phrase 'virtuous attachment' to describe the relationship 'was a view
for which there was much to be said' (12, 3, 419). In one way, seeing
Mme de Vionnet and Chad together is a plot, a 'plant' to depress
Strether and make him think reductively, in single terms, about the
sexual. In another way, there has been no conclusion, and the plant is
only a plant, an attempt to frame. There is no 'truth' to be learned in
the situation.

Woollett, manufacturing the 'vulgar' household product whose
name is never given (2, 1, 42), suggests a dour realism producing
its own casualties. In this novel, which is surely about America, Mrs
Newsome is 'an American invalid' (2, 1, 39) while Waymarsh's wife
is also an invalid who cannot live in America. Opposed to New
England's 'sacred rage' (1, 3, 32) epitomised in Waymarsh – the spirit
of Puritan-inherited protest against European tradition and deception, European betrayal – is the 'visual sense' of Paris (5, 1, 145). This
delights in the surface, in the 'vain appearance'. That last, as a
phrase, says that what is seen on the surface is not reality; but it
tells Strether to be content with that. The spirit that looks for truth,
for what things 'really are' – the Nietzschean or Foucauldian will to
truth – is laughed at as what the *femme du monde* at Gloriani's party,
Miss Barrace (rhyming with Paris) calls 'your Boston "reallys"' (5, 1,
146).

But Bostonian commitment to truth, to what things really are, is
also superficial. In *The Bostonians* (1876) James mocks advertising:
Selah Tarrant considers 'human existence...a huge publicity' (*The
Bostonians*, 13, 89) and Matthew Pardon believes in nothing but 'the
cultivation of the great arts of publicity' (*The Bostonians*, 16, 107).
Now, in 'our roaring age' (12, 4, 431), advertising is 'the great new
force'. Advertisers are ambassadors, in an 'art' like any other, and

infinite, like all the arts. 'The secret of trade' is the uncanny thing that disturbs the careful rules of commerce – it affects the sale of the object advertised 'extraordinarily, beyond what one had supposed'. There is no relation between reality and its representation in advertising, nor any relation between the worth of the object and its inflated status in word and image and in sales. Advertising, a product of New England industry, is the 'vain appearance' betraying the tradition of Bostonian sobriety and commitment, and meaning that art – like Strether's Review, which is financed by industry – becomes dependent upon a prior form of treachery within language, the ability to sell goods. Betraying that Boston, it shows it up as having been lightweight and selective in the way it chose to represent itself all along. The logic of betrayal means that *The Ambassadors* does not find advertising negative, for the trade that has taken off through being publicised was, historically, set up on mendacious grounds, as Strether intimates to Maria Gostrey.

Strether's learning of all this makes him 'the outgoing ambassador' (8, 1, 249) – no longer of service, who can no longer be an ambassador, because whatever Paris is, however much even its 'visual sense' – the clue to advertising – may deceive, there is no more reality to be found in Boston. Maria Gostrey was in Paris also as an ambassador, an 'agent for repatriation . . . to repeople our stricken country' (1, 3, 24) – to return Americans to America, to prop up genteel, business-orientated American ideology. Losing his ambassadorial position, Strether goes beyond Maria Gostrey, who hangs on to certain illusions.

Ambassadors need a double consciousness as much as bi-lingualism. At Gloriani's party, Mme de Vionnet speaks to a 'Duchesse', a *femme du monde*. Any Duchesse, however, needs ambassadors:

> One of the gentlemen . . . succeeded in placing himself in close relation with our friend's companion, a gentleman rather stout and importantly short, in a hat with a wonderful wide curl to its brim and a frock coat buttoned with an effect of superlative decision. His French had quickly turned to equal English, and it occurred to Strether that he might well be one of the ambassadors. His design was evidently to assert a claim to Madame de Vionnet's undivided countenance, and he made it good in the course of a minute – led her away with a trick of three words; a trick played with a social art of which Strether, looking after them as the four, whose backs were now all turned, moved off, felt himself no master. (5, 2, 151)

Strether, deputed by Mrs Newsome, the 'Queen Elizabeth' of Woollett (2, 1, 35), is no professional ambassador. Perhaps James had seen Holbein's *Portrait of Francis I's Ambassadors to the Court of Henry VIII, Jean de Dinteville and Georges de Selve* (1533), which the British National Gallery bought in 1890.[35] Holbein, the painter of Anne of Cleves, acted as ambassador and artist; painting does the work of an embassy. Adeline Tintner's suggestion that the painting of 'The Ambassadors' lies behind James's text and title seems good, but its importance is not so much in its attention to time and death and living all you can, as she argues, but in its anamorphosis, where 'the spectator must literally shape (*morphe*) again (*ana*) the image in order to see it correctly'.[36] The skull in the picture that rises up from the floor between the two furred and gowned ambassadors breaks the frame, and requires a double perspective and double consciousness to see it. It needs a realist 'take' – though this must also absorb allegorical details – and another, cancelling this one out. The skull, a *memento mori*, is the uncanny, the troubling detail in the picture which undoes everything else, as death betrays the worldly riches in the picture. It is the added thing interrupting the field of vision, but also constructing it, so that it takes dominion everywhere.

It is not enough to be committed to nothing but the 'vain appearance', for 'The Ambassadors' shows that appearance cannot be read in single terms. *The Ambassadors* shows no less that an appearance contains its own uncanny. The point applies to advertising, which exists in textual form so that, like Strether tipping the waiter and being told 'you give too much' (4, 2, 127), it too gives too much. Plotting – where nothing is certain, including the destinies of any of the major characters – and textuality go together. Working through the text, with its time-shifts, its recalls of memory ('our friend was to go over it afterwards again and again' – 3, 2, 95), its elusive viewpoints, its evasiveness in specifying, is to face and track the uncanny within its pages.

3

Histories of Sexuality in *The Portrait of a Lady* and *The Bostonians*

Could there be a slenderer, more insignificant thread in human history than this consciousness of a girl, busy with her small inferences of the way in which she could make her life pleasant? – in a time, too, when ideas were with fresh vigour making armies of themselves, and the universal kinship was declaring itself fiercely...?

What in the midst of that mighty drama are girls and their blind visions? They are the Yea or Nay of that good for which men are enduring and fighting. In these delicate vessels is borne onward through the ages the treasure of human affections.

George Eliot, Daniel Deronda[1]

...the wonder being, all the while, as we look at the world, how inordinately the Isabel Archers, and even much smaller female fry, insist on mattering. George Eliot has admirably noted it – 'In these frail vessels is borne onward through the ages, just as, in "Adam Bede" and "The Mill on the Floss" and "Middlemarch" and "Daniel Deronda", Hetty Sorrel and Maggie Tulliver and Rosamond Vincy and Gwendolen Harleth have to be...'

AN, 3, 49

In the Preface for the 1908 New York edition of *The Portrait of a Lady*, James affirms the novel's relationship to George Eliot. *Middlemarch* (1872) and *Daniel Deronda* (1876) raise issues of gender and sexuality which James picks up on in *The Portrait of a Lady* and *The Bostonians*, the texts I discuss in this chapter.[2] These, in turn, allow a re-reading of George Eliot, who in any case called forth one of James's most provocative ways of writing criticism, '*Daniel Deronda*: A Conversation'. In this trialogue, Theodora, whose name complements Dorothea in *Middlemarch*, discusses the possibility of tragedy associated with women that George Eliot writes, and that licenses both Isabel Archer, enticed into marrying disastrously, and Olive Chancellor, the Bostonian feminist:

> Gwendolen is a perfect picture of youthfulness – its eagerness, its presumption, its preoccupation with itself, its vanity and silliness, its sense of its own absoluteness. But she is extremely intelligent and clever, and therefore tragedy *can* have a hold upon her. Her conscience doesn't make the tragedy; that is an old story and, I think, a secondary form of suffering. It is the tragedy that makes her conscience, which then reacts upon it; and I can think of nothing more powerful than the way in which the growth of her conscience is traced, nothing more touching than the picture of its hopeless maturity.
>
> (Gard, p. 119)

The other woman in the trialogue is Pulcheria whose name recalls Pulchérie, the pleasure-loving sister in George Sand's novel *Lélia*. The French novel as a type poses other issues for James, which fit uneasily with George Eliot, so, in this chapter, which examines the texts Leavis in *The Great Tradition* made so much of in comparing James with Eliot, I want to proceed via Eliot and Hawthorne, closing with the alignments of *The Portrait of a Lady* with a different writer from either of these two: Flaubert.

I   *THE PORTRAIT OF A LADY*

Why does James substitute Rosamond Vincy for Dorothea Brooke when listing George Eliot's heroines in the Preface to *The Portrait of a Lady*? Dorothea would have been the 'natural' choice; Rosamond embodies everything Dorothea is not (and is unlike Gwendolen as described by Theodora). Rosamond marries the young doctor Tertius Lydgate and spoils his career. James is as critical as need be of her in his initial review of *Middlemarch*, saying that she 'represents, in a measure, the fatality of British decorum' (Gard, p. 79). The same review uses language suggestive for *The Portrait of a Lady* (written seven years later) in commenting on Dorothea. James refers to the 'eloquent preface' to *Middlemarch*, saying 'an ardent young girl was to have been the central figure' (Gard, p. 75).

So, Isabel Archer marries Osmond in 'ardent good faith' (*The Portrait of a Lady*, ch. 34, p. 294: the 1881 version reads 'passionate' for 'ardent'). Rosamond's instatement as a heroine in James's Preface complicates this reading, and it is a point to start with when noting that the other heroine of *Middlemarch* (Dorothea) and Gwendolen Harleth, the heroine of *Daniel Deronda*, are both in tears after or during their wedding-night. *Daniel Deronda* names the tears when Grandcourt, dressed for dinner, comes into her room on their first night of marriage: 'The sight of him brought a new nervous shock, and Gwendolen screamed again and again with *hysterical* violence' (31, 407, my emphasis). Hysteria, in the last thirty years of the nineteenth century, partly through the discourse of Charcot, Janet, Breuer and Freud, was in its 'heroic period' – 'la période héroïque de l'hystérie', as it was called in a conference in 1907.[3] This discourse labelled women as likely to become hysterical at some period, to be inherently unstable, and since hysteria, after 1860, was coupled with madness, suggested that women could not be separated from the category of madness.[4] This is part of the tendency at work in the modern period and symbolised in Pinel's lifting the manacles from the insane in 1795 – a scene rendered symbolic for this 'heroic' period by Robert-Fleury's famous 1878 painting of the incident – to collapse the distinction between the mad and the rest of society.

Gwendolen Harleth has been terrified by the jewels and by Lydia Glasher's letter, which proves that Grandcourt has no moral entitlement to marry Gwendolen, while she has chosen to marry him, repressing that information from herself (and her knowledge of it from him). She has lost a gamble. In *Middlemarch*, the bridegroom, Mr Casaubon, forty-seven, only seven years older than Osmond and not the old man he is sometimes thought to be, has decided before the wedding that 'the poets had much exaggerated the force of masculine passion',[5] and that asexuality corresponds to something in Dorothea ('Her mind was theoretic' – [1, 30]). In Rome, she weeps confronted with the city's 'stupendous fragmentariness': Rome's art, a revelation of sexual otherness, forces an awareness of the repressed onto the bride:

> Ruins and basilicas, palaces and colossi, set in the midst of a sordid
> present, where all that was living and warm-blooded seemed sunk in

the deep degeneracy of a superstition divorced from reverence; the dimmer but yet eager Titanic life gazing and struggling on walls and ceilings; the long vistas of white forms whose marble eyes seemed to hold the monotonous light of an alien world: all this vast wreck of ambitious ideals, sensuous and spiritual, mixed confusedly with the signs of breathing forgetfulness and degradation, at first jarred her as with an electric shock, and then urged themselves on her with that ache belonging to a glut of confused ideas which check the flow of emotion. Forms both pale and glowing took possession of her young sense, and fixed themselves in her memory even when she was not thinking of them, preparing strange associations which remained through her after-years....[I]in certain states of dull forlorness Dorothea all her life continued to see the vastness of St Peter's, the huge bronze canopy, the excited intention in the attitudes and garments of the prophets and evangelists in the mosaics above, and the red drapery which was being hung for Christmas spreading itself everywhere like a disease of the retina.   (20, 225–6)

Dorothea tells Ladislaw that she sees the art in Rome as 'often low and brutal', and that she rejects the mimetic since 'most of our lives would look much uglier and more bungling than the pictures, if they could be put on the wall'. Ladislaw replies:

You talk as if you had never known any youth. It is monstrous – as if you had had a vision of Hades in your childhood, like the boy in the legend. You have been brought up in some of those horrible notions that choose the sweetest women to devour – like Minotaurs.

(22, 253)

Not just Mr Casaubon's sexual deadness has caused Dorothea's tears. She is unable to look, so that the confrontation with Rome, a caesura which she recalls 'all her life', is a moment of recognition, rather than wholly new, a recall to emotions, and so linked with other memories which are not necessarily literal – coming back and being 'interwoven with moods of despondency', as Eliot says, describing how Peter Featherstone's funeral makes Dorothea lonely (34, 360). The tears in Rome are not isolated; Dorothea, who heard 'the great organ at Freiberg, and it made me sob' (7, 90), sobs for a night after she has surprised Ladislaw and Rosamond together, in chapter 77. The 'loud-whispered cries and moans' which 'subsided into helpless sobs' (80, 845) on account of Ladislaw, whom Dorothea feels she has lost, are not called hysterical: the chapter sublimates that assertion of the woman's sexuality, revealed in her body's uncontrollable behaviour, because it justifies her desire as the grounds for duty and altruism: 'She yearned towards the perfect Right, that it might make a throne within her, and rule her errant will' (80, 846). So she feels in the morning after her weeping. But Rosamand, displacing Dorothea's emotion after the scene with Ladislaw, who, after Dorothea's exit, breaks into self-reproaches and accusations, returns to Lydate and falls 'into hysterical sobbings and cries' (78, 838). Rosamond stands in for Dorothea and enables the sobbings of the heroine to be sublimated, to be not officially recognised as hysterical. That seems to be a textual repression which repeats Dorothea's own; the aetiology of the sobs (overdetermined by the point that Dorothea is still in mourning and in mourning dress) cannot even be explained fully by the fact that she feels she has been betrayed by Ladislaw, though it is significant that what makes her lose 'self-possession' (77, 832) is that she has been compelled to look.

In *Daniel Deronda* Gwendolen is also afraid to look. She sees in the house at Offendene, in a hinged panel set in the wall, 'the picture of an upturned dead face, from which an obscure figure seemed to be fleeing with outstretched arms'. Gwendolen's reaction (compared with that of her younger sister Isabel, whose name makes her part of the pre-history of *The Portrait of a Lady*) is extreme, as also when she unexpectedly sees the picture again – when with a piercing cry she is frozen, unable to move, 'a statue into which a soul of Fear had entered' (6, 91). Hysteria – which immobilises the body – produces allegory (no wonder Charcot's patients at the Salpêtrière were so photogenic), just as an allegorical figure itself – something like a Cain and Abel rendering – induces an allegorical response.

The upturned dead face reappears in Gwendolen's account of Grandcourt drowning when she and he were together in the boat, and how she saw 'the dead face – dead, dead' (56, 761). The memory of Grandcourt is overdetermined by the earlier face. It is not that the picture anticipates the end of Grandcourt, so that Gwendolen, describing herself in the boat as 'leaping away from my crime', makes herself the Cain of this accident, but rather that it memorialises an image which Gwendolen has already repressed, which accordingly reappears to haunt her. As she repeats, 'it can never be altered'. Her shock when Grandcourt enters the room on her wedding night suggests the repetition of the trauma: she has killed Lydia Glasher's hopes and has repressed the knowledge of that, and now is made to face seeing herself through the eyes of another (through Lydia Glasher's assessment) and is paralysed by it.

II 'GUESSING THE UNSEEN'

The Ambassadors, discussed in the previous chapter, illustrated James's obsession with the field of vision which yet contains something else not quite seen, and not wholly readable. In *The Portrait of a Lady* that obsession appears again under the direct influence of these scenes from George Eliot. Isabel in chapter 40 comes back from a walk in the Campagna and passes into her drawing-room:

> Just beyond the threshold of the drawing room she stopped short, the reason for her doing so being that she had received an impression.... Madame Merle was there in her bonnet, and Gilbert Osmond was talking to her; for a minute they were unaware she had come in. Isabel had often seen that before, certainly; but what she had not seen, or at least not noticed, was that their colloquy had for the moment converted itself into a sort of familiar silence, from which she instantly perceived that her entrance would startle them. Madame Merle was standing on the rug, a little way from the fire; Osmond was in a deep chair, leaning back and looking at her. Her head was erect, as usual, but her eyes were bent on his. What struck Isabel first was that he was sitting while Madame Merle stood; there was an anomaly in this that arrested her. Then she perceived that they had arrived at a desultory pause in their exchange of ideas and were musing, face to face, with the freedom of old friends who sometimes exchange ideas without uttering them. There was nothing to shock in this; they were old friends in fact. But the thing made an image, lasting only a moment, like a sudden flicker of light. Their relative positions, their absorbed mutual gaze, struck her as something detected. But it was all over by the time she had fairly seen it. Madame Merle had seen her and had welcomed her without moving; her husband, on the other hand, had instantly jumped up. (40, 342–3)

An 'impression' becomes an 'image'. According to Walter Benjamin, 'Anything about which one knows that one soon will not have it around becomes an image.'[6] An image is produced when something is disappearing; it is because the sight of Madame Merle and Osmond together – seen like a photographic shot – fades as it is seen (their relation is also coming to an end) that it impresses itself on Isabel, making her (like a novelist) 'guess the unseen from the seen', as 'The Art of Fiction' puts it (Gard, p. 195). What she guesses is something obscene, and it happens in chapter 42, when, as James put it in the Preface, 'she sits up, by her dying fire, far into the night, under the spell of recognitions on which she finds the last sharpness suddenly wait. It is a representation simply of her motionlessly *seeing*, and attempt withal to make her mere still lucidity of her act as "interesting" as the surprise of a caravan or the identification of a pirate' (*AN*, 57). In her night-time vigil, deriving from chapter 80 of *Middlemarch* as much as from seeing Osmond and Madame Merle together (which derives from Dorothea's seeing Ladislaw and Rosamond), the chapter closes as she 'stopped again in the middle of the room and stood there gazing at a remembered vision – that of her husband and Madame Merle unconsciously and familiarly associated' (42, 364). 'Associated' implies the sexual, as though Isabel is beginning to intuit as an image – something that cannot be described because it is not in what *can* be described – the sexual connection between the two. This is the power of the afterlife of the image, and it works in a temporal dimension.

The picture that yields an image which cannot quite be read, and remains to haunt is allegorical, and is at the heart of James's interest. *The Portrait of a Lady* flags its interest in allegory via Mrs Touchett, who says 'I could never understand allegories' (26, 235). This is the woman whose desire for complete self-possession, and lack of awareness of otherness, take the form of saying to Isabel after Ralph has died, 'Go and thank God you've no child' (55, 480), as a way of 'disengaging' herself from the other, and forgetting Isabel's own brief history of motherhood (Isabel gave birth to a boy, who died). The text wishes us to read otherwise than Mrs Touchett.

Dorothea's loss of self-possession is the discovery that Rosamond is in the place where she would like to be; similarly Gwendolen Harleth has wanted to supplant Lydia Glasher, but is removed from that place by Lydia Glasher's letter and the jewels, visible presence to everyone of her own lack of possession, of position. Lydia Glasher and Grandcourt reappear, with certain differences, as Madame Merle and Osmond in *The Portrait of a Lady*, and Isabel's half-awareness of her own lack of place – in chapter 40, she is on the threshold, in a liminal position – comes from seeing that Madame Merle, standing while Osmond sits, has no place. When Isabel stands in the middle of the room, in chapter 42, that space is invaded by, as it were, the ghosts of Madame Merle and Osmond. *The Portrait of a Lady*, since it ends with flight – Isabel running from Goodwood, and then returning to Rome, to the home where she has been displaced – dramatises a loss of position. In this novel, Grandcourt, who takes away Gwendolen's position in *Daniel Deronda*, has actually become a place – Gardencourt – and it is an aspect of Isabel's initial confidence in herself that she should feel it lodges no threat. Its danger is suggested when Isabel first hears the name of Gilbert Osmond there, in chapter 19, from Madame Merle; and it becomes the scene of hysteria at the end when she freezes – with 'set teeth' – before reacting with repulsion from Caspar Goodwood's attempts to kiss her. Before she is kissed she turns away from the phenomenon of Goodwood's love for her: she says she is going back to Rome and to her husband to get away from him:

> But this expressed only a little of what she felt. The rest was that she had never been loved before. She had believed it, but this was different; this was the hot air of the desert, at the approach of which the others dropped dead, like mere sweet airs of the garden. It wrapped her about; it lifted her off her feet, while the very taste of it, as of something potent, acrid and strange, forced open her set teeth. (55, 488)

Goodwood has not yet kissed her, but a moment later he does, and here James expands, in the revision, on what he wrote in 1881 – 'His kiss was like a flash of lightning; when it was dark again she was free':

> His kiss was like white lightning, a flash that spread, and spread again, and stayed; and it was extraordinarily as if, while she took it, she felt each thing in his hard manhood that had least pleased her, each aggressive fact of his face, his figure, his presence, justified of its intense identity and made one with this act of possession. So had she heard of those wretched and under water following a train of images before they sink. But when darkness returned, she was free. She never looked about her; she only darted from the spot. (55, 489)

In symmetry with this ending, *The Bostonians*, James's next novel, ends with Basil Ransom grabbing Verena 'by muscular force' and running with her into the street, away from Olive Chancellor. 'But though she was glad...she was in tears. It is to be feared that with the union, so far from brilliant, into which she was about to enter, these were not the last she was destined to shed' (42, 389–90). *The*

Bostonians closes with a comment on male power, and Verena's tears link with Dorothea's and Gwendolen's.

Caspar Goodwood exists in sexualised images in Isabel's consciousness. In terms anticipating the ending of the novel, she thinks early on that 'there was a disagreeably strong push, a hardness of presence, in his way of rising before her' (13, 105). This differs from the writing in 1881, which says 'There was something too forcible, something oppressive and restrictive, in the manner in which he presented himself.' The later version intensifies the phallicism, and contributes to the force of the 1908 self-assessment that Caspar Goodwood makes in relation to Isabel: 'I disgust you very much' (16, 137; the 1881 has 'displease'). The disgusting cannot be incorporated, taken into the system and swallowed, and Isabel has 'set her teeth' against it, as though fearing that the challenge from what she regards as disgusting comes to her mouth – the attempt to enter her body by the means of a kiss. James on Isabel's reaction, and Freud's discourse on hysteria in the 'Dora' case, have been linked. Commenting on the fourteen-year-old girl being kissed by Herr K—, a friend of her father's, and being made aware – in Freud's fantasies – of *his* 'hard manhood', Freud finds her disgust hysterical – 'I should without question consider a person hysterical in whom an occasion for sexual excitement elicited feelings that were predominantly or exclusively unpleasurable.'[7] Hysteria is the body's reaction to not fitting into the heterosexuality of the symbolic order, and Freud, at this moment in his discourse, aligns himself with the symbolic order.

If we linked Gwendolen Harleth's fear of the picture at Offendene, and its theme of running away, with the end of *The Portrait of a Lady*, it would seem that sexual intercourse and murder are being aligned. Gwendolen's repudiation of the sexual repeats her reaction to the allegory when, early on, she is the object of Rex Gascoigne's attentions:

> He [Rex] tried to take her hand, but she hastily eluded his grasp and moved to the other end of the hearth, facing him.
> 'Pray don't make love to me! I hate it.' She looked at him fiercely.
> . . . Gwendolen herself could not have foreseen that she should feel in this way. (7, 114)

Her hysterical reaction to Rex, paralysing, murderous, puts her outside the symbolic order, which dictates heterosexuality and marriage (as the social order pronounces that she has a choice: to marry or to be a governess). Similarly, Isabel, who wonders 'if she were not a cold, hard, priggish person' (12, 102), resists, in conversation with Ralph, the notion that she wants to 'see life' as 'young men' see it (i.e., in a sexually knowing way). 'But I do want to look about me,' she adds:

> 'You want to drain the cup of experience.'
> 'No, I don't want to touch the cup of experience. It's a poisoned drink. I only want to see for myself.'
> 'You want to see, but not to feel,' Ralph remarked.
> 'I don't think that if one's a sentient being one can make the distinction.' (15, 134)

What 'seeing' means – where seeing is learning to look at something allegorically, to read a situation for a content other than literal – appears when Isabel sees her husband and Madame Merle together. Seeing allegorically also means feeling, but what is to be taken in is analogous to the primal scene: a scene of sexual betrayal that is produced in the power of an image. The image confirms her earlier insight that the 'cup of experience', against which she 'sets her teeth', is sexual, the poison being experience of the man.

The sexuality of men is problematic in all the texts I have discussed. Grandcourt's sadism towards Gwendolen conveys some idea of sexual relations between men and women being violent, and James seems to side with the oppressiveness of the male by making Gilbert Osmond in *The Portrait of a Lady* a compound of the worst and the worst – both Casaubon and Grandcourt at once. When Isabel reflects that 'they were strangely married at all events and it was a horrible life. Until that morning he had scarcely spoken to her for a week; his manner was as dry as a burned-out fire' (42, 363), the marriage appears sexless. When Osmond puts his hand 'gently' on Goodwood's knee and says that he and his wife are 'as united, you know, as the candlestick and the snuffers' (48, 420), the conscious and unconscious implications of the phrase, following on that action of ambivalent sexuality, upsets gender-relations. Which is which in Osmond's comparison? Who annihilates whom? But it is not just that sexual possibilities between husband and wife are closed. Osmond, like Casaubon, is conventional and his thinking about art, like Casaubon's about mythology, unoriginal. Both fit the title 'sterile dilettante' (34, 292), as Ralph Touchett calls Osmond. Isabel's fault – 'she had effaced herself when he knew her; she had made herself small, pretending there was less of her than there really was' (42, 357) – is analogous to Dorothea's with Casaubon's in that she has denied her desire. As Casaubon is frightened of Dorothea, Osmond is not 'comfortable' (49, 436) with his marriage. And Grandcourt's egotism and narcissism continue from elements of Casaubon.

There is a difference between Grandcourt and Osmond: *The Portrait of a Lady* and *The Bostonians* associate violence with *American* men making love. Caspar Goodwood, the cotton-mill manufacturer from Massachusetts, is described in *The Portrait of a Lady*, chapter 13, as a Harvard graduate, and Harvard after the Civil War was America's gymnasium for the cultivation of masculine values and the new quality of 'masculinity' (a word which came into play by 1890).[8] Goodwood at Harvard 'gained renown rather as a gymnast and an oarsman than as a gleaner of more dispersed knowledge' (13, 105). Even this recalls *Middlemarch*: Goodwood's American education parallels Lydgate's English one (*Middlemarch*, chapter 15) while Goodwood's industrial patent (13, 106) echoes Lydgate's ambition to become an original researcher. Lydgate's sexual values, going for the actress Madame Laure, recur in Basil Ransom. In *The Bostonians*, Ransom, interrogated by Olive Chancellor, his feminist cousin, 'couldn't believe that he was one of *her* kind; he was conscious of much Bohemianism – he drank beer in New York cellars, knew no ladies, and was familiar with a "variety" actress' (3, 18). Reviewing *Middlemarch*, James comments that 'towards the end, these two fine characters [Dorothea and Lydgate] are brought into momentary contact so effectively as to suggest a wealth of dramatic possibility between them' (Gard, p. 78). This contact is played out in James between the Southerner and the feminist: Dorothea becoming Olive Chancellor – the intellectual who, unlike Casaubon, reads German.

III *THE BOSTONIANS*

While Isabel Archer absorbs features of Dorothea and Gwendolen, and reads 'the prose of George Eliot' (4, 42), she looks forward to the feminist of *The Bostonians*, Olive Chancellor – she and Verena being the two Bostonians of the title – whose house at Marmion 'had all George Eliot's writings' (36, 309). The passage which links the two is where Isabel Archer meets the sisters of Lord Warburton, the two Miss Molyneux, two unmarried ladies, not in their first youth, and evidently destined to remain unmarried:

> 'They're not *morbid*, at any rate, whatever they are,' our heroine said to herself; and she deemed this a great charm, for two or three of the friends of her childhood had been regrettably open to the charge (they would have been so nice without it), to say nothing of Isabel's having occasionally suspected it as a tendency of her own.
>
> (9, 73; my emphasis)

When Ransom meets Olive Chancellor, 'this pale girl, with her light-green eyes, her pointed features and nervous manner was visibly *morbid*; it was plain as day that she was *morbid*' (2, 11, my emphasis). Not long after that, he calls her 'a signal old maid. . . . There are women who are unmarried by accident, and others who are unmarried by option, but Olive Chancellor was unmarried by every implication of her being' (3, 17). What is the choice? If English, a woman and unmarried, is there nothing else but to become like one of the Misses Molyneux? Or, if American, is it to be like Isabel Archer, who has the potential to become Olive Chancellor – proving her kinship to Olive Chancellor by her hesitancy about the heterosexual throughout, in her drawing back from the poisoned cup?

James's review of *Nana* will be recalled. Written during the serialisation of *The Portrait of a Lady*, it said that 'half of life is a sealed book to young unmarried ladies', and that 'the novel is addressed to unmarried women, or assumes them to be a large part of the reading-public'. Yet Dorothea Brooke and Gwendolen Harleth suggest that, being unmarried, they are not outside sexuality, but rather they are faced with it as a trauma that they cannot work through, and that haunts them in and after their weddings. Actual virginity, or its loss, is not the point; hysteria is embedded in fantasmatic and real relationships to the symbolic order, and as much male as female. What are the influences behind Olive Chancellor's perception of male sexuality when she tells Verena (as if she had read about Isabel Archer): 'there are gentlemen in plenty who would be glad to stop your mouth by kissing you' (17, 119)? Since hysteria is also male, males are guilty of a displacement when they project it onto women. Olive Chancellor is dubbed morbid by Basil Ransom, but who is he to talk? He sounds off to Verena in Central Park (chapters 33 and 34) about 'the age', saying he wants to save it:

from the most damnable feminization!... The whole generation is womanized, the masculine tone is passing out of the world; it's a feminine, a nervous, hysterical, chattering, canting age, an age of hollow phrases and false delicacy and exaggerated solitudes and coddled sensibilities, which, if we don't soon look out, will usher in the reign of mediocrity, of the feeblest and flattest and the most pretentious that has ever been. The masculine character, the ability to dare and endure, to know and yet not feel reality, to look the world in the face and take it for what it is – a very queer and partly very base mixture – that is what I want to preserve, or rather, as I may say, to recover, and I must tell you that I don't in the least care what becomes of you ladies while I make the attempt! (34, 290)

This, in comparison, is Olive Chancellor: she is presented at this moment by a George Eliot-like narrator:

Olive had a standing quarrel with the levity, the good-nature, of the judgements of the day; many of them seemed to her weak to imbecility, losing sight of all measures and standards, lavishing superlatives, delighted to be fooled. The age seemed to her relaxed and demoralized, and I believe she looked to the feminine element to make it feel and speak more sharply. (16, 109)

Olive's complaint about laxness of judgements is a complaint about the weakness of the symbolic order and lack of phallic authority – so women must become more intense in upholding standards. Olive and Basil fight with their backs against the same wall, both agreeing on what is wrong with the age: the difference is their means of settling the problem, which both see as a lack of masculinity. Olive cannot bear the idea of men not being masculine: she tells Verena that 'there are men who pretend to care for [feminism]; but they are not really men, and I wouldn't be sure even of them! Any man, that one would look at – with him, as a matter of course, it is war upon us to the knife' (17. 119). The 'feminist' male would not be a proper man. The 'logic' of this compels lesbianism as a political choice, a way of negotiating relationships between the sexes.

Both Olive's and Ransom's reactions seem, in terms of late nineteenth-century discourse, hysterical (Carylean proto-fascism as hysteria in Basil Ransom's case), and judging from the end, likely to promote hysteria in Verena, the woman whose voice – powerful and oratorical – seems disassociated from her body, as though in a psychic splitting of the subject redolent of hysteria itself. The conservative marriage Basil wants, and the lesbian attraction to Verena Olive feels, are hysterical: near the end, Olive, like Gwendolen Harleth, has a morbid fantasy of Verena drowning (39, 356). Olive's lesbian feelings – if to put them into those terms is not to make them too determinate – are sublimated, finding sexual expression outside marriage 'disagreeable' – she is not in favour of free unions (11, 74). An Isabel Archer who had stayed on in America might, James implies, also have become such a sublimated lesbian: if the Jamesian texts find that problematic, they go in that direction.

James commented on what he intended to do in *The Bostonians*:

> The subject is very national, very typical. I wished to write a very *American* tale, a tale very characteristic of our social conditions, and I asked myself what was the most salient and peculiar point in our social life. The answer was: the situation of women, the decline of the sentiment of sex, the agitation on their behalf. (*Notebooks*, p. 20)

Does 'the decline of the sentiment of sex' mean that feeling has now become violence? That sex no longer has the protection of fine feelings behind it? Or that women no longer feel sexually towards men? Or that men no longer respect women? Or that sex is no longer a binding force in society (between women and men, or between women)? The passage is obscure, like Basil Ransom's 'profane question':

> The deepest feeling in Ransom's bosom in relation to [Verena] was that she was made for love.... She was profoundly unconscious of it, and another ideal ... had interposed itself; but in the presence of a man ... this flimsy structure would rattle to her feet, and the emancipation of Olive Chancellor's sex (what sex was it, great heaven? he used profanely to ask himself), would be relegated to the land of vapours ...
> (34, 287)

In asking what sex Olive Chancellor possessed, is Ransom questioning whether women have sexuality, or asking what the value of women ('the sex') is, or is he asking whether Olive Chancellor is a man or a woman (perhaps lesbian)? These questions fit with the word 'morbid', which provides my point of contact between Isabel and Olive. What does that word mean when it is used in 1881 by Isabel Archer about herself, and in 1886 when Basil Ransom uses it about Olive Chancellor?

In the *Saturday Review* of 1891, a notice of W. E. Henley's book of verse for boys, the reviewer hoped it would 'keep the blood of many English boys from the wretched and morbid stagnation of "modernity"'.[9] The pairing of morbidity with modernity fits with Olive's feminism and recalls Ransom's Carlylean rage against modern conditions. William Greenslade's discussions about morbidity, which I draw on, use John Stokes's book *In the Nineties*, which gives evidence for the linking of the word 'morbid' to 'egotism' and then for the application of this term to the New Woman; he also says that it could serve as 'a provocative euphemism for homosexuality':

> 'morbidity' linked the artistic minority [in the 1890s] with those other social outsiders whose insidious activities corrupted the whole – the lunatics, criminals and sexual deviants of scientific treatise. Modern artists may not all have been, as Nordau was to argue, literally insane, but the lunatic still provided the best model as an anomaly.[10]

Stokes quotes from the 1895 edition of Henry Maudsley's *The Pathology of Mind* on the lunatic as an alien in the social body, 'a morbid kind', and cites Wilde in 1891 in 'The Soul of Man Under Socialism' on 'morbid' as a hate-word used by philistines, Wilde saying, in its defence, 'what is morbidity but a mood or emotion that one cannot express[?].'[11]

If Wilde could write thus in 1891, perhaps 'morbidity' had a currency in the 1880s as expressing a frame of mind outside the bourgeois formation or unable to express itself in the terms of that formation. Voicelessness contrasts with Verena's speech-making, with the public feminism whose values can be articulated in the existing terms of the social and symbolic order (and therefore belongs to a politics that James does not relate to). What there is of lesbianism, however, must remain voiceless, as when, in chapter 39, Olive and Verena lie back together for an hour, neither speaking, in a state of virtual despair, which is called 'shame' – an emotion felt because the relationship is actually ending, a victim of (compulsory) heterosexuality. Walter Benjamin, discussing Baudelaire, calls the lesbian the heroine of modernism (Benjamin, p. 90). Even though the lesbian, in James, does not have survival-value, the unconscious knowledge of her heroic status is at the heart of Ransom's dislike of 'the age'.

IV AMERICAN MASCULINITY

'Morbid' is a loaded term. When Isabel applies it to herself, and Ransom applies it to Olive Chancellor, it implies the naming power of the dominant discourse. The word tends to misrecognition, to the attempt to code women within the symbolic order. Though 'morbid' applied on both sides of the Atlantic, James thinks of American women's power of transgression as greater than that of English women – the Misses Molyneux, for instance. The other Bostonians that James did not write about are the hegemonic sort, and to pick up on this, I turn to Hawthorne.

James comments on Hawthorne's 'curious aversion to the representation of the nude in sculpture' (p. 148). Referring to Hawthorne's *Notebooks*, he sees Hawthorne's dislike in terms of his defective 'plastic sense'.[12] *The Marble Faun*, Hawthorne's last romance, opens with four people – two Americans, Hilda and Kenyon, with one non-American, Miriam, and one Italian, Donatello – looking at Praxiteles's nude marble satyr (called a faun, as if to diminish the sexual implication). But nudity in paintings becomes a subject of the text, when Hawthorne has an account of Hilda, 'this pure and somewhat rigid New England girl' (James, *Hawthorne*, 6, 154), walking through art galleries in Rome. The incident compares with Dorothea's experiences in Rome: Hilda also suffers from hysteria, where this can be codified as melancholia,[13] and 'that icy demon of weariness who haunts great picture galleries':

> The remainder of the gallery comprises mythological subjects, such as nude Venuses, Ledas, Graces, and, in short, a general apotheosis of nudity, once fresh and rosy perhaps, but yellow and dingy in our day, and retaining only a traditionary charm. These impure pictures are from the same illustrious and impious hands that adventured to call before us the august forms of Apostles and Saints.... They seem to take up one task or the other – the disrobed woman whom they call Venus, or the type of highest and tenderest womanhood in the mother of their saviour – with equal readiness, but to achieve the former with far more satisfactory success. If an artist sometimes produced a picture of the Virgin ... it was probably the object of his earthly love to whom he paid thus the stupendous and fearful homage of setting up her portrait to be worshipped.... And who can trust the religious sentiment of Raphael, or receive any of his Virgins as heaven-descended likenesses, after seeing, for instance, the Fornarina of the Barberini Palace, and feeling how sensual the artist must have been to paint such

a brazen trollop of his own accord, and lovingly? Would the Blessed Mary reveal herself to his spiritual vision, and favour him with sittings alternatively with that type of glowing earthliness, the Fornarina?   (*The Marble Faun*, 37, 268)

The text continues that Hilda 'had a faculty (which fortunately for themselves, pure women often have) of ignoring all moral blotches in a character that won her admiration'. Raphael, therefore, goes uncriticised by her, but Hilda – a copyist not a painter, an example of American gentility – suggests how much of experience and of otherness (Donatello's criminality and Miriam's Jewishness, and the sexuality of both of them) Kenyon must repress in marrying her and becoming one of America's pure products. Hilda represents a product of American ideology that preserves the woman as separate, and America as pure, having no 'shadow' (Preface to *The Marble Faun*). Hilda's whiteness (her tower, her doves) makes her a woman without a shadow: 'She dwelt in her tower, as free to descend into the corrupted atmosphere of the city beneath, as one of her companion doves to fly downward into the street: all alone, perfectly independent, under her own sole guardianship, unless watched over by the Virgin, whose shrine she tended; doing what she liked without a suspicion or a *shadow* upon the snowy whiteness of her frame' (6, 44, my emphasis). So anxious is Hawthorne to protect American whiteness, he makes Hilda's purity the virtual condition of reading European art, since 'the adequate perception of a great work of art demands a gifted simplicity of vision' (37, 267).

Hawthorne must construct for the American ideology, which he is also part of, the woman who cannot be corrupted by sexuality. The male writer's attitude to the nudes becomes tendentially hysterical, like the construction of the pure woman. In Hawthorne's *The Blithedale Romance* (1852), often seen, since the work of Marius Bewley, as a formative text for *The Bostonians*,[14] the interest oscillates between two women, Zenobia, the feminist, and Priscilla. At the end, Zenobia kills herself, while Priscilla marries Hollingsworth, the egocentric reformer, and settles down to a life of domestic care. Consumed with guilt over Zenobia's death he has now 'a depressed and melancholy look, that seemed habitual; the powerfully built man showed a self-distrustful weakness, and a childlike, or childish tendency to press close, and closer still, to the side of the slender woman whose arm was within his' (*The Blithedale Romance*, 29, 223).[15]

If this makes American masculinity a neurotic formation, the narrator is an anatomy of American male double standards towards women. He is fascinated by the question of whether Zenobia has been married, marriage being 'the great event of a woman's existence' (6, 43). Her freedom of deportment is 'not exactly maidenlike'. 'Her unconstrained and inevitable manifestation, I said often to myself, was that of a woman to whom wedlock had thrown wide the gates of mystery.' Priscilla in contrast is pale, conventional and has much less character, yet the narrator ends his book with the confession 'I – I myself – was in love – with – PRISCILLA!' (29, 228). The words re-read the situation at Blithedale from an asexual position (he has never hinted at his love during the narrative; Priscilla is now safely married so that nothing can come of the statement), and whatever the intention, they define the narrator as both timid and eager to assert a heterosexual position within the social order. They are, indeed, virtually hysterical. Nor in this is the narrator so different from Hawthorne, whose vexation at the success of women writers in the 1850s produced a strange description of women, and prescription for them. Discussing Fanny Fern's *Ruth Hall* (1855), he concedes that he likes it because

> The woman writes as if the devil was in her, and that is the only condition under which a woman ever writes anything worth reading. Generally, women write like emasculated men, and are only to be distinguished from male authors by greater feebleness and folly; but when they throw off the restraints of decency and come before the public stark naked, as it were – then their books are sure to possess character and value.[16]

It is again hysterical writing, from the author who makes Priscilla and Hilda models of the pure American woman. Here is male unease within the symbolic order – the subject-matter of James's *Daisy Miller: A Study* (1878), the text that immediately preceded *The Portrait of a Lady*.

Daisy Miller is the 'American girl' Americans throw off: innocent, while being a 'flirt'. she challenges by flirting the notion that half of life is a sealed book to unmarried ladies, and she has no conventional 'maidenlike' quality to lose. *She* could never be a Priscilla, or Hilda. Yet she is defeated by an order whose centre is always displaced – the expatriate Americans refuse to know her because of the way they will be perceived by the Europeans:

> They [the expatriate Americans] ceased to invite her, and they intim-
> ated that they desired to express to observant Europeans the great
> truth that, though Miss Daisy Miller was a young American lady, her
> behaviour was not representative – was regarded by her compatriots as
> abnormal. (4, 43)

This 'Daisy' is 'cut' like any flower by the American socialite Mrs
Walker at her party because of her association with the unattached
Italian male (4, 39), and again 'cut' by Winterbourne, when he sees
her out at night. Winterbourne then cuts her with his words (4, 48),[17]
so she says 'in a strange little tone' – reduced at last by the 'stiffness'
of the American whom she actually loves – 'I don't care whether
I have Roman fever or not', and goes home to die. Her death is
induced by physical causes, but the 'cut' that destroys her is the
power of words – words as wounds, words that annihilate her
identity. In that this is crucial, the illness is itself partly hysterical.

Daisy Miller is killed by the 'stiff' aspects of American patriarchy,
and not allowed to be a viable alternative to Hawthorne's Hilda.
When W. D. Howells wrote *The Rise of Silas Lapham* (1885), Daisy
Miller had become the name for a transgressive womanhood that
readers of the fictional newspaper 'The Events' must be warned
against. Bartley Hubbard, the journalist, writes about Silas Lapham
the industrialist in a manner protecting nineteenth-century genteel
family values:

> We may say that the success of which he is justly proud he is also proud
> to attribute in great measure to the sympathy and energy of his wife –
> one of those women who, in whatever walk of life, seem born to
> honour the name of American Woman, and to redeem it from the
> national reproach of Daisy Millerism. Of Colonel Lapham's family,
> we will simply add that it consists of two young lady daughters.[18]

Lapham's daughters both read *Middlemarch*. Irene asks young Tom
Corey what he thinks of Rosamond Vincy; he replies that 'I can't say
I liked her. But I don't think I disliked her so much as the author does.
She's pretty hard on her good-looking... girls', to which Irene replies
that her sister, Penelope, agrees: 'She says she doesn't give her any
chance to be good. She says she should have been just as bad as
Rosamond if she had been in her place' (*Silas Lapham*, 9, 97–8).
Daisy Miller, banished from the ideology of the Bostonian middle
class – which reads the novel 'Tears Idle Tears', a love-story about

'self-sacrifice' (14, 174) – comes in via an appreciation of Rosamond Vincy, rather than Dorothea, who does believe in self-sacrifice (which hystericises her).

I have returned to *Middlemarch*, and Howells' point about Rosamond Vincy suggests an answer to my initial question: why James gives place to her in the Preface to *The Portrait of a Lady*, enlarging her importance. None the less, there is comparatively little of Daisy Miller's freedom in Isabel Archer, and nothing of her in the social comedy of *The Bostonians*. The element of freedom in Isabel, who is 'very fond of her own ways' as Mrs Touchett says, when telling her that in England 'young girls . . . don't sit alone with the gentlemen late at night' (7, 67), is, so Isabel says, so that she can 'choose' whether to go her own way or whether not. The desire to choose, however, pushes her towards Osmond, the man who is 'convention itself' (29, 265) – whose 'worship for propriety' is akin to the expatriate Americans in *Daisy Miller: A Study*. These Americans feel they are under the eye of 'observant Europeans'. What sentences Daisy Miller is, ultimately, the rudeness of the American she is attracted to – Winterbourne – a man whose secret sexual freedom in Geneva does not affect his conventionality. There is, then, a move in James whereby he implies how Daisy Miller, Isabel Archer and Olive Chancellor are all possible developments of each other, all differently betrayed and learning to fear betrayal, and all of them the record of a history.

V ISABEL ARCHER

Late in *The Portait of a Lady*, as a replay of the scene between Osmond and Madame Merle which Isabel entered in on, and this time in Madame Merle's apartment, we see how their alliance is cracking:

> [Osmond] took up a small cup, and held it in his hand; then, still holding it and leaning his arm on the mantel, he pursued: 'You always see too much in everything; you overdo it; you lose sight of the real. I'm much simpler than you think.'
>
> 'I think you're very simple.' And Madame Merle kept her eye on her cup. 'I've come to that with time. I judged you, as I say, of old; but it's only since your marriage that I've understood you. I've seen better what you have been to your wife than I ever saw what you were for me. Please be very careful of that precious object.'

'It already has a wee bit of a tiny crack,' said Osmond drily as he put it down. (50, 436)

This recalls James's interest in George Eliot's 'delicate vessels' – what he misquotes as 'frail vessels' – and his putting these at the heart of his narratives. I have suggested that Isabel Archer stands between Daisy Miller and Olive Chancellor, as the possibility of both. But she is still opaque. The novel puzzles because of its evasiveness – recognised since the book's first publication – and its inability to create a portrait of Isabel:

> [Ralph's] cousin was a very brilliant girl, who would take, as he said, a good deal of knowing; but she needed the knowing.... He surveyed the edifice from the outside and admired it greatly; he looked in at the windows and received an impression of proportions equally fair. But he felt that he saw it only by glimpses and that he had not yet stood under the roof. The door was fastened, and though he had keys in his pocket he had a conviction that none of them would fit. (7, 63–4)

Ralph Touchett feels he lacks a way to sum Isabel up. But as with so many Jamesian architectural images, the problem lies in the governing metaphor. Isabel is a house whose inside is inaccessible, only a façade. Architectural images give a sense of wholeness, of unity. They do not, any more than the image of a 'portrait' does, allow for splits and contradictions, or for tiny cracks.

The assumption that obtains in Ralph and his choice of images is of inner coherence, or of the unified subject. But the cup Osmond handles already has a crack – a gap, a *béance*, an originary absence at its centre, which is caught in Osmond's yonic image. The cup belongs to a collection of cultural artefacts, which are fetish-like – both Marx's commodity fetish and Freud's fetish, which covers up a sense of the woman's castration, to allow patriarchal disavowal of the castration fear. The fetish here is inscribed by the very lack it must conceal.

The narrator records Isabel herself as unsure of her own coherence, in a passage of thought after Osmond has proposed: a moment when 'the tears came into her eyes: this time they obeyed the sharpness of the pang that suggested to her somehow the slipping of a fine bolt – backward, forward, she couldn't have said which' (29, 263). Inside or outside: which is she? Is marriage freedom or a prison, one which none the less stabilizes the subject? Isabel wishes to see, as she tells

Ralph, but her 'imagination' – her power of forming images – fails to let her see everything, and thus challenges the power of centred perception Isabel had assumed she possessed:

> What had happened was something that for a week past her imagination had been going forward to meet; but here, when it came, she stopped.... The working of this young lady's spirit was strange, and I can only give it to you as I see it, not hoping to make it seem altogether natural. Her imagination, as I say, now hung back: there was a last vague space it couldn't cross – a dusky, uncertain tract which looked ambiguous and even slightly treacherous, like a moorland seen in the winter twilight. But she was to cross it yet. (29, 265)

But *how* she crosses it, James gives no suggestion – for though chapter 30, which follows, describes Isabel visiting Pansy in Florence as she had promised, chapter 31 begins with Isabel returning to Florence 'after several months', and awaiting the arrival of Goodwood. It then moves back in time to cover what she has been doing in the interval, so that when chapter 32 begins, she resumes her present waiting, acknowledging Goodwood by the 'bright, dry gaze with which she rather withheld than offered a greeting' – 'dry' being something of a keynote amongst these Americans. In their conversation, the reader learns, for the first time, of the engagement. The time-sequence then runs on till the end of chapter 35, but chapter 36 begins 'one afternoon in the autumn of 1876' – America's Centennial year – and it starts, not with Isabel, but with Edmund Rosier and Madame Merle, where the reader learns that Isabel has been married, had a baby and lost it, and so has been 'a lady' – i.e., a married woman – for some four years. James, unlike George Eliot, evades the honeymoon, and Isabel's experiences of motherhood. Not until chapter 37 does Isabel reappear. If the subject is not unified, is marked by a crack, it should be noted that there is no attempt within the text to unify it through a narrative that would fill in the gaps: it leaves the reader with its own elegance of ellipsis. In one way, this makes the text minor art, since there is so much that it cannot handle, and so much that its art protects from being seen.

The title *The Portrait of a Lady* draws attention to the art as representation, not even as attempting to give an unmediated picture, but deliberately smoothed out into the artistic and fetishistic coherency of a 'portrait', an image which announces its smoothness and its covering over of elements that do not fit. The scene of Isabel's midnight vigil is that kind of stabilizing art. But there is more to it than that, hinted at in the word 'morbid'. If Isabel feels herself morbid, then representation contains its own difficulty, for it includes misrecognition and misnaming, internalized by the subject herself. And morbidity is the name for something unrepresentable. The portrait has to work by concealment and evasion, has to have a crack, because it deals with moods and emotions that cannot be expressed. In that problem we see James's need to go on, and become the writer of evasion, tacking and weaving: not the writer who succeeds George Eliot but the writer of late James.

But staying with *The Portrait of a Lady*, I want to conclude by discussing the text in relation to George Eliot's contemporary, Flaubert. Isabel tells Henrietta Stackpole that she does not want to know where she is 'drifting'. 'I haven't the least idea, and I find it pleasant not to know. A swift carriage, of a dark night, rattling with four horses over roads that one can't see – that's my idea of happiness.' Henrietta replies that she speaks 'like the heroine of an immoral novel' (17, 146). There seems a critical consensus that the novel would be Flaubert's *Madame Bovary*.

Janet Beizer's *Ventriloquized Bodies: Narratives of Hysteria in Nineteenth-Century France* discusses Flaubert's correspondence with Louise Colet, from 1846 to 1854, finishing as *Madame Bovary* neared completion. From the letters, a stress on nerves emerges, 'la maladie de nerfs', and a fear of fluidity in women, fear that they may be characterised by a loss of boundaries or borders. Another tendency deprives Louise Colet of her sexuality, wishes her to be 'a sublime hermaphrodite', which may be associated with Flaubert's wish for an Art showing a 'liberation from materiality'. The letter discussing this (James reviewed Flaubert's correspondence when it was published in 1893) shows Flaubert's attempt to free himself from bourgeois thought – called *bêtisement* – and to fill the gap, the nothingness, with art:

> What seems beautiful to me, what I should like to write, is a book about nothing, a book dependent on nothing external, which would be held together by the strength of its style . . . a book which would have almost no subject, or at least in which the subject would be almost invisible, if such a thing is possible. The finest works are those that contain the least matter; the closer expression comes to thought, the closer language comes to coinciding and merging with it, the finer the result. I believe that the future of Art lies in this direction. I see it, as it

has developed from its beginnings, growing progressively more ethereal.... This emancipation from matter can be observed everywhere...there is no such thing as subject, style in itself being an absolute way of seeing things.[19]

The desire to lapse out from materiality (to writing) may be compared with Flaubert's fainting fit of January 1844, as though his body was refusing a law career. Flaubert's language identifies women with disgust and materiality, associated also with the bourgeoisie, to write about whom makes him suffer from 'hystéries d'ennui' (letter of 8 April 1852) – disgust linking with the 'abjection' Julia Kristeva describes.[20] Abjection violently refuses the feminine as that which breaks down borders, and threatens the ability of the subject to form any separate being. It is a melancholia whose violent repudiation of substances identified with the feminine and materiality means, in Flaubert's case, that he wants to throw up contemporary France. As he says in a letter of 30 September 1855, 'Je sens contre la bêtise de mon époque des flots de haine qui m'étouffent. Il me monte de la merde à la bouche.... Mais je veux la garder, la figer, la durcir. J'en veux faire un pâte dont je barbouillerais le XIXe siècle. [The stupidity of my age moves me to waves of hatred that smother me. Shit rises in my mouth.... But I want to keep it, to congeal it, to harden it. I want to turn it into a paste with which I will smear the nineteenth century' (Beizer's translation, p. 163)].

Baudelaire takes *Madame Bovary*'s subject to be hysteria. Flaubert, to write it, relinquished his actual sex and made himself into a woman,[21] but Baudelaire also sees Emma Bovary as gender-crossing, 'a virile soul within the body of a beautiful woman'. The adulterous woman 'is almost masculine, and...perhaps unconsciously, the author [has] bestowed upon her all the qualities of manliness'. Discussing her convent education, he says:

> she becomes intoxicated with the colour of the stained-glass windows, with the Oriental shades that the ornate shadows cast on her schoolgirl prayer book; she gorges herself on the solemn music of Vespers and obeying the impulse of her nerves rather than of her mind, she substitutes in her soul for the real God a God of pure fantasy, a God of the future and of chance, a picture-God wearing spurs and moustaches. This is characteristic of the hysterical-poet.

Emma Bovary and Flaubert are indistinguishable in this figure of the 'hysterical poet', which leads Baudelaire to specify his sense of art –

with its search for style, for immateriality, and its freedom from the constraints of gender-positioning – as produced from hysteria:

> The Academy of Medicine has not, as yet, been able to explain the mysterious condition of hysteria. In women, it acts like a stifling ball rising in the body (I mention only the main symptom), while in nervous men it can be the cause of many forms of impotence as well as a limitless aptitude at excess. Why could this physiological mystery not serve as the central subject, the true core, of a literary work?[22]

This makes hysteria the text's subject, while also suggesting, since it is both 'le fond et le tuf', that it is born out of hysteria, for instance, from men who cannot manage a sexual relationship (all forms of impotence are covered). After Emma Bovary has committed adultery with Léon, she suffers from fears where 'a dark shapeless chasm would open within her soul' and she ends 'shattered, exhausted, frozen, sobbing silently, with flowing tears'. This hysteria she describes to her maid Félicité as 'nerves':

> 'Ah! Yes,' Félicité went on, 'you are just like La Guérine, the daughter of Père Guérin, the fisherman at le Pollet that I used to know at Dieppe, before I came to see you. She was so sad, so sad.... Her illness, it appears, was a kind of fog she had in the head, and the doctors could do nothing about it, neither could the priest. When she had a bad spell, she went off by herself to the sea-shore, so that the customs officer, going his rounds, often found her flat on her face, crying on the pebbles. Then, after her marriage, it stopped, they say.'
> 'But with me', replied Emma, 'it was after marriage that it began.' (2, 5, 78)

The 'fog in the head' makes the absence of marriage productive of hysteria. To James's reference to young unmarried ladies, with half of life a sealed book to them, involving a tract of land their imaginations cannot pass over, sexuality as uncharted, it may be added that hysteria, fear of non-differentiation and loss of sense of connection with the body (Olive Chancellor has 'fits of tragic shyness, during which she was unable to meet even her own eyes in the mirror' (2, 10)), is in *Madame Bovary* associated with the state of knowing. For Emma Bovary, there is no Cartesian clarity about knowledge. The married condition, not the unmarried, is the split state; there is no privilege in sexual knowing, or knowledge becomes awareness of a split, which goes across gender as constituted in the symbolic order. The woman suffering from a fog in the head cannot be contracted into a single 'portrait of a lady' though she may imagine such a depiction in fantasy. Walter Benjamin cites Baudelaire's passage about Flaubert and Emma Bovary as evidence of his interest in lesbianism (Benjamin, p. 92). If lesbianism fits for discussing *Madame Bovary*, sexual distinctions become fog, or what James calls, restrainedly, morbidity.

Marriage as a split state is Isabel's discovery when she realises that she has been betrayed, that her husband and Madame Merle have been lovers and that Pansy is their daughter. It leaves Isabel as an ambiguous consciousness at the centre of her text; centred in her motionless seeing in chapter 42. Yet, if we recall that for Freud 'hysterics suffer mainly from reminiscences',[23] even that calm going over of her past reveals that centring as problematic. She thinks about Osmond's opinions, ambitions and preferences. He has been insistent to her about tradition, as the American who despises what America has to offer in favour of a servitude to a past which is European. She reflects, in her vigil, how 'he had an immense esteem for tradition; he had told her once that the best thing in the world was to have it, but that if one was so unfortunate as not to have it, one must immediately proceed to make it. She knew that he meant by this that she hadn't it ... though from what source he had derived his traditions she never learned.' When she has argued about being dominated by traditions, Osmond has replied that he knew she had none (42, 361–2). The passage continues:

> But there were certain things she could never take in. To begin with, they were hideously unclean. She was not a daughter of the Puritans, but for all that she believed in such a thing as chastity and even as decency. It was clear that Osmond was far from doing anything of the sort; some of his traditions made her push back her skirts. Did all women have lovers? Did they all lie and even the best have their price? (42, 362)

What Isabel means is elliptical, not spelled out. Perhaps she is thinking that her husband wants her to make love to Lord Warburton to secure Warburton for Pansy (this being the sense of his last remarks in chapter 41). But the plural of 'certain things' and 'they' does not fit that idea in its singularity, and 'to begin with' is otiose if the things are 'hideously unclean' – a phrase that would imply that there is something in the way Isabel is thinking which is leading her towards abjection. In the sentence, 'It was clear that Osmond was far from doing anything of the sort', what is Osmond not doing? If it is believing, which is demanded by the previous sentence, why is that verb not used? What does 'made her push back her skirts' mean? If you wear skirts you pull them back; to push them back means you are outside them (if that makes sense). The phrase could imply a tightening of the skirts by putting pressure on them from the hands, but the slippages in the text, centring round sexuality, about things Isabel cannot articulate, makes it more likely that the passage is a version of Emma Bovary's 'fog in the head'; 'some of his traditions' – what traditions other than the unspoken request that she commit adultery could Isabel think of to make her want to 'push back her skirts'? Again, the vigil is evasive – though it seems again that tradition and betrayal go together, as was commented on in relationship to *The Ambassadors*, since the tradition to be followed is that Isabel should betray herself, betray Warburton and Pansy. (And Isabel does continue to notice that the Countess Gemini's deceptions were 'assumed among Osmond's traditions', as if identifying tradition with betrayal, in an example of words meaning both what they say and the opposite.) None the less, the plural use of 'traditions' is puzzling, as if Isabel is not quite in charge of her language, and as with the reference to 'skirts', it seems that she is both inside and outside the skirts at once. She is not simply in one place, her subjectivity is not assured, so that she cannot speak univocally, cannot say one thing clearly.

These splits are at the foundations of hysteria. Lacan comments on the split the subject feels on being held inside the symbolic order, where there is a discord between the subject's thinking and meaning and those other things that create the subject, which Lacan calls 'thought' – unconscious thought, discourse, ideology. For Lacan, 'I think where I am not, therefore I am where I do not think',[24] Isabel reveals, in the parapraxes of the quotation from chapter 42, a split between her being and what she can articulate. Lacan says 'I do not think' because thinking is already happening in me, through unconscious discourse. Here it is worth recalling Wilde on the morbid as the inexpressible: morbid symptoms appear when there is no chance for new articulation.

Isabel as the subject wants to push back her skirts, as though these were choking her, like Osmond's traditions, in an abject gesture which is also self-hatred – they are, after all, her skirts which she pushes at, in a position of disgust, or refusal, which none the less fails to establish her subjectivity. Emma Bovary discovers in adultery with Léon 'all the platitudes of marriage':[25] she discovers that sexual passion is only repetition, kitsch romanticism, conducted on the same lines as marriage; it is impossible to escape out of the circle of 'thought' – i.e., the discourse of the bourgeois symbolic order. Hysteria – including hysteria in love-making – is a reaction to the world of bourgeois received ideas, violent rejection of them, which cannot succeed in letting the subject stand clear and independent, and can only produce further disgust: which in the case of Madame Bovary is completed by the horror of poisoning (vomiting asserts the materiality of the body), in a text which feels increasingly abject, in an hysteria linking Emma Bovary and Flaubert.

James resists this kind of argument by implicit denial, in the Preface, of Isabel's split state, centring her by his self-appreciative comments on the vigil in the Preface (AN, 3, 57). In relation to Flaubert, while noting that 'certain passages in his correspondence make us even wonder if it be not hate that sustains him most',[26] he idealises Madame Bovary, saying that 'the dignity of its substance is the dignity of Madame Bovary herself, as a vessel of experience' – the language of Daniel Deronda and the Preface to The Portrait of a Lady with its adaptation of George Eliot. 'Emma interests us by the nature of her consciousness and the play of her mind, thanks to the reality and beauty with which those sources are invested.' But James adds that 'our complaint is that Emma Bovary, in spite of the nature of her consciousness and in spite of her reflecting so much that of her creator, is really too small an affair' (Gard, p. 382). She is not representative – 'Representative of what? he makes us ask even while granting all the grounds of misery and tragedy involved' (Gard, p. 385).

Following George Eliot, James wrote about noble heroines. The idealisation is inseparable from class. Isabel Archer is proposed to by an English lord; Olive Chancellor belongs to a cultured Bostonian context which she sees as problematic: it characterises her response to meetings at Miss Birdseye's house at Boston's South End. Benjamin points out that by masculinising Emma Bovary, which gives character to all her dreaming, 'Baudelaire raises Flaubert's petty-bourgeois wife to the status of a heroine' (Benjamin, p. 92). She becomes the heroine of modern life. Because of their privileges, James's heroines in The

Portrait of a Lady and *The Bostonians* do not have to function in quite such unprotected circumstances. And perhaps this is James's limitation in relation to Flaubert, and perhaps, too, it shows an awareness of a kind of imprisonment.

Yet James shields neither Isabel, left with 'the middle years' and 'the grey curtain of her indifference' (53, 466), nor Olive, who, at the end of *The Bostonians*, fears that she will be hissed and hooted and insulted by the crowds in the Boston Music Hall who have come to hear Verena (the professional, not so respectable figure) and must now have to hear her instead. In this context, James stresses the vulgarity of the Boston crowd, its coarseness and materiality.[27] It is what Olive Chancellor must shrink from, as the abject, as she shrinks from seeing her reflection, not wanting to confirm her own identity, because even that contains its own otherness. But she faces the crowd in a desire for shame, wishing to negate her subjectivity. As *Daniel Deronda* can imagine nothing else for Gwendolen Harleth in her remorse save enduring after the death of Grandcourt, so there is no future for Olive, unless she makes something of public speaking, and so of living with the modern. Perhaps she will; perhaps not, as Verena, leaving her to her fate of waiting, reflects:

> She had a vision of those dreadful years; she knew that Olive would never get over the disappointment. It would touch her in the point where she felt everything most keenly; she would be incurably lonely and eternally humiliated. (38, 334)

4

Monomania and the American Past: *The Aspern Papers*

In *The Portrait of a Lady* and *The Bostonians*, it was hysteria largely focused on women. In *The Aspern Papers*,[1] hysteria is in the American narrator – unnamed, not even his alias given. He is trying to obtain papers to bring him closer to the dead American Romantic poet Jeffrey Aspern. He is deprived of a sight of them – assuming they exist – by Miss Juliana Bordereau and Miss Tina Bordereau, who may be her niece (perhaps her sister was the mother of Tina by Aspern) – or her grand-niece, or even possibly her daughter.[2] Tina finally burns them.

We start with James's notebook entry for 12 January 1887, written in Florence, and musing a year after *The Bostonians*. James muses on the story of Captain Silsbee, Boston art-critic and Shelley-worshipper, trying to obtain letters of Shelley belonging to Claire Clairmont, who had been Byron's mistress. The narrative of her death and the niece offering to give them if Silsbee married her, fuses with another, in the same entry (*Notebook*, pp. 33–4), of Countess Gamba, who had married a nephew of Byron's last mistress, Teresa Guiccioli (Byron met her in 1819).[3] James saw this couple in Florence, and heard how she had burned one of Byron's letters. She represented the letters as discreditable to Byron.

In the Preface to *The Aspern Papers*, James picks his way through the 'romantic' interest of the relationships and writes of how: 'that Jane Clairmont . . . should have been living on in Florence, where she had long lived, up to our own day, and that in fact, had I happened to hear of her but a little sooner, I might have seen her in the flesh. The question of whether I should have wished to do so was another matter – the question of whether I shouldn't have preferred to keep her preciously unseen, to run no risk...of depreciating that romance-value which, as I say, it was instantly inevitable to attach...to her long survival' (*AN*, 9, 161). Mary Jane Clairmont (1798–1879), who, to separate herself from her parents' influence, re-named herself Claire in 1814, was daughter to Mary Jane Clairmont, who, widowed, married William Godwin in 1801. (Mary Wollstonecraft, the earlier wife, died in 1797.) Claire Clairmont's schooling prepared her for life as a French teacher and governess. Mary Godwin and Percy Shelley eloped to France in 1814, and Claire joined them. They returned to England that autumn, when it is speculated that she had an affair with Shelley.[4] In April 1816, Claire Clairmont became Byron's mistress, in the year of his exile from England. In May, Mary Godwin, Shelley and their baby son William, and Claire Clairmont travelled to Geneva where they met Byron. The party returned to London. Harriet Shelley, Shelley's wife, committed suicide and Mary Godwin married Shelley. In January, Claire Clairmont gave birth to her daughter by Byron, Allegra Alba. In March 1818, the Shelleys and Claire Clairmont travelled to Italy. Allegra Alba went to join Byron in Venice; but he put her into a convent, where she died in April 1822.

In July 1822, two years before Byron's death, Shelley drowned. Mary Shelley returned to London, dying in 1851. Claire Clairmont joined her brother Charles in Vienna, and spent much of the rest of her life in Europe, as a governess and companion. (John Cumnor, the English enthusiast for Aspern, speculates that Juliana Bordereau, the Miss Clairmont of *The Aspern Papers*, had been a governess in some family which the poet Aspern visited (*The Aspern Papers*, 4, 76). Her last home was Florence, where her niece Pauline Clairmont (1825–1891) was housekeeper.

The lives of Mary Wollstonecraft, Mary Shelley and Claire Clairmont act out a Gothic narrative, with suicides, deaths of children, and parents disowning their own children, and the appearance of feminism, expressed in *Frankenstein*'s critique of the myths of male power which appeared in Byron's and Shelley's behaviour. The detail of the niece, who, to paraphrase the narrator of *The Aspern Papers* (1, 48), 'flung herself at the head' of Silsbee, and therefore repeated the actions of Claire Clairmont with regard to Byron, suggested to James 'a final scene of the rich dim Shelley drama played out in the theatre of our own "modernity"' (*AN*, 9, 163), an independence of action that left the confident Shelley-worshipper still running (Silsbee '*court encore*', as Lee-Hamilton told James). Silsbee is the hero who comes to take possession, and ends, non-Shelleyan, running away. James thinks of the women, then of 'the plot of the Shelley fanatic – his watchings and waitings – the way he *couvers* the treasure'. 'Couvers' means 'broods over', resonating with 'covers' and 'covets' – Silsbee's activity is projected as obsessive, crazy.

I THE AMERICAN UNCANNY

In the Preface, James writes about Italy as unknowable: 'we peep at most into two or three of the chambers of their hospitality, with the rest of the case stretching beyond our ken and escaping our penetration. . . . So, right and left, in Italy – before the great historic complexity at least – penetration fails; we scratch at the extensive surface, we meet the perfunctory smile, we hang about in the golden air' (*AN*, 9, 160). In the face of such impossibility of access, James dreams of 'a palpable imaginable *visitable* past – in the nearer distances and the clearer mysteries, the marks and signs of a world we may reach over to as by making a long arm we grasp an object at the other end of our own table' (*AN*, 9, 64). His interest centres on what he calls – three times on one page – 'the Byronic age' (*AN*, 9, 165). So, in 'old' New York, he asks, 'could a recognisable reflexion of the Byronic age . . . be picked up on the banks of the Hudson?'

> the impulse had more than once taken me to project the Byronic age and the afternoon light across the great sea, to see in short whether association would carry so far and what the young century might pass for on that side of the modern world where it was not only itself so irremediably youngest, but was bound up with youth in everything else. There was a refinement of curiosity in this imputation of a golden strangeness to American social facts.

To make strange American social facts, and to make them Italian ('golden'): this would try to create an uncanny. James says he wants an 'American Byron' to match 'an American Miss Clairmont'. James's friend Herbert Pratt (Edel, II, 445–6) rejected the idea:

these people 'couldn't possibly have' existed in that New York. 'The stricture was to apply itself to a whole group of short fictions in which I had, with whatever ingenuity, assigned to several so-called eminent figures positions absolutely unthinkable in our actual encompassing air.' James summarizes the case against himself, 'I foist upon our early American annals a distinguished presence for which they yield me absolutely no warrant' (*AN*, 9, 165–8). The critique is of romance, which James writes about in the Preface to *The American*. There, James asks 'by what art or mystery...does a given picture of life appear to us to surround its theme, its figures and its images, with the air of romance while a picture beside it may affect us as steeping the whole matter in the elements of reality?' (*AN*, 2, 30). James pauses over the definitions of romance, saying its 'general attribute' is 'experience liberated, so to speak; experience disengaged, disembroiled, disencumbered, exempt from the conditions that we usually know to attach to it, and... drag upon it, and operating in a medium which relieves it, in a particular interest, of the inconvenience of a *related*, a measurable state, a state subject to all our vulgar communities' (*AN*, 2, 33). This is a plea for allegory, and for a sense that the way things are is contingent, not necessary. Once the cable is cut that ties the balloon to the earth (connecting imagination to experience), 'we are at large and unrelated' (*AN*, 2, 34). 'Related' is a key term in James[5] – the word appears three times in this paragraph – and it links narrative and knowledge. What can be narrated – related – is what is known. The unrelated escapes the *déjà vu*, the sphere of bourgeois ideology where everything is already known. It is what cannot be put into a narrative. Herbert Pratt's objections to James are those of realism which is also literalism, and this realism is at the service of a memory which belongs to the official versions of things: it has no room for a counter-memory.

The Preface makes an initial distinction between the historian and the dramatist. The historian 'wants more documents than he can really use'. That is an implicit explanation of the character of the 'publishing scoundrel' who tells *The Aspern Papers*, and indicates the futility behind his dream of possession. The narrative ironises the narrator, but James, in the Preface, aligns himself with him, for like him, James, as dramatist, not historian, 'only wants more liberties than he can really take'. A permissible liberty that could be taken seems to be offered by James's sense that there is a 'visitable [a ghostly] past'. His wish – the creation of a Freudian 'family romance', replacing America's real past by a superior origin[6] – is that America's youth might have contained a Byron, and he also needs the friend of the Preface as a superego to make this an impossibility. The friend, by being part of the Jamesian discourse, enables the Jamesian fantasy. The James who is *not* the friend says that his interest is 'the visitable past', and 'visitable' suggests the desire to haunt the past, to give it some quality of the present. But to the historian all pasts are the same: unvisitable, and this gives the narrator's text its romance quality and Americanness. The liberty the dramatist wants is to make 'old' New York (not, remembering *The Europeans*, Boston) Byronic. Pratt is made to give the evaluation Henry Adams would give, when he wrote the letter to James about his biography of William Wetmore Story (see p. 5 above), that:

> The painful truth is that all of my New England generation, counting the half century 1820–1870, were in actual fact only one mind and nature. . . . One cannot exaggerate the profundity of ignorance of Story in becoming a sculptor, or Sumner in becoming a statesman, or Emerson in becoming a philosopher. Story and Sumner, Emerson and Alcott, Lowell and Longfellow, Hillard, Winthrop, Motley, Prescott and all the rest, were of the same mind, – and so, poor worm, was I! God knows that we knew our want of knowledge! The self-distrust became introspection – nervous self-consciousness – irritable dislike of America, and antipathy to Boston. . . . Improvised Europeans, we were, and – Lord God! – how thin![7]

James defends his idea that there might have been a Byronic moment in early nineteenth-century New York by asking 'whether the false element imputed would have borne that test of further development which so exposes the wrong and consecrates the right'. From no foundation at all, could something be built up whose development would indeed act as a justification for inventing something initially? Can the present be used to create a past, to say that it must have been like that? Jay Gatsby thinks you can repeat the past (*The Great Gatsby*, ch. 6); James thinks you can redo it. This approach to history would find *any* historical documents more than could be used, and in *The Aspern Papers*, none appear. The text comments on its own impossibility; wanting the verification that papers might be able to provide, but denying the narrator a sight of them, issues are neither confirmed nor denied.

II THE AMERICAN BYRON

On 13 April 1833, Emerson in Rome wrote in his journal: 'Rome fashions my dreams. All night I wander amidst statues and fountains, and last night was introduced to Lord Byron!'[8] Truly, 'Rome is as the desert, where we steer / Stumbling over recollections' (*Childe Harold's Pilgrimage*, canto IV, stanza 81, ll. 6–7). Byron, eleven years after his death, had colonised the New England consciousness, formed its perception of Rome and got into its recollections. Byron's appeal was to women and to men alike. And Emerson's homoerotic feelings towards the Harvard student Martin Gay, when Emerson was nineteen, may also suggest the ghost of Byron.[9]

Shelley said of Byron in Venice in 1818, that

> he hardens himself in a kind of obstinate and self-willed folly. . . . He associates with wretches who seem almost to have lost the gait and physiognomy of man, and who do not scruple to avow practices which are not only named but seldom even conceived in England. He says he disapproves, but he endures . . .[10]

Ruskin said that 'my Venice, like Turner's, had been chiefly created for us by Byron'.[11] *Childe Harold's Pilgrimage*, canto IV, romanticises and mythicises Venice for the nineteenth century, and makes it a place of oppression – 'A palace and a prison on each hand' (canto IV, stanza 1, l. 2), but it is worth noting that Byron also twice, abjectly, or censoriously, refers to Venice as 'the sea-Sodom' – once in a letter of December 1819, after he had left, and once at the end of his play *Marino Faliero* (V.3.99).[12] But as Venice ghosted Byron by seeming as a city to be sexually corrupting, or bisexual, so Byron ghosted Emerson in Rome, and ghosted the consciousness of Henry James in relation to both Venice and New York. And at this stage, I turn to Byron's ghost in *The Aspern Papers*.

At the end of Part 4 of the text, the narrator speculates on what might have been the case between Aspern and Juliana Bordereau. Cumnor, his offstage friend, the other, the English admirer of Aspern, the narrator's 'fellow-worshipper' (1, 47), he reports as thinking that the American Juliana Bordereau at the age of twenty (the date 1820 is mentioned) might have been a governess in some European family which the poet had visited (which would make Aspern Mr Rochester-like, or would anticipate *The Turn of the Screw*),[13] and that the poetry was written to her on the occasion of his second absence from America (the first absence, the originating one, not being mentioned). The narrator, however, thinks she might have been a daughter of a widowed American artist with a second daughter, and in this second possible narrative, which shows the desire to take liberties, the text wanders off into different and irreconcilable fantasised wishes:

> It was incontestable that, whether for right or for wrong, most readers of certain of Aspern's poems (poems not as ambiguous as the sonnets – scarcely more divine, I think – of Shakespeare) had taken for granted that Juliana had not always adhered to the steep footway of renunciation. There hovered about her name a perfume of impenitent passion, an intimation that she had not been exactly as the respectable young person in general. Was this a sign that her singer had betrayed her, had given her away, as we say, to posterity? ... It was part of my idea that the young lady had had a foreign lover – and say an unedifying tragical rupture – before her meeting with Jeffrey Aspern. She had lived with her father and sister in a queer old-fashioned expatriated artistic Bohemia. ... When Americans went abroad in 1820, there was something romantic, almost heroic in it, as compared with the perpetual ferryings of the present hour, the hour at which photography and other conveniences have annihilated surprises. ... It was a much more important fact, if one was looking at his genius critically, that he had lived in the days before the general transfusion. It had happened to me to regret that he had known Europe at all: I should have liked to see what he would have written without that experience, by which he had incontestably been enriched. But as his fate had ruled otherwise, I went with him – I tried to judge how the old order would have struck him. It was not only there, however, I watched him; the relations he had entertained with the special new had even a livelier interest. His own country after all had had most of his life, and his muse, as they said at the time, was essentially American. That was originally what I had prized him for: that at a period when our native land was nude and crude and provincial, when the famous 'atmosphere' it is supposed to lack was not even missed, he had found means to live and write like one of the first; to be free and general and not at all afraid; to feel, understand and express everything. (4, 76–8)

This passage wanders through several possibilities which it cannot unite – so it could have no use for historical documents. The history he gives Juliana Bordereau aestheticises a passion which will get the better of the narrator in the end, and so it is ironic, but what is the passion? It is complicated by the reference to Shakespeare's Sonnets, which are declared 'ambiguous', when that ambiguity could only imply their homosexual or bisexual content, being addressed to a man and a woman – which would tie up with Byron. But if these poems are not so ambiguous as Shakespeare's, why does the narrator assert that they are not? Was it necessary to state a negative, to issue a disavowal?[14] By the mid-nineteenth century, there could have been no ambiguity about being ambiguous. Tennyson writes about Hallam in *In Memoriam* (LXI) 'I loved thee, Spirit, and love, nor can / The soul of Shakespeare love thee more.' Accordingly, the review of *In Memoriam*, which was probably by Manley Hopkins, the father of the poet, and which appeared in *The Times* in late 1851, commented: 'very sweet and plaintive these verses are, but who would not give them a feminine application? Shakespeare may be considered the founder of this style in English.' It refers to Tennyson 'transferring every epithet of womanly endearment to a masculine friend – his "master – mistress" as he calls him by a compound epithet as harsh as it is disagreeable'.[15] If James was familiar with this kind of debate, as seems likely, disavowal of ambiguity in Aspern – double meanings gathered round a sexuality that is double in being bisexual – will work in either of two ways. It may represent the narrator's own position as American in contrast to the European, asserting that there is no homoeroticism at work in the poetry of nineteenth-century America, or it may be actuated by his own ambiguous position, as though he were Tennyson to Aspern's Hallam. Homoeroticism is suggested, lightly. It is significant that the poet has been painted by Miss Bordereau's father (7, 110), implying his attractiveness to men, and further, he appears to the narrator, a like a ghost, take his part in relationship to the woman, Miss Bordereau, adding, 'meanwhile, aren't we in Venice together, and what better place is there for the meeting of dear friends?' (4, 73). Aspern and the narrator 'together' in a kind of wish-fulfilment focus America's own homoeroticism – whether this is affirmed as being specifically American, part of what an American Byron would have provided, or denied under the claim that American poetry lacks Shakespeare's ambiguity.

A second set of contradictions opens up in the way the text curls round from talking about Americans abroad, and the heroism of travel in the moment just after the Napoleonic wars, especially the heroism of a woman's travel, in order to discuss what the publisher takes as the more compelling case of Aspern abroad. The reference to America's provinciality and the atmosphere 'it is supposed to lack' (the narrator being equivocal on this, because after all, he, more certainly than James in the Preface, *does* believe in the American Byron) takes in Hawthorne's Preface to *The Marble Faun*, and James on Hawthorne (2, 65), and the lack of 'the items of high civilization' that James refers to. Perhaps there is something of Hawthorne in Aspern: Hawthorne, who, born in 1804, was only twelve years younger than Shelley, nine years younger than Keats.[16] Perhaps envy of Aspern may be read autobiographically: for James felt he had to expatriate himself to write, and felt ambivalent about that. The public history of the period after 1812, the Byronic age, when America emerged from war with England, and began to think about a national literature, is where the English could feel total superiority: 'The Americans have no national literature and no learned men' (*The British Critic*, 1818).[17] Wishing Aspern to have stayed in America makes the narrator like the author of *William Wetmore Story*, which concludes that art does best 'in some air unfriendly to the element at large' (II, 225–6), and Story should have stayed in Boston, not relocated to Rome. (The biography speaks about the price that expatriation exacts from the subject.) The narrator indicates that much of Aspern's putative work was composed in America. The status of Aspern's relationship with Juliana and the question of provinciality becomes more puzzling when the narrator insists that she must have had an affair prior to the one with Aspern, suggesting that she has not been the innocent (almost as though Aspern were that, as though he were like Isabel Archer). This speculation seems to reverse an earlier thought, that Aspern had seduced several women around 1825, including Juliana Bordereau (1, 47), or it further mythicises Aspern, as a figure of the unconscious, where, as Freud suggests, there can be no unconscious no, no negative.

If Aspern 'treated [Juliana] badly' (1, 47) – and has treated other women so too – betrayal is at the heart of the narrative: Aspern betrays women while making one woman – Juliana Bordereau – as his 'muse'. If a muse is betrayed, especially an American one, so is the poetry, and Aspern cannot have the unambiguous identity of the American writer that the narrator invests so much time in. (The narrator is bound to the same pattern of repetition, since he plans to betray both the Misses Bordereau.) If the point is that Europe's influence has led him to betray Miss Bordereau, and his muse, then single American identity proves impossible: Europe as the other must be desired and the seas crossed for it, and Miss Bordereau is betrayed in favour of Europe. In the same way, early America is mythicised by being called 'nude', which implies freedom from duplicity: Aspern, however, succeeded by duplicity, just as this narrator says of himself that 'hypocrisy, duplicity are my only chance' (1, 51).

And what is to be made of the final claim that Aspern was 'free and general' – as Macbeth aspired to be 'broad and general as the casing air' (*Macbeth*, III.4.23) – and had been able in 'nude' American civilisation to express everything? (Presumably, with no ambiguity.) Emerson in 1839 did not feel that this freedom obtained, at least with America's visual arts. He comments that '[Washington] Allston's pictures are Elysian; fair, serene but unreal. I extend the remark to all the American geniuses. Irving, Bryant, Greenough, Everett, Channing, even Webster in his recorded Eloquence, all lack nerve and dagger.'[18] The lack of 'dagger' accuses American art of lack of masculinity. In contrast to Emerson, a *fin de siècle* text set in Europe comments on another case: an American Aspern having been 'not only one of the most brilliant minds of his day – and in those years, when the century was young, there were, as one knows, many – but one of the most genial men and one of the handsomest' (1, 47). America allows the family romance, a reinvention of the past, and of youth, where the word 'young' suggests that there is no past; America is ready to be invented.

The passage makes Aspern different things at once, and in lacking the papers at the end, does not need to resolve the ambiguities between innocence/vulnerability and sophistication, between America's background as confident, allowing writers to speak, and America as provincial, or between Aspern's reputation as a womaniser and his other status as appealing to the masculine, 'not a woman's poet' (1, 48). Such equivocation needs the European signifier, Byron. An American narrative needs an Italian setting to give it 'dagger'. James's arguments about Italy before which 'penetration fails' (*AN*, 9, 160), insulate the dramatist from being the historian: even if the novelist wanted to be the historian, he couldn't: the city's 'perfunctory smile' refuses to help, by giving no papers. Venice is what he would like to make old New York: a place that evades yielding a history. American openness and ability to express everything can only be achieved in an atmosphere of secrecy, impossible to map.

III   THE 'IDÉE FIXE'

The passage I have quoted suggests that Aspern's masculinity, and his assertive nationalism in his poetry, which the narrator is also near to, are problematic, but *The Aspern Papers* seems built on two irreconcilables – the desire to bring to life an American Byron, which contrasts as a positive, however impossible, and the character of the narrator, who is in no position to bring anything to life. As the American Byron project involves James in contradictions, wish-fulfilments not quite articulated, so the second issue – the narrator's character, which further contradicts everything – ensures that the text can resolve nothing singly nor state it openly.

Like Silsbee, whose Shelley-worship meant that the women were only instrumental for him, until Pauline Clairmont turned the tables on him, the narrator has time only for a dead male poet, who is also his creation. He summons up, in an act of prosopopoeia, the dead poet he so much admires. 'The revived immortal face – in which all his genius shone' appears before him:

> I had invoked him and he had come; he hovered before me half the time; it was if his bright ghost had returned to earth to assure me he regarded the affair as his own no less than as mine, and that we should see it fraternally and fondly to a conclusion.   (4, 73)

'Fraternally' evokes the narrator's self-deception, and casually points to the exclusionary world of male Romantics. But the narrator is also self-aware. When he gets the portrait, '[Aspern] seemed to smile at me with mild mockery; he might have been amused at my case' (9, 134), in a moment of 'unsatisfactoriness' which perpetuates itself down to the last line, when, in the present time, the narrator looks up at his picture: 'When I look at it I can scarcely bear my loss – I mean that of the precious papers' (9, 142).[19] The mask fails: the narrator becomes aware of what and how much he has fictionalised in creating Jeffrey Aspern.

Hillis Miller makes the point that if the narrator acquired possession of the papers by marrying Tina Bordereau, then, as she says, 'it would be the same for you as for me' (9, 135). He would, as she says, 'have no responsibility' if he then divulged what would be family secrets.[20] The dream of having the letters *and* being able to publish them is impossible. The past is the past because it is not visitable, not usable in the present, in the conditions of modernity.

At the beginning of the novel, the narrator thinks about the puzzle that such 'self-effacement' as Juliana Bordereau showed could be 'possible in the latter half of the nineteenth century – the age of newspapers and telegrams and photographers and interviewers' (1, 48). The narrator's desire is to 'bring to light' what Jeffrey Aspern had written (4, 73). When Miss Bordereau sees him purloining the papers, she calls him 'you publishing scoundrel' (8, 125). The line might be compared with Emily Dickinson's lines, equally anti-modernity in their self-protectiveness, and which, because they also protect whiteness, are also ambivalent:

> Publication – is the Auction
> Of the Mind of Man –
> Poverty – be justifying
> For so foul a thing
>
> Possibly – but We – would rather
> From Our Garret go
> White – Unto the White Creator –
> Than invest – Our Snow –...[21]

For the narrator to publish the papers – the record of a love-affair? – would be like putting the scarlet 'A' upon Hester Prynne in *The Scarlet Letter*: publication (A for auction) would be selling the woman in public (prostitution), even if it was called an 'investment'. The woman wishes to leave life with her virgin page (her snow) not written upon, not the object of male writing (even if the man makes her his muse), or with her writing – if her 'snow' is that – not published, or edited, or glossed, kept in its integrity.

The ambiguity of the narrator/editor's role in *The Aspern Papers* is his love for Aspern's poetry which makes him a 'fine case of monomania' (1, 46), but his research into the history of the poet takes place within the conditions of modernity: he wants to sell Aspern, betraying him, revealing him by compromising him. This 'selling' Aspern would feminise the poet, who is already his muse (his picture hangs above the desk), by shaming him. Putting him into a newspaper or coffee-table book narrative, he would 'relate' him, which James sees the romance form as not doing: *not* relating. His romantic project produces the literality of realism. In this, the gender-issues return: the structure of fetishising another – as muse, as privileged poet, as the spokesperson for young America – leads to a feminisation, by a reduction of the subject in the act of reifying him.

Collecting in modernity, the age of the commodity, shows 'monomania'. The narrator's 'living on' makes him ghostly, haunting the Bordereau palazzo, and living on ghosts, on fragments, relics and tokens and spoiled things. He is like Frankenstein, who collects together the fragments of dead bodies to construct the being of his imaginary. Tina Bordereau says that Miss Bordereau had the idea that the narrator was capable of 'violating a tomb' to get what he wanted (9, 136). A vicarious life creates monsters, including the Aspern who betrayed Juliana – which is his own narrative about him, his own fantasisings, an historical 'impression' (1, 47). He never sees the Aspern papers, but writes *The Aspern Papers*, as though continuing the fantastic hero's existence, making him live on in his own narrative. He not only makes Juliana Bordereau a figure of witch-like monstrosity, but Tina Bordereau, whom he pushes into convulsive behaviour, he makes monstrous, at least to herself. 'Her sobs resounded in the great empty hall', the narrator says (9, 137). To see the narrator as an echo of Frankenstein picks up on the 'feminist' critique of male Romantics which Mary Shelley writes, and connects the narrator to those scientists in Hawthorne deriving from Frankenstein: Chillingworth, Rappaccini,[22] and the scientist of 'The Birthmark'. 'Do you pry into his life?' Tina asks of his relation to Aspern (5, 88). In prying, he is a detective with the will to truth, mad collector, publisher and Frankenstein, as anti-woman as Mary Shelley's scientist, when he says of his researches, 'I pursued nature to her hiding-places.'[23] Working by endless 'strategems' (9, 139, 141), he finds he has been ensnared, rather than doing the ensnaring.

In the 1888 version, his interest in the papers is not 'a fine case of monomania' (New York edition) but 'a fixed idea'. Six years later, in 1894, Pierre Janet writes on 'Les idées fixe' in his *État mental des hystériques* in which he argues that the cause of hysterical symptoms is an unconscious 'idée fixe'. This, followed through, would convict the narrator of hysteria, which gives an interesting pairing: near the end, he reduces Tina Bordereau, who is in love with him, to an hysterical reaction, which she resolves by burning the papers 'one by one' (9, 142), in an act of working-through which settles, for her, her relationship to a past which blocks her to the extent of not allowing her to be sure of her parentage. The narrator, however, becomes hysterical when the proposal of marriage is made. He revolts from the papers – 'a bundle of tattered papers' (9, 138) – then 'swings back to a passionate appreciation of Juliana's treasures'.

That abject state appears in his direction to the gondolier – 'Go anywhere – everywhere – all over the place' (9, 139). He is schizoid and hysterical at that moment.

If the narrator has a fixed idea, he may be hysterical; if he is 'a fine case of monomania' he is crazy. Monomania was derived from the researches of Jean Esquirol, Pinel's student, and seems to have been first used around 1810. By 1870, it seems to have lost its force as a description, taken over by the term hysteria.[24] The notion of the *idée fixe* as a medical term in association with monomania followed very soon: acording to Goldstein, around 1812. Monomania was defined by Esquirol in contrast to melancholia, which he re-named lypemania. 'Monomania is the type intermediate betweeen mania and lypemania; it shares with lypemania the fixity and concentration of ideas and with mania the exaltation of ideas and the phsyical and mental activity.'[25] Whereas mania corresponded to general delirium, lypemania and monomania were both partial forms of insanity, and Esquirol insisted on the discreteness of the monomanic's delusion – 'he reasons well on all other subjects' – and on what Goldstein calls his 'high level of excitation and even audacity'. Esquirol tied monomania to the dominant passions of each era: monomania was the disease of each stage of civilisation. Frankenstein's monomania ('my enthusiasm was checked by my anxiety....Every night I was oppressed by a slow fever and I became nervous to a most painful degree' [4, 316–17]) is scientific, part of a will to truth, like the narrator's desire to know by owning papers. Both connect with Hawthorne's obsessives: the Minister with the black veil, Wakefield or Ethan Brand, and to equivalents in James – the narrator in *The Sacred Fount*, or John Marcher or Spencer Brydon. Since James hovered between notions of fixed ideas and monomania in his writing, one as a term used earlier in the century and placed in opposition to melancholia, and the other as a term linked to hysteria, perhaps both should be used to consider the narrator. Freud's dictum from *Studies in Hysteria*, that 'hysterics suffer mainly from reminiscences',[26] means reminiscences are not memory, but a fake memory, coming about from a failed reaction to the past. One reaction the narrator has to Juliana Bordereau calls her 'too sacred for trivial modernisms – too venerable to touch' (6, 91). Dealing with the romance of Jeffrey Aspern, the narrator, to get back to that past, which is also the past of America, performs his own Gothic romance. He describes himself in terms of laying siege as if to a Medieval castle; he virtually allegorises himself as the devil entering the Garden of Eden, and tempting the lady with flowers. Perhaps he copies Hawthorne's madmen. The move from realism to romance to allegory is monomaniacal, a sign that reality has been replaced by the reduction of life to one 'unrelated' idea. The romance structure of the narrative suggests that the romance form, however necessary, may also be a madness. The failure implied in contracting life to an allegory produces feelings of loss – the name for which is melancholia.

Juliana Bordereau does live in the past with perhaps hysterical symptoms in her life and body, like those of Dickens's Mrs Clennam or Miss Havisham. Like the latter, she is calculating and engineering in her relationship to the narrator, who she wants to marry Tina Bordereau (9, 135), to assure her future. Her attitudes are dissimilar from those of Dickinson's poem, in treating things as commodities. When she takes the green shade off her eyes, or when she tries to burn the papers, she reveals both that she is not wholly in thrall to that past, and that there is a concealed aggression towards it, and its patriarchal implications.

IV   JAMES AND WHITMAN

The narrator gives one narrative: another is implied in the aim to give an American Byron. The absence of papers at the end is the sign that no other narrative can be given, in the conditions James was given to think under. Perhaps Venice, as home to a form of death, is wrong for Aspern, and so is Byron. Byron in Venice takes the form of projecting not Aspern-like youth, but ruin, personal and European:

> But my soul wanders: I demand it back
> To meditate amongst decay, and stand
> A ruin amidst ruins...
> (*Childe Harold's Pilgrimage*, IV, 25)

Obsessiveness and a fixed idea induce the narrator to obtain in the papers a past to connect with the present – one whose prior value cannot be assumed, only fantasised. Venice, rather than a present, represents the ruins of past experience.

Perhaps the missing name that James needed for his American Byron was the American poet whose purpose was, according to

James, 'to celebrate the greatness of the city of New York' (*LC* II, 631) – as Byron celebrated that of Venice. James was then reviewing Whitman's *Drum-Taps* negatively. But in Lenox in America in 1904, James was reading aloud and enthusiastically from 'Song of Myself', 'When lilacs last in the doorways bloomed' and 'Out of the Cradle'. In 1909 in conversation 'he maintained that it was impossible for any woman to write a good criticism of Whitman or get near his point of view' (Edel, V, 225, 395). Whitman sounds like Aspern, 'free and general and not at all afraid' in his poetry. And James could hardly have been unaware of Whitman's status as the poet of male love.[27]

If Whitman is in any sense the Aspern of *The Aspern Papers*, he must have been more so for James at the time of the New York edition than at the time of the tale's first appearance. He would have enabled, in James's mind, a connection between the American and American literature, as a New York poet, not needing Europe (James regretted to Edith Wharton Whitman's 'too-extensive acquaintance with the foreign languages'), with a way of writing about the city, the body and the erotic, both non-'queer' and free of the negativity of Byron's connections with Europe as old, as the ruin. Whitman, born in 1819, was too late to be Aspern, yet could have given the signal that someone like him could have been a poet in New York. Yet there is no hint that Whitman – pushed back in time – could become a figure in the Preface to *The Aspern Papers*. Which suggests several possibilities, one of which was that between Byron and Whitman, James could only see Byron, so that in some way and at some level of consciousness screening out Whitman, he selected the larger impossibility. As if fitting with this commitment to the impossible, the American narrator fails in realising this particular aspect of an American's dream. He comes away with only the too dearly bought portrait of Aspern.

The narrator's inability to bring Aspern to life by his papers is explained in two ways by the tale: first in relation to his character as an historian – he is doing the wrong thing throughout – and then secondly in terms of the idea of him being foiled by the power of Venice, the old traditional power where the Americans (i.e., the Bordereaus) have been almost wholly taken over by the city's European character, so that Juliana Bordereau is more than a match for the American. The tale gives many reasons to explain the failure of the narrator to procure documents, but one never articulated is that had he secured them, they would have been found to have had the ambiguity the narrator thinks Aspern's poems lacked – they would have been interpretable as letters to a man. Whether James saw the logic of that position is not calculable; as historian, he would have seen that they would have provided him with more documents than he could really use. *The Aspern Papers*, as a title of considerable interest, conceals another interest: the Aspern papers. Another displacement to add to the others.

5

Allegorical Autobiography: *The Turn of the Screw*

James's autobiography recalls the Louvre's picture of the Princes in the Tower by Paul Delaroche (1797–1856):

> 'Les Enfants d'Edouard' thrilled me ... and I couldn't doubt that the long-drawn odd face of the elder prince, sad and sore and sick, with his wide crimped sidelocks of fair hair and his violet legs marked by the Garter and dangling from the bed, was a reconstitution of far-off history of the subtlest and most 'last word' modern or psychologic kind. I had never heard of psychology in art or anywhere else – scarcely anyone then had, but I truly felt the nameless force at play.
>
> *(Autobiography*, I, 194)

Its modernity is to show the power of anxiety. The elder boy sits, pensive. The younger has been reading with him, but looks away as though he heard something; as the spaniel stands with its back to the viewer, looking out of the picture as if sensing an arrival. What can be seen in the picture does not explain the narrative. There is no visible threat: a 'nameless force' is at play, working on lives by psychological pressure, filling them with dread so that they are as good as dead before they are murdered. What affects the self isn't visible to any spectator. This is indirect source-material for *The Turn of the Screw*,[1] which culminates in the death of one of two privileged yet orphaned children. The New York edition placed it next to *The Aspern Papers*, written ten years earlier, whose 'fine case of mono-mania' has often been taken as a way into *The Turn of the Screw*. But since *The Turn of the Screw* mixes a possible ghost-story with the power of anxiety, it evokes hysteria all round.

The unnamed governess has her autobiographical narrative framed, for the unknown narrator of uncertain gender writing the first, untitled, section (henceforth the Introduction) has transcribed it from an original manuscript which she wrote out for the benefit of Douglas (a first or last name?). He or she gives the transcript plus an autobiographical account of the circumstances in which Douglas read out the manuscript, including a record of Douglas's 'few words of prologue' (Introduction, 148). The prologue Douglas gives before reading the manuscript aloud is necessary because 'the written statement took up the tale at a point after it had, in a manner, begun' (Introduction, 149). Thus the governess's narrative has *two* prologues: Douglas's oral one by Douglas, recreated by the narrator, and the whole Introduction, saying how Douglas came to tell the story. The last words are the governess's, not a return to the scene when Douglas reads out the story, leaving the narration unedited by anyone else's words, though in a way it circles back to the beginning ('The story had held us, round the fire, sufficiently breathless' (Introduction, 145)), though this beginning reacts to a previously told 'strange tale'.

This unknown story deals with *one* child being haunted. Douglas says that 'the child gives the effect another turn of the screw' (Introduction, 145). Where one child means *another* turn, there is no knowing what the *first* turn would have been (or if it was the first). But one child means two turns, so two children mean not two turns, as 'somebody' says, but *three*. The governess's narrative, dealing with the corruption of *two* children, leaves the assumption that her story would prologue the next, the corruption of *three* children... and so on. *The Turn of the Screw* was published serially, and its content implies serial turnings, like serial killings. And in seriality, like Freud's sense of the uncanniness of repetition, there is a doing away with the notion of the origin. So there is no first turn, no beginning: narrative must start in the middle and incrementalise its horrors, to achieve status, to attain possession, to exist at all. The title is 'about' narrative spirallings, narrative as a form of increasing torture, increasing sensation, in order to enter the condition of autobiographical narrative – at all. Only on the basis of unmeasured trauma can there be any beginning of an autobiogaphical life.[2]

The title applies both to the governess's narrative (untitled), and to the procedures of the whole text, the frame plus the woman's narrative. The governess's narrative postpones the beginning, since that has already happened: one child has already been ruined in a previous narrative. Remembering that James was supposed to have heard the source for the story from E. W. Benson, the Archbishop of Canterbury (*Notebook*, 12 January 1895, p. 109), this could be called James's Canterbury Tale, where 'The Governess's Tale' follows on from a link-narrative. Like Chaucer's *Canterbury Tales*, which joins together pilgrims for them to tell stories on their journey, or like Boccaccio's *Decameron*, which puts people together in a house telling stories over ten days, the structure of this text is people telling stories to each other to pass the time at a house-party. The movement structure is in fact two-fold, with a *fort–da* sequence: an opposition between turning the screw (one tale following another) and its contrary, 'postponement' (Introduction, 146), deferral succeeding what is called 'the mere opening of a serial' (Introduction, 148).[3] Interestingly, too, the house narratives are not self-contained, for Douglas compensates for his 'postponement' of the narration by writing 'by the first post' to get the manuscript sent to him at the house-party. The order of the house turns out to be insufficient, it must be supplemented by the outside. In contrast, the governess in the house can live by and work by nothing except the order of the house – with disastrous consequences. She is forbidden to write to the master.

Douglas has kept the story locked up for years in a drawer. He must send for it, rather than tell it second-hand: 'It was to me in particular that he appeared to propound this – appeared almost to appeal for aid not to hesitate. He had broken a thickness of ice, the formation of many a winter; had had his reasons for a long silence. The others resented postponement, but it was just his scruples that charmed me. I adjured him to write by the first post' (Introduction, 146). He is like John Marcher in *The Beast in the Jungle*: he has done nothing for years. Hesitation has been his rule of life, as postponement is basic to this narrator, and to Marcher. But telling a narrative again avoids postponing, lifting repression, though that narrative will contain in itself in its itinerary to the last word, 'stopped', its own *fort/da* movement. The governess begins with a *fort/da* movement: 'I remember the whole beginning as a succession of flights and drops, a little see-saw of the right throbs and the wrong' (1, 152). What happens to Douglas – telling the story, after so long a postponement, then dying – relates narrative to death, which maps onto the serial structure implied in the title. Identity can only be by a pattern of repetitions supplemented by an incremental intensity (which because it is repeated is also diminishing intensity).

Thus, after Griffin's male narrative about a ghost appearing to a boy and to his mother, and another tale which succeeds it, called 'not particularly effective', it is the governess's turn, in a narrative which has been buried for years, and which is now brought out – framed – by Douglas. The difference from Chaucer is that there has been no prior portrait of a governess, no General Prologue to this Canterbury Tale. But there is no beginning for the governess because she is only one of a line of impersonal nineteenth-century governesses, and if she has no beginning, she is already lost, caught in a process that 'turns' her, as a screw keeping together parts of the social machine. The machinery produces gender, class and imperialism (the children's parents lived in India), but an uncanny emerges out of the mechanistic, fully predictable world, where identity is guaranteed/betrayed by mechanistic repetition.

I 'THE GOVERNESS'S TALE'

To listen to 'The Governess's tale' – and to her narrative voice, which is autonomous in trying to come close to Douglas, and is also making a 'statement' (3, 164), an official document, a confessional autobiography for the police, so lacking autonomy – I start with the episode which recalls Strether by the river in *The Ambassadors*, where the governess first sees the ghost of Peter Quint. Strolling one afternoon, she thinks it would be 'as charming as a charming story' to meet someone. The unspecified person, associated with literature, with stories, becomes male in the next sentence: 'I only asked that he should *know*; and the only way to be sure he knew would be to see it, and the kind light of it, in his handsome face. That was exactly present to me – by which I mean the face was – when, on the first of these occasions, at the end of a long June day, I stopped short... what arrested me on the spot – and with a shock much greater than any vision had allowed for – was the sense that my imagination had, in a flash, turned real. He did stand there!' (3, 164).

'The first of these occasions' implies that she continued to have such thoughts about seeing a man who seems to be also 'the person to whose pressure I yielded', as she says in the previous paragraph (3, 163). Though frightened on this occasion by the sight of the ghost, she continued at other times to have the same fantasy. It is a sign of the difficulty of giving a chronology to the events which are described, and of how much autobiography must be a rationalisation into one account of several different occasions. The narrative of the governess gives more and less than can be used. Though she is referring to the Master, and is unrepressed about being in love with him, her words do not join up the 'person', 'someone' and 'he', leaving that to the reader to construct a narrative; at the same time it implies other things happening in excess of what it explains:

> It produced in me, this figure, in the clear twilight, I remember, two distinct gasps of emotion, which were, sharply, the shock of my first and that of my second surprise. My second was a violent perception of the mistake of my first: the man who met my eyes was not the person I had precipitately supposed. There came to me thus a bewilderment of vision of which, after these years, there is no living view that I can hope to give. An unknown man in a lonely place is a permitted object of fear to a young woman privately bred; and the figure that faced me was – as little any one else I knew as it was the image that had been in my mind. I had not seen it in Harley Street – I had not seen it anywhere. The place, moreover, in the strangest way in the world, had on the instant and by the very fact of its appearance become a solitude. To me, at least, making my statement here with a deliberation which I have never made it, the whole feeling of the moment returns. It was as if, while I took in what I did take in, all the rest of the scene had been stricken with death. I can hear again, as I write, the intense hush in which the sounds of evening dropped. The rooks stopped cawing in the golden sky and the friendly hour lost for the unspeakable minute all its voice. But there was no other change in nature, unless indeed it were a change that I saw with a stranger sharpness. The gold was still in the sky, the clearness in the air, and the man who looked at me over the battlements was as definite as a picture in a frame.   (3, 164–5)

Something extraneous is in the picture: the field of vision cannot be fully described. But comparing this with *The Ambassadors* is to note a reversal. Strether thinks of himself in a picture, then the perception is cancelled out when the picture as it were becomes animated and Madame de Vionnet and Chad appear in the boat. The governess comes round the corner into view and sees someone standing on top of one of the towers of the house. He appears with the clarity of a picture, in a definition which seems unnatural. He demands attention: when he is seen, all sounds die down. The rooks were heard when she first arrived at the house (1, 152), but now everything is mute though to the eye everything is as before. Ear and eye are disassociated. She has been taken out of a lived situation and is abstracted, looking at a picture, where, as one form of attention goes, another takes its place: a '*stranger* sharpness' brightening colours, and increasing the sense of a picture in a frame, everything, including his position on the top of the tower, giving him a firm silhouette, bringing him out.

In the governess's second view of him (4, 169) he is framed by the window, as he looks from outside into the room, as though supplementing the order of the house. Only once is he seen inside (10, 198), and as the governess says that this was the only time, the question is open whether his appearance on the tower is to be regarded as inside or out. Quint, on the tower, questions the distinction between inside and outside; the inside being the place of power, but shown by this blurring to be dependent on the outside. Yet Quint's framing means that he does not stand in his own space; he is part of the field of vision of another. Analogously, a frame narrative encloses the governess's narrative, she being a ghostly presence as she stands out in these pages ('she has been dead these twenty years' (Introduction, 146)). Her text lacks autonomy, the power to tell, because it is framed by something else. But Douglas, in the frame text, is also dead, and has been replaced by another narrator. Quint – the governess – Douglas: it is a sequence of turns of the screw, where each turn indicates another framing. The vision of each lacks authority to make its perception tell.

As the governess writes, the feel of the moment *returns*, as at the end of the vision, 'he *turned* away; that was all I knew' (3, 165 – my emphases). As the moment returns, like Freud's 'return of the repressed', she says 'I can hear again, as I write, the intense hush.' For Freud, memory is present-tense, creating its own past, and trauma is a present-day fear which necessitates creating and interpreting the past. The governess's memory may be accurate: seeing the man may make everything different as 'the friendly hour lost for the unspeakable minute all its voice'. It would suggest a moment of being outside history, outside continuity, as though the governess needs to separate the moment off as in a picture, as though she was telling herself that this was not the truth of the situation; the truth being that of 'the *friendly* hour'.

Yet the hour is not friendly. For the governess has been imposed on in an unfriendly manner by the master, as Miles will separate himself

from her class with the line 'I want my own sort' (14, 217). Unfriend-
liness links with muteness. The governess fears silence, which she
finishes on with the words: 'We were alone with the quiet day, and
his little heart, dispossessed, had stopped' (24, 262). Not even the
heart to give a beat, a rhythm, like the ticking of a clock: everything
of seriality has 'stopped', like Douglas's voice, drawn attention to at
the end of the frame narrative. He says 'stopped' and then he stops:
and since he is dead, silence and stopping become preclusive to death,
as another turn of the screw. There are no more narrative postpone-
ments to ward off death. This last sentence of the tale fuses silence
and being 'dispossessed' a word that resonates. Shoshana Felman
links it to the notion of grasping at meaning, holding it.[4] The ability
to control, to read things one way, is a loss. The last paragraph is full
of synonyms for grasping and holding:

> But he [Miles] had already jerked straight round, stared, glared again,
> and seen but the quiet day. With the stroke of the loss I was so proud of
> he uttered the cry of a creature hurled over an abyss, and the grasp
> with which I recovered him might have been that of catching him in his
> fall. I caught him, yes I held him – it may be imagined with what a
> passion; but at the end of a minute I began to feel what it truly was that
> I held. We were alone with the quiet day and his little heart, dispos-
> sessed, had stopped.   (24, 261–2)

A possessed person is held by a devil (compare Miles's last words,
'Peter Quint – you devil' (24, 261)), but to be dispossessed is not the
contrary of that, since it implies the loss of the subject's self-possession; to be possessed entails being dispossessed, to be dispossessed
implies possession by another. Possession and dispossession are
switch-words, reversible. 'Dispossessed', having lost possession,
works in several ways through the text. When a lady listening to
Douglas telling the story asks him 'What's your title?' (Introduction,
151), and Douglas says he hasn't one, this suggests a lack of entitlement which fits with dispossession,[5] and both senses link with the
lack of a title for the governess. When Miles dies, the family is
dispossessed, since there is no male heir, the family line stopping
with the end of the sentence and the end of the narrative. To have
possession, or self-possession, so undermined, suggests the power of
betrayal.

Betrayal becomes a clue in relation to what the narrative will tell,
confessionally, as if to the police. 'Who was it she [the governess] was

in love with?' is the question asked before the governess's narrative is read out. The narrator replies 'The story will tell', but Douglas responds 'The story *won't* tell...not in any literal vulgar way' (Introduction, 147). Mrs Griffin, who asked the question, says about Douglas, 'Well, if I don't know who she was in love with I know who *he* was' (Introduction, 148). For her, Douglas's actions have betrayed his affective state. Douglas's fear that narrative betrays pushes him towards the tale as allegory – the tale must not tell 'in any *literal* vulgar way' (my emphasis). Shoshana Felman analyses the force of 'tell'. Miles says things to the people he liked at school, and he speculates that they must have repeated them to those that they liked. These things came to 'the masters' Miles thinks, 'But I didn't know they'd tell.' She replies to him 'The masters? They didn't – they've never told' (24, 260). Felman says of this, picking up on the association of the school masters with the Headmaster of the school from which Miles is dismissed and the master in Harley Street, and the idea of 'mastery' as in the governess's statement 'I seemed to myself for the instant to have mastered it, to see it all' (21, 248), that the word 'master' 'comes to signify, in James's text, at once the principle of authority and the principle of repression – the very principle of the *authority to repress*: to repress at once mentally and physically, in a psychoanalytical but equally in a political sense'.[6] The principle of mastery is not to tell, not to have to confess, or, oppositely, not to betray: mastery and betrayal are antitheses, unless being a master is a method of betrayal (as perhaps the Master in Harley Street betrayed Miss Jessel, and may in another way betray the governess).[7] The tale cannot be mastered (interpreted) since a narrative that does not tell who the governess loved, as Douglas says, will not betray her in an atmosphere where everyone is ready to betray the other by knowing their secrets.

Issues of mastery and possession intersect with the governess's own marginality. The point may be made by comparison to another text of 1898, *In the Cage*. The attention in this narrative focuses on an unnamed working-class woman, a young person who works in the section of a local Mayfair post office where telegrams are sent off. She spends her time 'in *framed* and wired confinement' (my emphasis) serving the people who come in to conduct their affairs – mainly extra-marital affairs – with the aid of telegrams. Dealing often with the rich, but from a marginalised, personally unrecognised position, she soon develops an 'eye for types' – 'There were the

brazen women, as she called them . . . whose squanderings and grasp-
ings, whose struggles and secrets and love-affairs and lies, she
tracked and stored up against them, till she had at moments, in
private, a triumphant, vicious feeling of mastery and ease [power,
1898], a sense of carrying their silly, guilty secrets in her pocket, her
small retentive brain, and thereby knowing so much more about
them than they suspected or would care to think.' Her position is
ambiguous: on the one side, she could easily become a blackmailer,
something she fantasises about with the aid of the cheap fiction
('ha'penny novels') that she reads (11, 417); on the other hand, she
is fascinated by what she sees, and by the life from which she is
excluded, but which she ghosts. An adulterous affair is afoot between
Captain Everard and Lady Bradeen: her fascination is with that other
life, which the nature of her work leads her to haunt. The other
narrative is nowhere detailed; it remains offstage, as a fascinating
possibility of what she is excluded from. At one point she has a
meeting with Captain Everard after office-hours, on her way home
(chapters 14–17), on an occasion where she enters his life as though
she is haunting it. After this, she remains fascinated and frightened;
she does not want to see him:

> That was what, the night before, at eight o'clock, her hour to go, had
> made her hang back and dawdle. She did last things, or pretended to
> do them; to be in the cage had suddenly become her safety, and she was
> literally afraid of the alternate self who might be waiting outside. *He*
> might be waiting; it was he who was her alternate self and of him she
> was afraid. (21, 469)

Here, Everard is the ghost whom she fears, though in a sense, the
explanation that 'he was her alternate self' (a phrase that activates
The Jolly Corner) does not satisfy or explain enough. She has an
alternate self in the character of the woman who runs away with the
aristocrat, or who lets herself be seduced. At the end, she goes back
into the 'cage', safe marriage to Mr Mudge, her friend of long-
standing: 'reality for the poor things they both were [her and her
friend Mrs Jordan – the widow of a vicar] could only be ugliness and
obscurity, could never be the escape, the rise' (26, 499). The irony is
that she also discovers that her fantasies about the aristocratic
adultery are not real: Everard is poor, and it seems that he is to
be forced into marriage to the newly widowed Lady Bradeen at
the end.

In the Cage dramatises the woman's lack of 'position' – with two meanings, 'status', and 'job'. The governess and the telegraphist are condemned to be little more than ghosts. Only at the house does the governess get the chance to see herself from head to foot in 'long glasses' (1, 153). She has not been able to acquire an identity, as now she cannot quite write an autobiography, cannot authenticate an identity, while the ghosts disconfirm her identity, leaving no place for her, as when she sees Miss Jessel writing at her own table (15, 221). In another way, they confirm her status. In the relay of looks, whereby all looking at the other proves unsatisfactory in terms of confirming the identity of the self,[8] it is too easily assumed that it is possible to make a distinction between the living and the non-living. The servant class acts as the ghost in relation to the upper class – the Mayfair set in *In the Cage*, or the Harley Street and Bly set – and perhaps women are always ghosts in culture. The dead governess, whose place has been taken by numerous other governesses, has never had an existence, and the first line of her narrative – 'I remember' – while it puts emphasis on recall, also puts into play the point that not only may she be unreliable, telling the story so many years after it had happened, but she shows no memory of anything beforehand in her life, nor any sign in her writing that the experience is other than end-stopped for her afterwards. The events seem to have happened forty years prior to Douglas telling them, and Douglas has died before the narrator begins. The governess seems to have been 21 at the time of her narrative, to have told the story to Douglas ten years later, and to have written it out before dying at around the age of 50. Douglas is 60 when he reads out her narrative: how long a time has elapsed between Douglas's death and the narrator's act of writing is not given, but if we are to assume that the narrator of the frame text is writing in 1897, and if Douglas has just died, then the events are datable to 1847.

After seeing Peter Quint the first time, the governess asks, 'Was there a "secret" at Bly – a mystery of Udolpho or an insane, an unmentionable relative kept in unsuspected confinement?' (4, 166).[9] Her mind is filled with literature, literary ghosts. If the events are of 1847, it might be argued on the basis of this reference that the governess has been an early reader of *Jane Eyre: An Autobiography*, which appeared that September. Her imagination fits with her reading: she has read about the governess who marries the master, Mr Rochester, and she knows about madwomen in the attic. If the events at Bly are earlier than 1847, the half-reference to *Jane Eyre* is a secondary revision put in after she has lived and thought through the events, which have undergone unconscious mental editing. But what of the reference to Ann Radcliffe's *The Mysteries of Udolpho* (1794)? Jane Austen used it as an intertext in *Northanger Abbey*, which is usually dated between 1798 and 1803, though it was published posthumously, in 1818. The relevance of this connection would be that the governess, 'one of several daughters of a poor country parson' from a 'Hampshire vicarage', is akin to Jane Austen, confronted with more intense, Charlotte Brontë-like situations (another turn of the screw). She lives within the sphere of literature like the telegraphist of *In the Cage*, the difference being that the polite governess reads English literature (e.g., *Amelia*), the former, cheap fiction. The distinction, however, turns out to be minimal, since the governess's references are to literature as 'a charming story.' The governess likes being part of a Gothic romance, even if it means mis-reading, for *The Mysteries of Udolpho* is not about the triumph of the irrational over the heroine, but the triumph of rationality (the castle's mysteries are each explicable). Similarly, the hero of James's tale *The Birthplace* (1903) is fascinated by the prospect of becoming curator of a famous dead poet's birthplace; he wants the place to be haunted, to discover the poet through the house. But the haunted house must be sold commercially to tourists visiting the birthplace: there is no room for the ghostly in this atmosphere of the vulgar-popular and the kitsch. The governess loses status throughout, as she learns that she is not in 'possession' of her position; that she has no position, and this is not a house of romance. At the centre is the question of whether the ghosts or the governess are ghostly. The governess assumes that there is no question, and that the ghosts are evil. She cannot see that she may be the same as them.

Dispossession and castration are metaphors for each other. Returning to the muteness the governess is aware of when she first sees Peter Quint, that may be seen as a form of loss, a deprivation. Seeing the ghost is equivocal, disempowering, that the increase of vision is also a mutilation. The name 'Quint' sounds Dickensian, but it has other resonances. I have already quoted James on Hawthorne, that he saw 'the quaintness or the weirdness, the interest *behind* the interest, of things' (*LC* II, 471). Looking for the interest behind the interest means looking for the 'nameless force at play' in the picture by Delaroche: becoming obsessed with what is and is not there. It is what happens to the governess when she sees the ghost in the scene, as she moves from seeing the familiar to discovering the unfamiliar in it. She thinks she has found the force, but the 'quaint' links at the level of the signifier to the Chaucerian 'queynte' (vagina). Through Freud's essay on 'The Uncanny', a link would be possible from the weird to the uncanny itself – the *unheimlich* – with this as the mother's genitals or her body.[10] Seeing a male whose name evokes the feminine, the vaginal, in the context of the woman's thinking about the superior power of the master, would suggest not that the ghosts have power, but the idea of castration.

'The interest *behind* the interest' produces the obsessiveness of assuming that every appearance conceals another reality. The governess's pursuit of possession and confession, which will give her a sure knowledge ('If he confesses, he's saved' she says of Miles – 21, 248), makes this her danger. In Hawthorne's *The Blithedale Romance*, for comparison, the narrator returns from Blithedale to the city, staying at a hotel where he can observe the backs of houses (their fronts being always 'a veil and a concealment' (17, 138)). He wants to know, and 'that cold tendency, between instinct and intellect, which made me pry with a speculative interest into people's passions and impulses, appeared to have gone far towards unhumanizing my heart' (*The Blithedale Romance*, 18, 142). In this situation, he sees Zenobia and Westervelt together, at the window of another house. He is punished for his scopic drive by Zenobia's awareness that she is being spied on: her reactions severely mutilate the pretensions of a man who rejects the accusation that his looking is 'a mere vulgar curiosity'. 'Zenobia . . . should have been able to appreciate that quality of the intellect and the heart, which impelled me (often against my own will, and to the detriment of my own comfort) to live in other lives, and to endeavor – by generous sympathies, by delicate intuitions, by taking note of things too slight for record, and by bringing my human spirit into manifold accordance with the companions whom God assigned me – to learn the secret which was hidden even from themselves' (19, 148). These are the weak justifications of someone whose present blindness to himself is continued in James, in *The Aspern Papers*, resulting in as much a feeling of terminal 'loss' in the narrator as might be suggested by castration or mutilation.

The temptation of this type of knowing is fullest in *The Sacred Fount* (1901), whose first-person narrative is devoted to discovering a possible 'interest behind the interest' at the price of missing the actual sexual goings on at the weekend house-party it depicts. The 'I' narrating pursues a question which leads him into conversation with the artist Ford Obert. He speculates that Guy Brissenden, Grace Brissenden's husband, who is twelve years younger, seems to be 'paying' to make Grace Brissenden appear younger and more attractive; but on that analogy (i.e., that one partner suffers while the other feeds, vampire-like off them), who has made Gilbert Long appear more witty and intelligent than normal? The choice seems to lie between two guests at the house-party: Lady John Lutley and May Server. The narrator describes himself as 'nos[ing] about for a relation that a lady has her reasons for keeping secret' and Obert declares this looking about for a narrative 'positively honourable, by being confined to psychologic evidence':

> I wondered a little. 'Honourable to whom?'
> 'Why, to the investigator. Resting on the *kind* of signs that the game takes account of when fairly played – resting on the psychologic signs alone, it's a high application of intelligence. What's ignoble is the detective and the keyhole.' (*The Sacred Fount*, 4, 40)

The 'ignoble' fits with the 'vulgar' ('the story won't tell, not in any literal vulgar way'). James is the contemporary both of Sherlock Holmes and of Freud, who use 'the detective and the keyhole', though differently, the first to back up the values of the dominant order, the other taking those values as symptoms. The narrator holds to the illusion that his methods are not ignoble. But that, which, like Douglas's rejection of the vulgar, puts him on the side of the genteel and of refinement, limits his reading-power. He can be sidelined by Mrs Brissenden – who may be having an affair with Long herself, if her denial (14, 171) that he has grown any more intelligent is her way of putting the narrator off the scent. Her last comment, castrating enough, is 'My poor dear, you *are* crazy, and I bid you good night!' (14, 186).

As in *The Blithedale Romance*, the narrator in *The Sacred Fount* has ways of self-justifyingly protecting his nobility:

> I know not what heavy admonition of my responsibility had thus suddenly descended on me; but nothing, under it, was indeed more sensible than that it practically paralysed me. And I could only say to myself that this was the price – the price of the secret success, the lonely liberty and the intellectual joy... the special torment of my case

was that the condition of light, of the satisfaction of curiosity and of the attestation of triumph, was in this direct way the sacrifice of feeling. (14, 173)

The narrator's consolations in the loss of feeling and emotional ties situate him as turned to stone, outside all affect. He compares with Douglas in *The Turn of the Screw*, whose 'thickness of ice', as the tale's Introduction calls it, suggests that something in the tale has paralysed him; the tale won't tell, because there is nothing beyond its last word 'stopped' – no commentary to break the silence.

Douglas is repressed, silenced, reduced by a narrative: the terms are all synonymous for the loss of the power of signification suggested in 'castration'. The governess embodies that state of powerlessness and it renders her hysterical. Indifference and hysteria are two turns of the screw.

II   POSSESSION AND HYSTERIA

If 'another' turn of the screw is given by a narrative showing one child being haunted, then, as someone says to Douglas, two turns are 'of course' given by two children being haunted. Yet the common-sense answer can be questioned in more than one way, and symmetry is spoiled. Two children here raise questions of gender, and it is not one ghost here, but two. In addition to the governess, at least four people are involved, with however many gender-positions may be implied in the various forms of possibly sexual wickedness perpetrated between them. The simultaneous haunting of two people brings in questions of telepathy, feelings that are felt together – like the sudden violence of the Papin sisters when they murdered their employers in the incident which alerted Lacan to the study of aggression[11] – and also questions notions of single identity.

Similar turns of the screw were experienced in the James family's hysteria. In *Society the Redeemed Form of Man* (1879), Henry James, Senior (1811–82), describes a moment in England in May, 1844, when

> fear came upon me, and trembling, which made all my bones to shake. To all appearance it was a perfectly insane and abject terror, without ostensible cause, and only to be accounted for, to my perplexed imagination, by some damnèd shape squatting invisible to me within the

precincts of the room, and raying out from his fetid personality influences fatal to life. The thing had not lasted ten seconds before I felt
myself a wreck, that is, reduced from a state of firm, vigorous, joyful
manhood to one of almost helpless infancy.[12]

The incident compares with his son's 'most appalling yet most admirable nightmare' centred on the Galerie d'Apollon in the Louvre,
experienced 'one summer dawn'. The date is indeterminate – assuming that a dream with such resonances throughout all his fiction, in a
place with such significance for his life, could ever have had a discrete
form renderable autobiographically, as if it was not already a secondary revision of some other event unentitled to narration. Its
climax

> was the sudden pursuit, through an open door, along a huge high
> saloon, of a just dimly descried-figure that retreated in terror before
> my rush and dash... out of the room I had before been desperately,
> and all the more abjectly, defending by the push of my shoulder against
> hard pressure on lock and bar from the other side. The lucidity, not to
> say the sublimity, of the crisis had consisted of the great thought that
> I, in my appalled state, was probably still more appalling than the
> awful agent, creature or presence, whatever he was, whom I had
> guessed, in the suddenest wild start from sleep, the sleep within my
> sleep, to be making for my rest. The triumph of my impulse... forcing
> the door outward, was the grand thing, but the great point of the
> whole was the wonder of my final recognition. Routed, dismayed, the
> tables turned upon him by my so surpassing him for straight aggres-
> sion and dire intention, my visitant was already but a diminished spot
> in the long perspective, the tremendous, glorious hall, as I say, over the
> far-gleaming floor of which, cleared for the occasion of its great line of
> priceless vitrines down the middle, he sped for *his* life, while a great
> storm of thunder and lightning played through the deep embrasures of
> high windows at the right... what in the world were the deep embra-
> sures and the so polished floor but those of the Galerie d'Apollon of
> my childhood?[13]

After the Civil War, James's brother, William James (1842–1910),
went through a period of nervous depression, which was treated by a
time spent in an asylum in Massachusetts.[14] In 1869 he was still in a
'morbid state'[15] and in 1870 suffered a collapse which he describes in
The Varieties of Religious Experience – saying that 'the worst kind of
melancholy is that which takes the form of panic fear':

There fell upon me without warning, just as if it came out of the darkness, a horrible fear of my own existence. Simultaneously there arose in my mind the image of an epileptic fit whom I had seen in the asylum, a black-haired youth with greenish skin, entirely idiotic, who used to sit all day on one of the benches, or rather shelves against the wall, with his knees drawn up against his chin, and the coarse gray undershirt, which was his only garment, drawn over them inclosing his entire figure. He sat there like a sort of sculptured Egyptian cat or Peruvian mummy, moving nothing but his black eyes and looking absolutely non-human. This image and my fear entered into a species of combination with each other. *That shape am I*, I felt, potentially.... There was such a horror of him, and such a perception of my own merely momentary discrepancy from him, that it was as if something hitherto solid within my breast gave way entirely, and I became a mass of quivering fear.[16]

It seems that the Civil War and its aftermath produced a widespread nervous invalidism. Silas Mitchell derived his famous rest-cure for female patients from his treatment of nervous, battle-fatigued soldiers during the American Civil War.[17] On 15 April 1861, James's eighteenth birthday, Lincoln called for volunteers in the Civil War. On 28 October 1861, James, involved in pumping water for fire-fighting in Newport, and 'jammed into the acute angle between two high fences', – a jolly corner indeed – suffered 'a horrid even if an obscure hurt' whose future 'duration' he felt he could not doubt (*Autobiography*, II, 415). This compares with his father who, aged thirteen, had his right leg amputated after trying to stamp out a fire, and anticipates his brother, Garth Wilkinson (1845–83), wounded in action in 1863. The incident is discussed by Edel and Kaplan.[18] Castration or a back injury,[19] real, fictional or psychic, it suggests an hysteria where body, masculinity and gender, and cultural positioning in regard to the war, cannot be reconciled, and the body reacts against an ideological placing of the man or woman in terms of sexual difference.[20]

In James's journal entry of his visit to America (29 March 1905), he describes the 'never-to-be-lost memory' of visiting the cemetery in Cambridge, when 'the moon was there, early, white and young':

But why do I write of the all unutterable and the all abysmal? Why does my pen not drop from my hand on approaching the infinite pity and tragedy of all the past? It does, poor helpless pen, with what it meets of the ineffable, what it meets of the cold Medusa-face of life, of all the life *lived* on every side. (*Notebooks*, p. 240)

The moon, death and the cold Medusa face of life evoke fears of the feminine as castrating,[21] paralysing, productive of a state analogous to Douglas's, and the emotionality is hysterical, willing the feminine as the castrated position. 'The infinite pity and tragedy of all the past' suggests Barthes's *Camera Lucida* – 'History is hysterical: it is constituted only if we consider it, only if we look at it, and in order to look at it, we must be excluded from it.'[22] History as hysterical differentiates it from tradition. As Benjamin writes, discussing the image of death – the skull – as it appears in German baroque tragedy. 'Everything about history that, from the very beginning, has been untimely, sorrowful, unsuccessful, is expressed in a face – or rather, in a death's head.'[23] Taking this into *The Turn of the Screw* makes history the record of buried, repressed hysterias, its allegorical emblem the death's head, which the governess intuits when feeling that the scene has been 'stricken with death'.

The context of James's comments at the cemetery in 1905 is the epitaph for Alice James, who suffered an hysterical breakdown in 1868. Another, ten years later, she wrote about it in her Diary, which she started writing three years before her death (6 March 1892): 'The fact is, I have been dead so long and it has been simply a such a grim shoving of the hours behind me as I faced a ceaseless possible horror, since that hideous summer of '78, when I went down to the deep sea, its dark waters closed over me, and I knew neither hope nor peace.'[24] Her depression lasted till she developed a breast-tumour and died, aged 44; as a form of hysteria, it may link to a sense of not belonging, sexually, within the symbolic order.[25]

Her diary entry for 26 October 1890 refers to William James's account of hysteria, 'The Hidden Self', which had just appeared. William James was engaging with Pierre Janet's accounts of hysteria, where one human being contains different personages, and 'the total possible consciousness may be split into parts which co-exist by mutually ignoring one another'. This also describes haunting, where the body is like the house inhabited by ghosts. William James said 'an hysteric woman abandons part of her consciousness because she is too weak nervously to hold it all together'. Agreeing, Alice James called her hysteria a battle between her body and her will:

> I used to sit immovable reading...with waves of violent inclination
> suddenly invading my muscles taking some one of their myriad forms

such as throwing myself out of the window or knocking the head off the benignant pater.... Conceive of never being without the sense that if you let yourself go... you must abandon it all, let the dykes break and the flood sweep in, acknowledging yourself abjectly impotent before the immutable laws.[26]

The hysterical body is 'abject' – the word used by Henry James, both father and son, and Alice James, and now given new accentuation in Julia Kristeva, where the subject's self-disgust makes whole subjectivity unachievable. Alice James's hysteria identifies her father with a patriarchy to be destroyed, and prompts thoughts of suicide by jumping. The governess at the end of *The Turn of the Screw* treats Miles as though she was saving him from falling (24, 261). He has not literally fallen, but he is dead, and that spells also the governess's death, though the timing of that event may be postponed. Alice James's move towards destruction, of the self or another, makes identities interchangeable. The governess diabolises or apotheosises Quint as 'the author of our woe' (24, 260): Miles's last words, 'you devil', may mean Quint or the governess: in his hysteria identities are confounded. All the subjects in the narrative are marked by loss, none can quite assert a separate being, all deputise for each other – the governess, Miss Jessel, Peter Quint, Miles, Flora. The governess, however, wants to preserve distinctions, by identifying the 'author'. As Alice James became aggressive towards her father, so here. Patriarchal power – the author of our woe – is unreachable, nameless, invisible, unlike the ghosts. The governess's aggression is unconsciously directed towards the master – the narrative does *not* show who she was in love with – and is displaced onto Miles who burnt the letter, written against patriarchal interdiction. At the end, he tells her he told things to those he liked:

> Those he liked? I seemed to float, not into clearness, but into a darker obscure, and within a minute there had come to me out of my very pity the appalling alarm of his being perhaps innocent. It was for the instant confounding and bottomless, for if he *were* innocent, what then on earth was I?   (24, 259–60)

At that vertiginous moment she loses self-possession, and does not know what she is. Unnameable, she feels monstrous, less than the ghosts, who have names. (Only the next governess will get to know her name, when she appears as a ghost, in another turn of the screw.)

Loss of a name is a reminder that, as with the James family, hysterial hauntings are cultural, infectious, crossing the bounds of single identity, making identities interchangeable, none complete. The governess, Douglas and the narrator, all deprived, maimed personages, figure the James family, as they in turn figure them, making everything in this tale allegorical autobiography.

6

'Within a Modern Shade': Race, Sex and Class in *The Bostonians*, *What Maisie Knew* and *The Awkward Age*

I MODERNITY

'The awkward age' means, among other things, 'modernity', the subject flagged in the novel's Preface. James, thinking back to 1898, the period of writing, to the 'liberal firesides' of London where talk became open, says:

> The wide glow was bright, was favourable to 'real' talk, to play of mind, to an explicit interest in life, a due demonstration of the interest by persons qualified to feel it: all of which meant frankness and ease, the perfection, almost, as it were, of intercourse, and a tone as far as possible removed from that of the nursery and the schoolroom – as far as possible removed, even, no doubt, in its appealing 'modernity', from that of supposedly privileged scenes of conversation twenty years ago. (*AN*, 6, 102)

He compares that London to the one where he settled in 1876, a 'true lover and believer' in its values. Modernity in the Preface to *The Awkward Age* is part of a history of the nineteenth century that he writes, and two histories, English and American, needing to be connected. When James asks about *Middlemarch*, 'if we write novels so, how shall we write History?' (Gard, p. 81), it is worth recalling the social history in James's novels, starting from the *The Europeans: A Sketch* (1878) or *Washington Square* (1881), which turn back to the ante-bellum period with a challenge to read a history there, as Hawthorne had excavated one beneath the apparently shadow-free, traditionless America. James's interest in these texts is with establishing cultural difference: hence the place-name title in *Washington Square*, and the sense of a city on display in *The Bostonians*.

The Europeans opens 'upwards of thirty years since' – in the 1840s. *Washington Square* details a history of the geography of New York, one now almost hegemonic in accounts of the nineteenth-century city, and gives the history of the generation who settled in Washington Square, laid out in 1828. It is possible to work out a chronology whereby Dr Sloper, born around 1793, married in 1820, saw Catherine born in 1825, commissioned a home in Washington Square in 1835 and moved there from his earlier house, five minutes' walk from the City Hall, 'which saw its best days (from the social point of view) about 1820. After this, the tide of fashion began to set steadily northward, as, indeed, in New York... it is obliged to do, and the great hum of traffic rolled farther to the right and left of Broadway' (*Washington Square*, 3, 15). Dr Sloper moves as the houses around him are converted into 'offices, warehouses, and shipping agencies, and otherwise applied to the base uses of commerce'. The action effectively begins in the late 1840s (again, 'thirty years ago' – the opening of chapter 8). By that moment, as Dr Sloper says at the end of chapter 7, he has had 'thirty years of observation' behind him – and can read the stockbroker Morris Townsend, who lives in the 'neatest house in New York' but says:

> 'it's only for three or four years. At the end of three or four years we'll move. That's the way to live in New York – to move every three or four years. Then you always get the last thing. It's because the city's growing so quick – you've got to keep up with it. It's going straight up town – that's where New York's going.... we'll always have a new house; it's a great advantage to have a new house; you get all the latest improvements. They invent everything all over again about every five years, and it's a great thing to keep up with the new things. I always try and keep up with the new things of every kind.'
>
> (*Washington Square*, 5, 25)

Morris Townsend's language repeats what Dr Sloper has done, but implies more speed. Sloper sounds traditional, but his house is called modern, and 'embod[ies] the last results of architectural science' – looking back on it from forty years on – so that although it looks as though it had 'an established repose' and 'a social history' it has neither. These things are simulacral values, where what is real is moving 'up' both literally and metaphorically.[1]

James's third American novel, *The Bostonians*, compares Boston and New York, and shows something in its writing of the character of a tourist's guide to both, for instance in the description of the new Harvard Memorial Hall (1878). Since Reconstruction has finished (1877), its action is contemporary, assuming the deaths of Carlyle (1881) and Emerson (1882). Its New York scenes are set at a moment when New York's upward displacements have moved as far as Central Park, which Frederick Olmsted began laying out in 1857. Basil Ransom and Verena Tarrant go to Central Park via the new elevated railway, in chapter 33 (the Metropolitan Elevated railway began running up to Central Park in 1878), and wander through the park in a scene comparable to the 'pastoral' moment of *What Maisie Knew* when Maisie and Sir Claude stroll in Kensington Gardens. Basil Ransom's hysterical reaction to the present age is in response to the visible presence of a new underclass – an immigrant population, who make the division of the city into separate neighbourhoods, or into upward mobility, so much more compelling: 'Groups of the unemployed, the children of disappointment from beyond the sea, propped themselves against the low, sunny wall of the Park' (*The Bostonians*, 34, 295). New York's population had reached the million mark by 1875. Verena has asked Basil Ransom, 'those who have got no home (there are millions, you know), what are you going to do with *them*?' (34, 293). Her question is a reminder of the alternative history of New York tenements that Jacob A. Riss was to write in *How the Other Half Lives* (1890). The silent question or demand that comes from a disappointed immigrant population is the sign that the Southern Carlylean Ransom is not only politically reactionary, but anachronistic. He talks of 'unspeakable shams' and 'the modern cant about freedom and [he] had no sympathy with those who wanted an extension of it' (34, 284). There is no doubt what he would do with unemployed immigrants, the 'disappointed'. Verena Tarrant 'didn't suppose you could hear any one say such a thing as that in the nineteenth century'. Ransom's *ressentiment* (coming from a defeated part of the States, being virtually unemployed himself) explains his attitudes towards women and to the unemployed, and is a part of the conservative modernity which in the twentieth century found expression in fascism. Ransom, far from being part of the solution, is part of the problem, and to see the issues of modernity requires some different describing.

So what are these issues? In 1883, when working on *The Bostonians*, James wrote on Alphonse Daudet and on *L'Evangéliste: roman parisien*. In this novel, of which James said 'Daudet's *Evangeliste* has given me the idea of this thing [the subject-matter of *The Bostonians*]' (*Notebooks*, pp. 19–20), Daudet (1840–97) prompts James to read 'modernity':

> [Daudet's] elder brother, who has not his talent, has written a little book about him in which the word *modernité* perpetually occurs. M. Ernest Daudet, in *Mon Frère et Moi* insists upon his possession of the qualities expressed by this barbarous substantive, which is so indispensable to the new school. Alphonse Daudet is, in truth, very modern; he has all the newly-developed, the newly-invented, perceptions. Nothing speaks so much to his imagination as the latest and most composite things, the refinements of current civilization, the most delicate shades of the actual. It is scarcely too much to say that (especially in the Parisian race) modern manners, modern nerves, modern wealth and modern improvements, have engendered a new sense, a sense not easily named nor classified, but recognizable in all the most characteristic productions of contemporary art. It is partly physical, partly moral, and the shortest way to describe it is to say that it is a more analytic consideration of appearances.
>
> (*LC* I, 229)

This last line links Daudet with naturalism. In *L'Evangéliste*, Madame Autheman, 'an elaborate portrait of a fanatic of Protestantism, a bigot to the point of monstrosity' (*LC* I, 225) – Jewish in origin and with Jewish banking money behind her, so that the novel has anti-semitic assumptions within it – adopts Eline Ebsen, who leaves her mother and her fiancé, M. Lorie-Dufresne, who has motherless children she feels fondness for, to become a feminist evangelist, denying her 'natural' destiny to be a mother. James summarises the novel, before turning to his criticism of it – one he feels also fits Zola: that much of the material has been 'got up' from note-taking:[2] that it looks only at exterior appearances:

It treats of a young girl (a Danish Protestant) who is turned to stone by a Medusa of Calvinism, the sombre and fanatical wife of a great Protestant banker. Madame Autheman persuades Eline Ebsen to wash her hands of the poor old mother with whom up to this moment she has lived in the closest affection, and to go forth into strange countries to stir up the wicked to conversion. The excellent Madame Ebsen, bewildered, heart-broken, desperate, terrified at the imagined pernalties of her denunciation of the rich and poweful bigot (so that she leaves her habitation and hides in a household of small mechanics to escape from them – one of the best episodes of the book), protests, struggles, goes down on her knees in vain; then, at last, stupified and exhausted, desists, looks for the last time at her inexorable, impenetrable daughter, who has hard texts on her lips and no recognition in her eye, and who lets her pass away, without an embrace, for ever. The incident in itself is perfectly conceivable: many well-meaning persons have held human relationships cheap in the face of a religious call. (*LC* I, 247)

The novel was dedicated to Charcot (1825–93), who treated Daudet for spinal weakness, and worked on hysteria at the Salpêtrière, where Freud studied with him (1885–6). Invoking Charcot suggests the novel's pretensions to scientific objectivity in dealing with what James, in the review quoted above, calls 'modern nerves'. Associating together two discourses – one of modernity and another of neurosis – was possible in both France and America. The American psychiatrist George M. Beard gave the word 'neurasthenia' to the middle-class elite (especially male) at the end of the 1860s, and in *American Nervousness: Its Causes and Consequences* (1881) said it originated from 'modern civilization' characterised by 'steam power, the periodical press, the telegraph, the sciences and the mental activity of women'.[3] Gender displacement goes with modernity and neurosis, for Beard argued that the result of women's sex instinct being 'perverted' and them 'hating the opposite sex and lov[ing] their own', was that 'men become women and women men, in their tastes, conduct, character, feelings and behaviour'.[4] This is source-material for *The Bostonians*, where attention to women's sexuality itself is part of modernity, as much as a new reading of history:

> [Olive and Verena] read a great deal of history together, and read it ever with the same thought – that of finding confirmation in it for this idea that their sex had suffered inexpressibly, and that at any moment in the course of human affairs the state of the world would have been

so much less horrible (history seemed to them in every way horrible), if women had been able to press down the scale.   (20, 153)

History is hysterical indeed. This novel, several times called a 'history', suggests that an alternative woman's narrative could be given, though it does not ultimately do more than comment on the point. Its urbanity and superiority, which have inclined some readers to think that it aligns itself more with Basil Ransom than with women, means that *The Bostonians* has been attacked for its gender politics. Perhaps its tone is intended to stave off hysteria in the narrator, caused by a sense that all that the women say is true. The case of Catherine Sloper in *Washington Square* would bear out the point, suggesting that a history other than the public one of New York's prosperity is worked out in her silence. But *The Bostonians* qualifies the suggestion that it is all true by its suggestion of the hypnotic power Olive Chancellor holds over Verena Tarrant, a product of her hysteria and related to her 'morbidity'. Whereas Beard suggests that new female power produces male hysteria, or neurasthenia, *The Bostonians* suggests the opposite, that *male* history has produced hysteria, and this becomes particularly active when women come to knowledge of what they have been kept back from knowing – when they begin to read history together.

Yet the text can embrace the 'threat' of women's sexuality and the re-readings of male history it demands more easily than it can the South of Reconstruction. Ransom's discourse is 'pervaded by something sultry and vast, something almost African in its rich basking tone, something that suggested the teeming expanse of the cotton-field' (1, 6). In his speech, there is something equivocal. James wants to suggest the black presence, as something not to be assimilated to the reform movements of the north; outside, even, the world of European immigration to New York. It is as though something of this activates the *ressentiment* and makes the American and English experiences of modernity different. Coming in from the outside into the Northern states and dragging Verena Tarrant off is an action of utter violence.

As a text of modernity in Britain, *The Awkward Age*, focusing on London in the mid-1890s, specifically directs attention to changes focused on women. Race is mentioned: the text notes a persistent anti-semitism in smart society (see 2, 6, 71; 6, 23, 239), but the issue is wholly subordinate. It opens with the re-appearance in London of

Mr Longdon, who, at fifty-six (James's age), is Lambert Strether's age and Strether's type, though without his openness to other forms of consciousness. Longdon has not been in London for thirty years (1, 28). Assuming a contemporary dating for the novel, this would make him a contemporary of the world of *Our Mutual Friend* (1865), whose Mr Podsnap, epitome of middle-class snobbery and philistinism, pronounces on the literature young unmarried women can read:

> A certain institution in Mr Podsnap's mind which he called 'the young person' may have been considered to have been embodied in Miss Podsnap, his daughter. It was an inconvenient and exacting institution, as requiring everything in the universe to be filed down and fitted to it. The question about everything was, would it bring a blush to the cheek of the young person? And the inconvenience of the young person was that, according to Mr Podsnap, she seemed always liable to burst into blushes when there was no need at all. There appeared to be no line of demarcation between the young person's excessive innocence, and another person's guiltiest knowledge. Take Mr Podsnap's word for it, and the soberest tints of drab, white, lilac and grey, were all flaming red to this troublesome Bull of a young person.   (1, 11, 129–30)[5]

This passage, which recalls the discussion in Chapter 2, of life as a sealed book to young unmarried ladies, is discussed by Ruth Bernard Yeazell,[6] whose arguments I draw on. Using Darwin, she says that blushing points not to innocence, but knowledge. Mr Podsnap defends not his daughter's innocence, but her ignorance, to which may be added, following Blake, '*Unorganiz'd Innocence: An Impossibility.* Innocence dwells with Wisdom but never with Ignorance'.[7] Innocence – which may be what James's Maisie achieves – must be worked towards. The point may be developed by saying that if every utterance has to be policed in order not to bring a blush to the cheek of the young person, then the young person is defined as a blusher: her body is produced as characteristically blushing, which becomes something like an hysterical symptom; she is produced as guilty. If *anything* is likely to make the young person's cheek blush, all knowledge becomes sexual: the deepest forms of knowledge are sexual. But if all knowledge is thus codified, this is a plea for ignorance altogether. Nothing can be discussed. The prudery of the English novel, James's topic in, for instance, 'The Future of the Novel' (1899), where he says it gives rise to an 'immense omission' (Gard, p. 342) – leaving sexuality out – becomes not a matter of the sexual formation of the English, but an alibi for not talking about other things.

The English novel cannot talk about sex because that displaces other forms of knowledge. That Dickens knows this is hinted at in the chapter 'Podsnappery', where Mr Podsnap does not want to know things – 'I don't want to know about it, I don't choose to discuss it: I don't admit it', because to know certain things would cut at the ideology behind being 'English'. 'Not English!' is his way of getting rid of things he does not want to discuss: Dickens hints that this is related to British domestic and imperial rule; as the premise on which rule of the other can take place. At the end of one of Mr Podsnap's speeches, 'he put the rest of Europe and the whole of Asia, Africa and America nowhere' (1, 11, 133). The daughter is sacrificed to preserve the Empire's supremacy, whose imperial guilt is assuaged by a policy of deliberately not knowing. One of the apologies for the British · Empire was that it was acquired in a state of absent-mindedness.

Modernity is the place for production of knowledge: the ignorant (young women) are produced as the guilty, and the subject – i.e., the young person – is defined in relation to a sexuality equally produced. Producing sexual knowledge as the source of guilt constructs also a particular ignorance. But the knowledge disseminated through newspapers is a new form of knowing, out of Mr Podsnap's control, and hence the source of his anxiety and bluster. In *The Bostonians* James writes insistently about 'publicity'. Selah Tarrant, Verena's father in *The Bostonians*, thinks only of getting into the newspapers – 'the vision of that publicity haunted his dreams' (13, 89), and Matthias Pardon, the journalist he cultivates, makes no distinction between private and public: everything is there to be revealed. 'Indelicacy was his profession; and he asked for revelations of the *vie intime* of his victims with the bland confidence of a fashionable physician inquiring about symptoms' (17, 123). He nourishes 'the great arts of publicity. For this ingenuous son of his age all distinction between the person and the artist had ceased to exist; the writer was personal, the person food for newsboys, and everything and everyone were everyone's business':

> He was only twenty-eight years old, and with his hoary head, was a thoroughly modern young man; he had no idea of not taking advantage of all the modern conveniences. He regarded the mission of mankind upon earth as a perpetual evolution of telegrams; everything to him was very much the same, he had no sense of proportion or quality; but the newest thing was what came nearest exciting in his mind the sentiment of respect. (16, 108)

The telegraph (in place by 1866, when Western Union became America's first monopoly), it will be recalled, was blamed as causing neurasthenia. The production of knowledge at such a speed multiplies nodes of power and modes of surveillance, and destabilizes sexuality and gender roles. Matthias Pardon likes the speed at which things go, and everything being very much the same (the abolition of difference, including sexual difference), but no-one has liberty with the new modes of information, where even a crusade for women must be carried on with the arts of 'publicity', which means that Pardon envisages Verena Tarrant as the spokesperson for feminism, 'running' – like a Broadway show – for 'ten years at least', while he himself 'wants to make history' – instant history – by his journalism since feminism is 'the great modern question' (17, 125). Journalism and 'publicity' decide what is 'modern'. History is 'made' by a conscious accentuation dictated by the profit motive behind the arts of publicity; feminism relies on gossip-columns to carry its message. Distinctions between high and popular forms of culture cannot be sustained. Olive Chancellor looks out of date with her George Eliot, Comte, Goethe and other German authors, and Ransom's Carlyle no longer fits. It is one of the sources of Olive Chancellor's 'morbidity' and melancholia.

II DIVORCE

Meaning reversing into its opposite – indifference, everything meaning very much the same – happens in *The Awkward Age*, where James writes with Dickens behind him for the social observation. Book 2, chapter 7, opens with a Dickensian description of Lord Petherton and Mr Mitchett ('so little intrinsic appearance that an observer would have felt indebted, as an aid to memory, to the rare prominence of his colourless eyes and the positive attention drawn to his chin by the precipitation of its retreat from detection') and Mrs Brookenham tells him that most people 'are sticking fast in their native mud' (which is a recall of the opening of *Bleak House*, and of *Our Mutual Friend*). Mitchy calls the drawing-room 'remarkably charming mud':

> 'Well, that's what a great deal of the element really appears, today, to be thought; and precisely as a specimen, Mitchy dear, those two French

books you were so good as to send me and which – really, this time, you extraordinary man!' She fell back, intimately reproachful, from the effect produced on her, renouncing all expression save that of the rolled eye.

'Why, were they particularly dreadful?' – Mitchy was honestly surprised. 'I rather liked the one in the pink cover – what's the confounded thing called? I thought it had a sort of a something-or-other'. He had cast his eye about as if for a glimpse of the forgotten title, and she caught the question as he vaguely and good-humouredly dropped it.

'A kind of morbid modernity? There *is* that', she dimly conceded.

'Is that what they call it? Awfully good name. You must have got it from old Van!' he gaily declared.   (1, 7, 77–8)

She calls the book – *Nana*? or *A Rebours*? – 'abject, horrid, unredeemed vileness, from beginning to end'. She has, of course, read it through to the end.

'Morbid modernity' hooks this novel back to *The Bostonians*, but it suggests a development: the language of accusation that connects morbidity with decadence has now become that of the arts of publicity. 'Morbid modernity' sounds like a publisher's blurb. In the conditions of information, 'publicity' and the speed of the telegram, value distinctions collapse and everything becomes very much the same as everything else, so that even 'a morbid modernity' becomes neutralised into something like publicity, meaningless as a term of abuse, criticism or description. On the next page, Mitchy refers to 'old Randage' (names, like 'Cashmore', are allegorical) and to the erotica ('literary remains') which his executors found amongst his effects after he had died. The obscene is public, and a morbid modernity can no longer exist as a term of abuse or criticism.

The production of knowledge, promoted by the arts of publicity, appears when the Duchess refers to 'your amazing English periodical washings of dirty linen'. The statement is to be assumed as being made about the time of the Wilde trial (1895), and was certainly written after it, as well as several well-known divorce scandals. These were enabled by the Matrimonial Causes Act (1857), which made divorce a matter for civil, rather than ecclesiastical, proceedings, and kept the advantage to the husband, who could sue on grounds of adultery, while the wife had to sue on ground of adultery plus something else (incest, cruelty, desertion).

On 23 February 1870, Edward, Prince of Wales, appeared in the witness-box in the divorce case of Sir Charles Mordaunt (1836–97), a Conservative MP petitioning against his 21-year-old wife: his wife, by being declared insane – suffering from 'puerperal mania' or 'hysteria' – could not appear.[8] Edward had to deny in the witness box that he had committed 'any improper familiarity or criminal act'. Victoria feared trust on Edward's involvement would show in him 'an amount of imprudence which cannot but damage him in the eyes of the middle and lower classes, which is most deeply to be lamented in these days when the higher classes, in their frivolous, selfish and pleasure-seeking lives, do more to increase the spirit of democracy than anything else'.[9] The year 1885 saw the case of the radical Liberal MP Sir Charles Dilke (1843–1911), whom James had known, calling him 'a fortunate Englishman: born, without exceptional talents, to a big property, a place in the world, and a political ambition which – resolute industry and the force of social circumstance aiding – he is steadily *en train* to realise. And withal, not a grain of genius or inspiration' (Edel, II, 337). James gives a narrative of the court proceedings, writing to Grace Norton on 23 August 1885:

> The London mind is now absorbed in the great 'Dilke Scandal' – no very edifying chapter of social history. It is, however, by no means without a certain rather low interest if one happens to know (and I have the sorry privilege) most of the people concerned, nearly and remotely, in it. Donald Crawford has applied for a divorce from his wife on account of her relations with Dilke, the lady being the sister of Mrs Ashton Dilke, C.D'.s late brother's wife. Hearing of this, Mrs Mark Pattison, in India (staying at Madras with the Grant Duffs), heroically makes it known that she is engaged to be married to Dilke (by way of comfort to him), and the news is in all the papers. Meanwhile, another London lady, whom I won't name, with whom for years his relations have been concomitant with his relations with Mrs Pattison, and whose husband died (strangely enough) just at the moment as the Rector of Lincoln has had every expectation that he was on the point of marrying *her*! This is a very brief sketch of the situation, which is queer and dramatic and disagreeable. Dilke's private life won't (I imagine) bear looking into, and the vengeful Crawford will do his best to lay it bare. He will probably not succeed, and Dilke's political reputation with the 'great middle class' will weather the storm. But he will have been frightened almost to death. For a man who has had such a passion for keeping up appearances and appealing to the said middle class, he has, in reality, been strangely, incredibly reckless. His long, double liasion with Mrs Pattison and the other lady, of a nature to make it a duty of honour to marry *both* (!!) when they should become free, and the death of each husband at the same

time – with the public watching to see *which* he *would* marry – and he meanwhile 'going on' with poor little Mrs Crawford, who is a kind of infant – the whole thing is a theme for the novelist – or at least for *a* novelist. I, however, am not the one....

Edel glosses this: Mrs Pattison (Emilia Frances Strong, 1840–1904) was widowed in 1884; her husband, Mark Pattison, who she married at twenty-one, was thirty years older. Rector of Lincoln College, Oxford, he was a Casaubon lookalike – as James wrote to William James (26 April 1869): 'The Rector is a desiccated old scholar, torpid even to incivility with too much learning, but his wife is of quite another fashion, very young (about 28) very pretty, very clever, very charming and very conscious of it all. She is I believe highly emancipated, and I defy an English-woman to be emancipated except coldly and wantonly.' Mrs Pattison and Dilke married two months after James's letter. The other lady, whom James doesn't name, was another friend, Mrs James (Christina) Rogerson, married to an alcoholic, and Dilke's neighbour since 1869. James said of her, that 'had she been beautiful and sane, she would have been one of the world's great wicked women'. Dilke's most recent biographer, David Nicholls, adds, 'perhaps she was anyway – her mental instability feeding her wickedness'.[10] Nicholls concludes that Dilke was the victim of a conspiracy between Mrs Rogerson and Mrs Crawford, the first who had wanted to marry Dilke, and the second who wanted to free herself from her husband.

Dilke's trial was heard on 12 February 1886, Crawford giving evidence of his wife's confession about her relationship with Dilke. ('He taught me every French vice. He used to say that I knew more than most women of thirty' [Nicholls, p. 180].) Crawford got his divorce, but the case went to a second hearing, attempting to clear Dilke of the accusation that he had committed adultery with Virginia Crawford. She had been eighteen, straight from finishing-school at Lausanne, when she married a man twice her age in 1881: her later Catholicism, membership of the Labour Party and death in 1948 are detailed by Nicholls, who says that she 'wove a net of fabrications' (p. 193) and was already in an affair with an army officer, Captain Henry Forster. (Dilke himself had had an affair with Virginia Crawford's mother, Mrs Eustace Smith.) Nicholls thinks that Mrs Crawford was forced to marry Crawford, after rejecting two previous proposals and a first from Crawford, by being kept in her room on bread and water. 'Along with her elder sister, Helen, trapped in a similar unhappy relationship, she embarked on a series of amorous adventures. The one egged the other on. They hunted for lovers together among the medical students at St George's Hospital' (Nicholls, p. 205). Captain Forster was met at a house of assignation, in Mayfair.

A third scandal broke in 1886, and a fourth in 1890 (Captain William O'Shea sueing for divorce from Katherine (Kitty) O'Shea, on account of her association – since 1881 – with Charles Stewart Parnell, the Irish Nationalist leader. James attended some of the trial sessions). The third scandal divorce suit provided material for *A London Life* (1888): Lord Colin Campbell, Liberal MP for Argyllshire, named four co-respondents, including the Duke of Marlborough. His wife counter-petitioned, and accusations flew in the hearing, with both parties claiming to have been infected with syphilis by the other.[11] Calling it 'hideous', James wrote from Italy to Charles Eliot Norton at the end of 1886 that it 'will besmirch exceedingly the already very damaged prestige of the English upper class. The condition of that body seems to me to be in many ways the same rotten and *collapsible* one as that of the French aristocracy before the revolution – minus cleverness and conversation; or perhaps it's more like the heavy, congested and depraved Roman world upon which the barbarians came down'.[12] James uses the rhetoric of the decadence of the Romans, with a sense that these aristocrats cannot learn from history, but this is not his sole response. The morality of the American innocent and conventional Laura Wing over her married sister's adultery in *A London Life* is hysterical: that point persists through *What Maisie Knew, The Pupil*, and *The Awkward Age*.

III   *WHAT MAISIE KNEW*

Unsurprisingly, *What Maisie Knew* (1897) starts with a divorce – a middle-class one. In this trial, although the 'judgement of Solomon' is referred to, it is the reverse of that, for the child is not preserved whole by the 'real' (meaning here the loving) parent. She is 'divided in two' – in a cutting and a trauma which means that she will always be the expression of the *ressentiment* of both parents against each other in their concern for 'justice' and the sense that one is doing slightly better than the other. In this sense of imaginary injustice, which overcodes the sexuality of the parents and makes their sexual affairs after the divorce symmetrically equal, because it is a competition of acquisition with each other, even the child must be divided equally. The novel's first line is 'the litigation had seemed interminable' and it is, since it continues in the child's life. James only prevents the sense of the trauma spreading by ending the novel, and so his analysis, before Maisie reaches puberty, before she can be aware of trauma being a memory of the past which activates itself in the present – before the text can become a ghost narrative, like *The Turn of the Screw*.

But there are ghosts in *What Maisie Knew* – Mrs Wix's dead child, Clara Matilda, in both heaven and Kensal Green cemetery ghosts Maisie by being a reminder of the violent end of childhood which is now reified, made marmoreal. And another ghost haunts these pages: *David Copperfield* – referred to when Mrs Wix is declared to be like Mrs Micawber (14, 113). When Dickens appears within James's fiction, James writes within the archive of 'literature', for David Copperfield is the most famous example of a child orphaned and deserted, left to the mercy of a step-parent after his own mother has died, as Maisie is left to her parents by marriage after her own parents have finished with her – i.e., Sir Claude (who married Ida, the mother) and Mrs Beale (Miss Overmore, who married Beale Farange, the father). James writes in the Preface that he at once recognised 'that my light vessel of consciousness, swaying in such a draught, couldn't be with verisimilitude a rude little boy; since, beyond the fact that little boys are never so "present", the sensibility of the female young is indubitably, for early youth, the greater' (*AN*, 8, 143–4). The sentence alludes to George Eliot's 'delicate vessels', but *David Copperfield* is in view, for David gets a girl's name from Steerforth ('Daisy' – contrast Maisie) and Betsey Trotwood's reaction to him affirms the importance of being a girl.

Feminisation is at the heart of James's identifications (in contrast, Sir Claude calls Maisie a boy). James repeats the structure of Dickens's early chapters describing David's childhood, but with three changes. It is not a boy but a girl, and not first-person narration but third, so that Maisie is not both 'subject' and 'object' in the narrative (see the Preface to *The Ambassadors*, *AN*, 17, 321). Unlike David Copperfield she is not the ultimate guarantor of what she knows. Thirdly, James does not write a narrative assuming any final position. Copperfield writes as an assured bourgeois. Maisie is a child, pre-pubescent, a subject still in process. David Copperfield is not that; as an autobiographer, rather, his life is finished, completed. Thus James's title puts the stress on what Maisie *knew*: knowledge is always past tense, inapplicable to the present situation, since it is knowledge of the past. These changes are deliberate moves from a position of strength, assumed in the case of the Dickens, to a position of weakness.

Not only *David Copperfield*, but *Dombey and Son* haunts the book: Maisie recalls Florence Dombey, who does not exist for Mr Dombey. Something of that invisibility makes Maisie, to evoke James's term, 'more present'. Also from *Dombey and Son*, Susan Ash recalls Susan Nipper, and Beale Farange's teeth evoke Carker's. Dickens exists as a ghost for James, alongside Thackeray and that earlier archive of the English novel; for James, who, settling into 'small chambers in a small street that opened, at a very near corner, into Piccadilly and a view of the Green park' in 1876, said that 'the big human rumble of Piccadilly...was close at hand; I liked to think that Thackeray's Curzon Street, in which Becky Sharp...had lived, was not much further off: I thought of it preponderantly, in my comings and goings, as Becky's and her creator's, just as I was to find fifty other London neighbourhoods speak to me almost only with the voice, the thousand voices, of Dickens' (*AN*, 11, 211–12).

James's house for writing fiction looks out onto a London already fictionalised. His childhood American reading of Dickens and Thackeray produces a London experience in adulthood constituted by these ghosts. The past's hold makes modernity not new, but the past's felt weight. Writing, after Dickens and Thackeray, with their apparently unproblematic forms of fiction, must be in the ghostly archive the modern writer feels their work sets up. Further, this is the age of 'publicity', with the virtual impossibility of stepping out of the sphere of what is already known. In the language of this book's title, what does it mean to talk about individual knowledge? Knowledge presupposes having an identity outside the circulation of received ideas and instant information.

IV REPETITION

In chapter 16, Maisie, walking with Sir Claude, her new stepfather, in Kensington Gardens, meets her mother with her new friend, the

Captain. In chapter 17, Maisie goes with Mrs Beale, her new step-mother, to Earl's Court. At a sideshow, Maisie stops before an exhibition of 'the Flowers of the Forest', – a collection of black women: the title sounds like a proleptic parody of *The Beast in the Jungle* – and there meets her father with his new friend, an 'American countess', of whom Maisie says 'She's almost black' (18, 143). (The equivocation about the title of the woman is important: perhaps she is meant to suggest a South American figure. But it is also important that she is rich, and Beale is, like a shabby colonialist, living off her.) Only momentarily, however, do these issues of race cross other issues of modernity in the text, as with *The Bostonians*. They suggest how much more is to be 'known' within modernity than the text can talk about, how much more diverse appearances are; but the episode is presented as Maisie's father's nadir, for it leads to Maisie's last inter-view with him, when he virtually discards her. It is followed by a final leave-taking of her mother at Folkestone – she, by this time, has dumped the Captain. That is the theme of chapters 20 and 21.

The symmetry of events over these chapters, concluding with the loss of both parents, is striking, and it is interesting that Maisie's own reaction moves from being relatively passive – in her interview with the Captain – to being positive. She defends the Captain to her mother; with a 'vision' of her mother as walking into 'madness and desolation... ruin, darkness and death' (21, 177). At the heart of this learning is another perception which Leavis isolates in discussing the text.[13] The clue comes at the moment when Mrs Beale with Maisie sees her husband with his new woman, the 'American countess':

> Mrs Beale for a moment only looked after them. 'The liar! The liar!'
> Maisie considered. 'Because he's not – where one thought?' That was also, a month ago, where her mother had not been. 'Perhaps he has come back', she said.
> 'He never went – the hound!'
> That, according to Sir Claude, had been also what her mother had not done, and Maisie could only have a sense of something that in a maturer mind would be called the way history repeats itself. 'Who *is* she?' she asked again. (18, 143)

History as repetition is built into the three episodes that run from chapters 16 to 21, on several levels. (a) The husband repeats the actions of his wife, who then repeats those of her husband, in an incremental pattern like that of *The Turn of the Screw*, and equally machinic. (b) The symmetry allows us to think that the events of the divorce are being replayed, so that each affair is a displacement of the 'original' adultery, or adulteries – so that the real targets are the ex-husband and ex-wife, rather than the present partners. (c) Each partner repeats his or her previous conquests with another partner, so that adultery is repetition. (d) Reactions to these events are always the same with the same kind of lies getting told. Emma Bovary discovered this sense of repetition, that adultery is another form of cliché, another recirculation of the platitudinous, not anything new. This reading of repetition pairs with Marx, who begins *The Eighteenth Brumaire of Louis Bonaparte* (1852): 'Hegel says somewhere that all the great events and characters of world history occur, so to speak, twice. He forgot to add: the first time as tragedy, the second as farce.'[14] That they occur twice – history repeating itself – means no-one learns from history. Marx's sense of nineteenth-century history losing any narrative force and becoming a structure of repetition fits with the ascendancy of bourgeois taste, committed to counter-revolution. It gives an historical dimension to Lacan's identification of a structure of repetition running through Edgar Allan Poe's short story 'The Purloined Letter', in his classic seminar with that title.

James's narrative of repetition is reconcilable with Flaubert's. Beale Farange was destined for a colonial career, 'but contemporary history had somehow had no use for him and left him in perpetual Piccadilly' (Introduction, 8). He will keep his appointment with colonialism, by living off the American countess. In contrast to Dickens's sense of bourgeois success, which is marked out in the history of David Copperfield, or George Eliot's perception of 'human history' as that which claims adherents in the form of people enduring, fighting for ideas, history is here no more than a loop, or stasis; Piccadilly is Limbo, 1890s style.

The comic vision of *What Maisie Knew* involves the ghost of David Copperfield – in that James tries to write in it a girl who takes possession of her own life, without the benefit of a Betsey Trotwood (in fact, a distant relation of Maisie's does turn up at the beginning, as Miss Trotwood does the night David is born, but she never reappears). Mrs Wix is the nearest to Miss Trotwood here. Maisie, far more than David Copperfield, 'knows' things outside received ideas, bourgeois ideology, for which she is frequently described as monstrous. So James argues for the possibility of thinking outside the loop. At the beginning, Maisie sees images as in a phantasmagoria (1, 39), as in a magic lantern, and if 'phantasmagoria' is given its sense in Marx of illusion, the occulted way in which things – including things sexual (also part of commodity culture) – appear in the age of high capitalism, then the text argues for Maisie approaching innocence as she learns 'the art of not thinking singly' (21, 176). Thinking doubly – the divided child can have a Strether-like double consciousness – means being able to work with contradictions, or across aporias, working elliptically, so that

> Maisie had known all along a great deal, but never so much as she was to know from this moment on and she learned in particular during the couple of days that she was to hang in the air, as it were, over the sea which represented in breezy blueness and with a summer charm a *crossing of more spaces* than the Channel. It was granted her at this time to arrive at divinations so simple that I shall have no time for the goal if I attempt to trace the stages... (20, 162; my emphasis)

Maisie is tracking the uncanny, like Strether. Making these crossings in argument is allegorical thinking, by which I mean thinking other, thinking differently, not literally. To think singly is to be caught in history as repetition, or to be ensnared by Mrs Wix's demand that she think morally, the theme of the novel's chapter 26.

'Thinking morally' is the complacency enjoyed by Pemberton, the tutor in *The Pupil* (1891). Pemberton is ensnared by Mr and Mrs Moreen to teach their sickly son Morgan, for free. They are Americans on the make, but unsuccessful operators. In their meanness and willingness to use Pemberton, they resemble Skimpole in *Bleak House*, or the Micawbers. While they are to blame for trying to give Morgan to Pemberton (parents letting their child go, like Maisie's parents, or the Tarrants giving Verena to Olive Chancellor), so that Morgan dies when recognising that neither they nor Pemberton want him, the text also suggests Pemberton's complicity. He stays tutoring the boy free because he likes being able to say that he is sacrificing himself. He can rationalise the matter to himself:

> He had simply given himself away to a band of adventurers. The idea, the word itself, had a sort of romantic horror for him – he had always lived on such safe lines. Later it assumed a more interesting, almost a soothing sense: it pointed a moral and Pemberton could enjoy a moral. (4, 534)[15]

Having a moral sense stabilises the subject's sense of himself or herself, and encourages single thinking. Pemberton, an American who has failed to react against Puritanism in his years at Yale (2, 519), forgets his own complicity in the situation. Mrs Wix is the more urgent in her demands that Maisie think morally because she, under the influence of Boulogne and a hotel, is becoming de-stabilised herself with regard to Sir Claude, saying off-guardedly, 'I adore him' (26, 118). In such a moment, when Mrs Wix's own personality seems dispersed, like Maisie's at Folkestone, 'hang[ing] in the air over the sea' and she is blind to her own desire,[16] she must collect herself with talk of morality. Maisie knows she cannot think singly, and this may be because, psychoanalytically speaking, a girl's experience conveys a lesson of inner division more easily than a boy's. Every part of the title would then be problematic. 'What', because there is no single subject there, and 'knew', because know-ledge is not a matter of possession, not the property of the Cartesian subject, and because, being based on aporias and ellipses, it is not wholly separable from non-knowledge. Maisie knows but not as a matter of possession, unlike the governess in *The Turn of the Screw.*

V *THE AWKWARD AGE*

> London doesn't love the latent or the lurking, has neither time, nor taste, nor sense for anything less discernible than the red flag in front of the steam-roller. It wants cash over the counter and letters ten feet high.

So Vanderbank in *The Awkward Age* discusses modernity in London, but not correctly, as the not-uncanny, since he says nothing lurks there. It is the place of publicity and advertising, of the production of a certain type of knowledge – and it makes Nanda an allegory of what that London cannot see. 'How *will* she look, what will be thought of her and what will she be able to do for herself? She's at the age when the whole thing, speaking of her appearance, her possible share of good looks – is still, in a manner, in a fog. But everything depends on it' (1, 2, 43). Vanderbank, however, needs to make Nanda an obscure beauty and at an awkward age to project her difference from the modern: he would be appalled to know that Nanda says – in a statement connecting her with Maisie – 'there

was never a time when I didn't know *something* or other and that
I became more and more aware, as I grew older, of a hundred little
chinks of daylight' (10, 37, 371–2). What Nanda knew would make
this spokesperson of the modern age feel very awkward – awkwardness being a failed relationship with the uncanny.

When Longdon reminds Vanderbank that his conversation has just
given Mrs Brookenham away on a point of confidentiality, Vanderbank emphasises the differences between himself and Longdon: 'It
strikes you also as probably the kind of thing we must be constantly
doing: it strikes you that, right or left, probably, we keep giving each
other away. Well, I dare say we do. Yes, "come to think of it," as they
say in America, we do. But what shall I tell you? Practically we all
know it and allow for it and it's as broad as it's long. What's London
life after all? It's tit for tat!' (1, 2, 39). Betrayal dominates
London dialogue, or 'talk' (1, 1, 32) or tittle-tattle – 'tit for tat' –
which as a phrase implies that society is founded on the desire
for resentful revenge. (Tit for tat describes how Maisie's parents
operate.)

According to Vanderbank, 'everything depends on' Nana marrying. The Duchess complains that 'the way your people don't marry is
the ruin, here, of society and . . . of conversation and of literature' (5,
19, 187). The ideology of bourgeois society depends on it in its
fetishising of sexual ignorance, called innocence, not to protect
women, but to protect ideology. Betrayal, which everyone practises
if only through talk, suggests adultery, which everyone is supposed to
practise. In the novel, Mrs Brookenham is 41, at an awkward age
where she does not want her daughter to marry because it will
indicate her age. She does not want her to marry Vanderbank because
she wants him for herself, and designedly or not, she betrays Nanda
in conversation by showing that she has read a French novel (*Nana*?
– it fits with Nanda) – for, in this ideology, an unmarried woman
cannot respectably read a sexually explicit text. Being ignorant – in
this novel, this happens to Aggie till she marries Mitchy – or being
allowed to know are alternative forms of spoiling. Both forms are
tried on Maisie. Vanderbank, whose talk shows his total modernity,
or desire for it, turns out to be a traditionalist, not wanting Nanda
because she seems to be sexually knowing.[17] At the same time, he
does not want Mrs Brookenham now, telling Nanda 'she's booked
for my old age' (10, 36, 358). His talk is a betrayal, including of his
own modernity, which is no Rimbaud-like commitment to be

'absolutely modern', but an anxiety about his masculinity and his self-protection. He does not know it, but he is already at his old age. Even his Americanisms – Mrs Brookenham also has these (4, 14, 143; 9, 31, 316) – are a provinciality. They recall an alternative history, which is America, as a place of alternative possibilities, and show London not really modern in comparison with New York (or Paris). Harold Brookenham knows this when he is after 'an American girl with millions' (6, 23, 239). America is the place to be desired as somewhere smarter and slicker, and London's provinciality appears in its anti-semitism. Its racism – about Americans and Jews – and the cultivated ignorance about the sexual, go together.

The Awkward Age uses Dickens – the Veneerings in *Our Mutual Friend*, and, in the jokes in the first chapter about the new architecture of Whitehall, *Martin Chuzzlewit*, a text whose theme is antiarchitecture; but one ghost in it is Wilde, another writer who enables a re-reading of Dickens, so that, for example, Skimpole in *Bleak House* can be seen as proto-Wildean. The talk in *The Awkward Age* – which Vanderbank refers to at the beginning (1, 1, 32), drawing attention to its major feature as a 'dialogue novel' – is a tribute to Wilde. There is Vanderbank on the Duchess: 'She has bloomed in the hothouse of her widowhood – she's a Neapolitan hatched by an incubator' (1, 1, 35). Or Vanderbank on Mrs Brookenham referring to her daughter Nanda (probably nineteen) as only sixteen: 'She usually does! She has done so, I think for the last year or two' (1, 2, 38). These are lines reminiscent of *The Importance of Being Earnest*, like Mrs Brookenham telling the Duchess not to eat all the teathings before Lord Petherton arrives (2, 5, 63), or musing on how men like the girls they don't marry (2, 5, 65), or Mrs Brookenham telling her daughter that 'she dresses for herself' (6, 23, 232). Or Nanda describing Mitchy: 'People of no use, of no occupation and no importance' (10, 37, 364). Other examples could be given, for each part of the text yields the epigrammatic and shows the priority of style (Vanderbank's 'the high intellectual detachment' [6, 22, 225]) in the conversations of the Brookenham circle.

James met Wilde in 1882 in Washington when 'the first literary "celebrity", the first literary person who consciously sought to make his career by publicizing himself in the writing for the mass-circulation newspapers and women's magazines of the 1880s and 1890s',[18] was there publicising himself. James called him 'repulsive and fatuous' and his comments on Wilde throughout were appalling, perhaps abject: 'an unclean beast' – 'a fatuous cad' – 'the unspeakable one'.

I have referred to four famous trials, but a fifth challenged definitions of the 'obscene' as bourgeois hegemony, which had not been challenged by the previous four. *Guy Domville* opened on 5 January 1895 at St James's Theatre: James spent the evening at *An Ideal Husband* at the Haymarket. Four weeks later, *The Importance of Being Earnest* opened in the theatre where James's play had flopped. On 18 February the Marquess of Queensberry left his note for Wilde. James began making notes on 'Brada's' book *Notes sur Londres* at the end of February, especially on 'the masculinization of the women' and 'the demoralization of the aristocracy' (*Notebooks*, 117), and on 4 March began notes for *The Awkward Age*.[19] On 6 April, Wilde was arrested at the Cadogan Hotel, and on 27 April, a day after the first trial had begun, *An Ideal Husband* ended, while on 8 May, twelve days before the final trial, *The Importance of Being Earnest* was withdrawn.

James wrote to William James that Wilde's 'fall is hideously tragic – & the squalid violence of it gives him an interest (of misery) that he never had for me – in any degree – before. Strange to say I think he may have a "future" – of a sort – by reaction – when he comes out of prison – if he survives the horrible sentence of hard labour that he will probably get. His trial begins today – however – & it is too soon to say. But there are depths in London, & a certain general shudder as to what, with regard to some other people, may possibly come to light.' To Edmund Gosse, he wrote that the affair was 'hideously, atrociously dramatic and really interesting.... It is the squalid gratuitousness of it all, of the mere exposure, that blurs the spectacle. But the *fall*...to that sordid prison-cell & this gulf of obscenity over which the ghoulish public hangs & gloats – it is beyond any utterance of irony or any pang of compassion! He was never in the smallest degree interesting to me – but this hideous human history has made him so – in a manner.'[20] Noteworthily, James refused to sign a petition for Wilde's release. According to Jonathan Sturges, an American friend of James and Wilde, 'James says the petition would not have the slightest effect on the *authorities* here, in whose nostrils the very name of Zola and even of [Paul] Bourget is a stench, and that the document would only exist as a manifesto of personal loyalty to Oscar by his friends, of whom he was never one.'

In James's relations with Wilde, awkwardness appears, and *The Awkward Age* could be seen as a recognition of untimeliness marking everybody and everything. In this novel, everyone is at the wrong age, for there is no right age where knowledge, age and desire are punctual with each other. The Duchess says of Nanda, 'she's really any age you like: your London world so fearfully batters and bruises' (5, 19, 187). This is in the context of a discussion with Longdon, 'long done' but knowing London as Vanderbank does not. Longdon says Mrs Brookenham looks about thirty, to which she says she looks about three. Nanda the 'modern daughter' (4, 13, 133) recalls Lady Julia to Mr Longdon, her face being not 'a bit modern' (3, 12, 121) and seems older than her mother, of whom she says 'she's so fearfully young' (10, 36, 356). Mrs Brookenham says 'the modern has always been my own note' (4, 13, 133) and resents Mr Longdon as a voice from the past, and a reminder of her mother. Harold Brookenham, with 'the voice of a man of forty' (2, 4, 2), sounds no younger than his mother. Mitchy, married, is no longer what he is, in fact, a 'young thing' – 'he's as old as all time, and his [Aggie] who the other day was about six, is now practically about forty' (9, 31, 314). The dislocations of time veil the incestuous overtones (connecting Vanderbank/Mrs Brookenham/Nanda) and mask the sexuality that encircles gender, age and incest taboos: the Duchess with Petherton; Petherton with Mitchie; Aggie marrying Mitchie and having an affair with Pemberton.

'The awkward age' implies that lives cannot be written in terms of linearity. As Isabel Archer journeys to England, her mind goes through various possibilities, including death, renunciation, new happiness and hope, then the melancholia of 'she never should escape; she should last to the end. Then the middle years wrapped her about again and the grey curtain of her indifference closed her in' (*The Portrait of a Lady*, 5, 466). 'The middle years' – the title of a short story written in 1893, when James was fifty, and the projected title for part of James's autobiography – would be an example of an awkward age. These are the years Catherine Sloper and Olive Chancellor must face. They imply blankness, indifference.

In *The Awkward Age*, everything, in the dislocations of age already discussed, is likely to prove the middle years. In Aggie's case, the sexual was the source of ignorance, and now it is like the uncanny. Dislocation of her age is the price she pays for 'trying to find out...what sort of person she is. How can she ever have known? [asks Nanda]. It was carefully, elaborately, hidden from her – kept so obscure that she could make out nothing' (10, 37, 371). Perhaps in James's case, the Wilde trial had some unexpected clarificatory power. Fred Kaplan suggests that in the mid-1890s, James 'fell in love a number of times. He established intimate relationships, beyond his usual friendships, that for the first time provided him with the feeling of being in love' (Kaplan, 401). Kaplan says that all these relationships were with one or another young man. But this new access of feeling, if Kaplan records it aright, does not give the 'truth' about James, but suggests that the violent, hysterical reaction of disgust towards Wilde, for which James is not admirable, is rooted in the violence of a change of episteme, as homosexuality was newly invented – as a disposition of character, as an offence punishable by hard labour, as a new word, preceding the category of heterosexuality, which it thus shapes as a binary opposite – in the awkward age. Homosexuality here would not be the name of a settled disposition existing outside historical givens. In the production of sexuality Foucault discusses, the construction of homosexuality is an invitation for the self to misrecognise itself and turn away with loathing and a sense of inadequacy which will make it subject. The naming of the subject and the invitation to know itself in a particular way freezes it, it does not allow the subject to have any double consciousness. Yet *What Maisie Knew* and *The Awkward Age* imply that all sexual knowledge, like other forms of knowledge, should be seen as provisional, non-punctual in relation to human development, not the subject of a linear narrative of progression.

As a partial tribute to Wilde, *The Awkward Age* involves the sense that no-one in the text is happy with their sexual existence, though negatively, the talk never confronts anything uncanny within sexuality (the non-coincidence of being and discourse). Yet everyone is awkward and alliances are misalliances. James does not share the nostalgia of the figures of his text, whose resistance to sexual knowledge in Nanda allegorises their secret hostility to the sexual, because of its uncanniness. An equivalent resistance to the uncanny would account in part for the horror the public felt over the Wilde trial.

Positively, in *The Awkward Age*, the talk resists determinacy. At one point, Mr Longdon, talking to Vanderbank, expresses his surprise that Mrs Brookenham has declared her passion for Vanderbank: 'In my time women didn't declare their passion. I'm thinking of what the meaning is of Mrs Brookenham's wanting you – as I've heard it called – herself'. Mr Longdon doesn't comment on the major implications of what Mrs Brookenham means – that she is openly soliciting adultery. He goes for the minor – what is the 'meaning' of the perfectly obvious statement? It is a Wildean move, present in any interchange in *The Importance of Being Earnest.*

Vanderbank replies that 'we all call everything – anything. The meaning of it, if you and I put it so is – well a modern shade', to which Mr Longdon replies that 'you must deal then yourself with your modern shades' (5, 20, 205).

It is harder to know what Mrs Brookenham means after Vanderbank's explanation. 'A modern shade' is obscure, but includes (a) shady (unrespectable); (b) shadowy – vague, or ghostly, or containing a shadow, unlike America in the Preface to *The Marble Faun*; (c) containing shades of meaning, not black-and-white and not clear; and (d) shaded from view, not to be seen, not to be known. Perhaps the point about modernity is that it allows for gradations, differences, which include those of race and colour and gender, so *The Awkward Age* has ghostly implications in producing 'modern shades'.

Difficulty in making sense of that expression gives an instance of Todorov's point about the novel's dialogue: 'One might point out that the characters themselves have a curious habit...they refer to others not by constant names known to all but by locutions which vary from one circumstance to another, as if these characters were careful to assume nothing as to the existence of an immutable identity at the core of each being but were content to register their immediate perceptions, each one temporary and subject to change.'[21] While Nanda is trapped by this society, it also allows for a resistance to deep truth about the subject, and in this it corresponds to Wilde's practice in art and life, and partially accounts for the hatred he attracted. Wilde made homosexuality a *performance* – like his publicity-seeking. They went together, and if everything in Wilde, like the epigrams, was performed, that makes a resistance to analysing appearances. Wilde was put on trial, and a trial claims to know and constitute the subject, but Wilde resisted that will to truth. He weakened resistance, and, as James saw, his plays were popular: Oscar was 'raking in the profits' (Kaplan, 409). James called *Lady Windermere's Fan* a 'deliberate trap for the literalist'.[22] An audience for Wilde could not believe that Wilde meant just what he said. They could not have anticipated that he was as rude about them and the middle-class moral sense as he was. The letters might be 'ten feet high' as Vanderbank says about advertising, but they could not be read.

Something of this also lurks in *The Awkward Age*'s refusal to 'go behind' and comment on what lies behind the surface dialogue and appearances (*AN*, 6, 111). And perhaps James outdoes Wilde. Edel is unsure whether James ever read *The Picture of Dorian Gray*, but Dorian Gray is morally 'poisoned' by a book – perhaps a composite of *The Renaissance* and *A Rebours* – given by Sir Henry Wootton. The history of books corrupting goes back a long way, but *The Awkward Age* has no such illusions, and Zola's novel does not corrupt Nanda's mind. The belief it might is bourgeois ideology, whose literalist mentality means that it thinks influence works like that. James's modernism does not accept that there is a ready subject who is endangered in such a way, since the subject, to know, must think doubly.

7

Henry James's 'American Girl': *The Wings of the Dove*

Between the summers of 1900 and 1901 James worked on *The Ambassadors*. The first of the novels of F. O. Matthiessen's 'major phase' to be written, it was not the first to appear. From July 1901 to May 1902, James was busy on *The Wings of the Dove*, which 'ignominiously failed, in advance, of all power to see itself "serialised"' (*AN*, 16, 295), and was published that August. *The Beast in the Jungle* was written in the second half of 1902. *The Ambassadors* began serialisation in January 1903 and appeared in book form at the end of that year. *The Golden Bowl*, begun in the late summer of 1902, was finished by the beginning of 1904, and appeared in book form at the end of the year. *William Wetmore Story and His Friends* was begun at the same time as *The Golden Bowl*. This text, too, has intensely autobiographical implications, like all the novels of the 'major phase'. The self interrogated is American, and in *The Wings of the Dove* the gender of that self is also under question, being constructed as an 'American girl'.

I

The action of *The Wings of the Dove* runs through nearly a year, starting in early Spring. The year is after 1891, since Susan Stringham has read Baron Marbot, whose *Memoirs* appeared in that year. Susan

Stringham also refers to Maeterlinck, whose plays could be seen in the 1890s: he also becomes a cultural referent later in the text (7, 3, 317). Further, the title evokes the 1890s, since Pater, who died in 1894, added as an epigraph the words 'Yet shall ye be as the wings of a dove' for the fourth edition of *The Renaissance* (1893), giving that text an odour of sanctity its 1873 edition had lacked. The Biblical line runs, 'Though ye have lain among the pots, yet shall ye be as the wings of a dove covered with silver, and her feathers with yellow gold' (Psalms, 68: 13). It suggests the reversal of humiliation, the transmutation of the common into the rich and beautiful, or else the desire to aestheticise.

The Wings of the Dove opens in unfashionable Chelsea, in the Dickensian-sounding Chirk Street, with Kate Croy, dressed in mourning because her mother has just died, waiting to see her father, Lionel Croy, who has ruined the family through some misdeed. Her brothers are dead and her sister, Marian Condrip, widowed and the mother of small children, needs Kate Croy's financial help. Kate Croy has been taken up by her rich aunt, Mrs Lowder (the name suggests, apart from 'louder', 'London' plus 'power'). 'Britannia of the Market Place', as Kate Croy calls her (1, 2, 22), Mrs Lowder lives at Lancaster Gate and wants Kate Croy to make what Thackeray in chapter 31 of *The Newcomes* – a novel whose relevance will become clear later – satirises as a *mariage de convenance*: i.e., to marry into the aristocracy, to Lord Mark. Kate Croy, however, loves Merton Densher, a journalist (like the artist Clive Newcome in *The Newcomes* whom his cousin Ethel would like to marry, except that she has been taken up by her grandmother, Lady Kew, to marry into the aristocracy). Kate Croy and Densher conceal their love since Mrs Lowder does not approve, and they meet only in public places. They hope to square her and get some money to marry.

In the third of the novel's books, the millionairess Milly Theale, newly orphaned, alone in the world, and dressed in mourning (like Kate Croy), arrives in Europe with her companion Susan Stringham, a Bostonian romantic novelist and a former friend of Mrs Lowder's. Milly Theale is first seen in the book in the Alps, but her choice is to go to London. She has met Densher in New York while he was on a journalistic assignment, and is attracted to him; it is not clear to what extent she wants to go to London to see him, or to see a doctor.

When Milly Theale comes to London, the settings and characters already introduced are gone over again from the perspective of the

New Yorker, brought up on Victorian fiction and *Punch*. In the first chapter of Book 4, Milly is seen dining at Lancaster Gate, while the following two chapters give a past narration of her feelings about the characters she has met:

> Milly expressed to Susan Shepherd [Stringham] more than once that Kate had some secret, some smothered trouble, besides all the rest of her history.... But on the case thus postulated our young American had as yet no light: she only felt that when the light should come it would greatly deepen the colour; and she liked to think she was prepared for anything. What she already knew, moreover, was full, to her vision, of English, of eccentric, of Thackerayan character – Kate Croy having gradually become not a little explicit on the subject of her situation, her past, her present, her general predicament, her small success, up to the present hour, in contenting at the same time her father, her sister, her aunt and herself. It was Milly's subtle guess, imparted to her Susie, that the girl had somebody else as well, as yet unnamed, to content... (4, 2, 123)

The comparison makes Kate Croy like Becky Sharp in *Vanity Fair*, or Ethel Newcome.

Milly goes to Chelsea, 'the quarter of the famous Carlyle, the field of exercise of his ghost' (4, 3, 136), and meets Marian and realises how differently positioned sisters can be and how variegated London's 'social map'. Forced to make connections she reads the social differences in relation to 'literary legend', catching

> a mixed wandering echo of Trollope, of Thackeray, perhaps mostly of Dickens – under favour of which her pilgrimage had so much appealed. She could relate to Susie later on, late the same evening, that the legend, before she had done with it, had run clear, that the adored author of *The Newcomes* in fine, had been on the whole the note: the picture lacking thus more than she had hoped, or rather, perhaps showing less than she had feared, a certain possibility of Pickwickian outline. She explained how she meant by this that Mrs Condrip hadn't altogether proved another Mrs Nickleby, nor even – for she might have proved almost anything, from the way poor worried Kate had spoken – a widowed and aggravated Mrs Micawber. (4, 3, 137)

The scene seems more in debt to Thackeray and *The Newcomes* than to Dickens. *The Newcomes: Memoirs of a Most Respectable Family* (1853–5) satirises the English bourgeoisie by taking one family through three or four generations, rising to become wealthy London bankers and making wealthy marriages.[1] Seeing Kate Croy, Milly Theale suspects that Densher loves her, but thinks Kate Croy does not reciprocate. At a visit to Lord Mark's country house, Matcham (the name reappears in *The Golden Bowl*), she sees Bronzino's portrait of a Renaissance lady. The painting's perfection is that of death: it says of the woman, '"And she was dead, dead, dead." Milly recognised her exactly in words that had nothing to do with her. "I shall never be better than this"' (5, 2, 157). Milly will be called a dove by Kate (5, 6, 202), but she will not be like the person of Psalm 55: 6, 'then I said, O that I had wings like a dove! Then I would fly away and be at rest.'

The intuition of death, and of art as lifeless, and herself as being treated as simply a rich woman who is a financial asset, like a rich work of art, causes Milly Theale to identify with this portrait and to recoil from it. Victorian – perhaps especially Pre-Raphaelite-influenced – art made a cult of the beautiful dead woman, of Ophelia, of the Lady of Shalott. Edgar Allan Poe had written in 'The Philosophy of Composition' that 'the death of a beautiful woman is, unquestionably, the most poetical topic in the world'.[2] Milly Theale's reaction to this identification of death and the maiden makes her visit a doctor. The doctor is Sir Luke Strett, whose words, 'isn't to "live" exactly what I'm trying to persuade you to take the trouble to do?' (5, 3, 176) encourage her to live as an act of willpower. In the final chapter of Book 5, she walks into the National Gallery in London, returning, as with the Bronzino, to paintings, with their implications of lifelessness, and of frozen official culture. At home [in New York] the Gallery had seemed 'one of the attractions of Europe and one of its highest aids to culture' (5, 7, 205). In this atmosphere of deadness, copying and of tourist culture, she has the same kind of vision Strether has by the river. She sees Merton Densher, newly arrived from America, in the company of Kate Croy (5, 7, 209). The scene of aesthetic culture becomes a way of underlining what is fake in their relationship, and it produces falseness everywhere. In these circumstances, being in love with Merton Densher and uncertain about his relationship with Kate, she acts the part of the 'American girl' (5, 7, 211) – the spontaneous figure of 'comicality' who seems unconcerned by the situation, not making any claim upon Densher, rather denying her own emotions, which otherwise would lead her to 'live'.

In the second part, as the New York edition prints the text, Kate and Densher join in a conspiracy about Milly Theale on the assumption that she is dying. As they have been silent to Mrs Lowder about themselves, their silence towards Milly about their relationship means that they can successfully deceive her (6, 4, 266). Kate persuades Densher to 'make up to her' because, without love, Milly Theale has nothing, and is, it seems, dying. Kate's motivations at this stage are opaque. Milly, after another conversation with Sir Luke Strett, who has made it clear that she must be made 'happy' (presumably through love), leaves London for Venice, scene of Shakespearian intrigues and of Jamesian betrayals (*The Aspern Papers*). Kate Croy and Densher follow. It gradually becomes clear that Kate Croy's plan is for Densher to reciprocate Milly Theale's attraction so that she will die and leave him her fortune. Like Mrs Lowder, she tries to arrange a *mariage de convenance*, whose implications go beyond Thackeray's. She spells these out at a party given by Milly Theale in Venice, where Milly is dressed in white, no longer in mourning (8, 3). Densher agrees on the condition that Kate comes to him in his rooms in Venice, which she does in an episode the text passes over narrating. She leaves Venice to return to London, so that Densher is alone with Milly. But, in this ninth book, Sir Mark, who also wants to marry Milly Theale, tells her that Densher is deceiving her, and this causes her to 'turn her face to the wall' in a gesture which suggests she is giving up on living; none the less she sees Densher again in a meeting engineered by Sir Luke Strett, the contents of which are not recorded. Before dying, she makes him her heir. Her death is not described, but in Book 10, set again in London, the news of it arrives on Christmas Day. Densher on Christmas Eve receives a letter from her, which he does not open but gives to Kate. She burns it before him, unread. Kate and Densher are together, but she realises that he is in love with Milly's memory (he has been back in England for a fortnight without contacting her), while his guilty feelings make him unable to take the money as well as Kate Croy. She, who had begun the novel thinking 'she hadn't given up yet, and the broken sentence, if she was the last word, *would* end with a sort of meaning' (1, 1, 3), does indeed have the last word. Densher says he will marry her in an hour 'as we were' – i.e., not enriched by Milly Theale.

'As we were?'
'As we were.'

> But she turned to the door, and her headshake was now the end. 'We shall never be again as we were!' (10, 6, 509)

It is the 'end' of the engagement, the end of the text and the end of the future ('never').

II 'LITTLE MISS THEALE'

> As for [English] women I give 'em up: in advance . . . I revolt from their dreary deathly want of – what shall I call it? – Clover Hooper [later married to Henry Adams] has it – intellectual grace – Minny Temple has it – moral spontaneity. They live wholly in the realm of the cut and dried. . . . I should vastly enjoy half an hour's talk with an 'intelligent American.' (To William James, 8 March 1870, *Letters*, I, 208–9)

Like *The Portrait of a Lady*, *The Wings of the Dove* looks at the American heiress, and writes the 'international theme', contrasting 'the distinctively American and the distinctively European outlook' (*AN*, 11, 198) as this cross-cuts with emotional issues, with sexuality, and differences between English and American women. James said that comparisons displayed 'the comparative *state of innocence* of my countryfolk'. The American in Europe was 'almost incredibly *unaware of life* – as the European order expressed life', but the American had to represent for him, James said, 'the *whole* exhibitional range; the particular initiation on my own part that would have helped me to other apprehensions being absolutely bolted and barred to me. . . . I was reduced to studying my New Yorkers and my Bostonians . . . under the queer rubric of their more or less stranded helplessness' (*AN*, 10, 187).

The 'American girl' speaks in James's fiction because she ghosts James, who explains that the 'other apprehension' from which he felt 'bolted and barred' was of the American male, who was only thinkable as 'the American "business-man"'; and from him 'I was absolutely and irredeemably helpless, with no fibre of my intelligence responding to his mystery. No approach I could make to him on his "business-side" really got near it' (*AN*, 10, 193). Frances Cogan in *All-American Girl* discusses the expansion of business in the second half of the nineteenth-century, and refers to its problems, which were unknown in Europe: 'the sheer economic size of the country and attendant transportation problems, the absence of a bureacratic middle-management class...and the lack of government regulation' which led to a 'violently overheated economy...characterised by depressions, recessions and periodic boom–bust cycles'.[3] This was the world James senior had broken with (*Autobiography*, I, 109–10). And the son felt his difference in relation to both the American business-man and the European. On the occasion of Thackeray's first lecture-tour in America (1852–3), James, then nine, had been introduced to him, and had shown him the buttons on his jacket. Thackeray made fun of these, saying that he would be called 'Buttons' in England (as a servant in livery) and – 'it had been revealed to me thus in a flash that we were somehow *queer*' (*Autobiography*, I, 5, 52).

As the American boy, so also the American girl. In Paris in 1857, the Jameses again met Thackeray, when he again singled out the children's clothing, laying his hand on James's seven-year-old sister (Alice James), and exclaiming with 'ludicrous horror' – 'Crinoline? I was suspecting it! So young and so depraved!' (*Autobiography*, I, 5, 52). In the joke lies the sense of endless sexual superiority enjoyed by the European. Hence the frailty of Daisy Miller, introduced by her brother as 'an American girl!' W. D. Howells' context for saying that James had discovered 'the Daisy Miller type of American girl' was that readers of James would be feminine, including male James readers.[4]

James's autobiography makes Mary Temple an American girl. In the first section of *A Small Boy and Others*, with its echoes of the Albany house used for *The Portrait of a Lady*, he ends with Henry James senior's sister Catherine, who married Mary's father, Captain Robert Temple (*Autobiography*, II, 1, 10). In *Notes of a Son and Brother*, section 4, treating of the circle in which they moved when Mary Temple was seventeen, he speaks of 'those who knew and loved, I was going to say adored her' (*Autobiography*, II, 4, 282). She dominates the final section of *Notes of a Son and Brother* (section 13), where she is 'Minnie' (515) – compare Daisy Miller and Milly (Mildred) Theale – and her letters are transcribed, and her death described, in an allusion to *The Wings of the Dove*:

> She did in fact cling to consciousness; death at the last, was dreadful to her; she would have given anything to live – and the image of this, which was long to remain with me, appeared so of the essence of

tragedy that I was in the far-off aftertime to seek to lay the ghost by wrapping it, a particular occasion aiding, in the beauty and dignity of art. (*Autobiography*, II, 544)

She stands in for Jamesian vulnerability, but she was not the only woman he knew marked for death: compare Alice James, and Constance Fenimore Woolson. She and James kept up a friendship by correspondence for fourteen years till her suicide in 1894, jumping from the window of the Casa she had rented in Venice.[5] To Francis Boott, James wrote of her 'chronic melancholy' which in illness would deepen into 'suicidal mania' (*Letters*, III, 460, 463), and he travelled to Venice to help wind up her affairs, and take away letters: the year of planning in his notebook *The Wings of the Dove*.[6]

If something of these women enters into the portrait of Milly Theale, who like Woolson, dies in Venice, the 'ghost' to be laid becomes complex. The difference between Mary Temple and Milly Theale is that the latter is not in any clear sense ill at all – Kate Croy denies that there is anything wrong with Milly's lungs, adding – it indicates how much she belongs to the 1890s discourse of aestheticism – that when Milly dies 'she won't smell, as it were, of drugs. She won't taste, as it were, of medicine. No one will know' (6, 4, 254, 255). Kate may be unreliable, and callous, but the statement about Milly that 'she worked – and seemingly quite without design – upon the sympathy, the curiosity, the fancy of her associates' (3, 1, 83) suggests an ambiguity. The woman who 'turns her face to the wall' may be complicit in her own death, even suicidal. James wrote about Mary Temple that 'no one who ever knew her can have failed to look at her future as an absolute problem – and we almost all had imagination enough to say, to murmur at least, that life – poor narrow life – contained no place for her. How all her conduct and character seem to have pointed to this conclusion – how profoundly inconsequential, in her history, continued life would have been!' (*Letters*, I, 228). Writing to Grace Norton, he confided that he was 'really the happier for knowing her at absolute peace and rest. Her life was a strenuous, almost passionate *question*, which *my* mind at least, lacked the energy to offer the elements of an answer for' (*Letters*, I, 231–2).

That letter affirms that James could not have married Mary Temple (it can be compared with one to Grace Norton (1880) saying he was 'unlikely ever to marry', since 'one's attitude toward marriage is

a fact – the most characteristic part doubtless of one's general attitude towards life . . . . If I were to marry I should be guilty in my own
eyes of inconsistency – I should pretend to think better of life than
I really do' (*Letters*, II, 314)). His version of Mary Temple helps
justify such nihilism: he does not think she could have survived
marriage. American 'youth' cannot move into anything else. Daisy
Miller dies; Isabel Archer marries an American 'sterile dilettante', as
another American, the invalid Ralph Touchett, calls him (*The Portrait of a Lady*, 2, 34, 292). And Milly Theale, less analysed in the
text than is Isabel Archer, is seen as 'strange'. Writing on the novel,
Virginia Fowler refers, in disagreement, to Robert C. McLean's essay,
'attempt[ing] to prove that a "sexually frustrated Milly Theale"
commits suicide "most probably by leaping to her death from the
balcony of the Palazzo Leporelli"'.[7] This – which presumably does
not allow for the possibility of anything sexual between Densher and
Milly Theale before the end of her life – fuses Milly with Constance
Fenimore Woolson, and perhaps evokes the suicide of another 'American girl', Grace Mavis, who jumps from the *Patagonia* in the 1888
story of that name. It connects the death of Milly Theale with the
first time she appears, where Mrs Stringham sees her seated at the
edge of a precipice in the Alps, and wonders if there is a 'horrible
hidden obsession' which will lead her to suicide, until she sees her as
'more in a state of uplifted and unlimited possession that had nothing
to gain from violence' (3, 1, 89). Roderick Hudson's death is also
recalled. But 'nothing to gain from violence' is Mrs Stringham's
reading. However she dies, Milly, by calling herself the American
girl (5, 7, 211–12), and letting herself be seen as the peaceful
loving dove, so that even her death is reduced in its reporting to
the aesthetic, even kitsch image of her folding her wings (10, 3,
473), in some sense does commit suicide, unable to survive within
the role she has assigned for herself and which has been given to
her.

Mrs Stringham asks Milly, before she has seen Densher in London,
if she wants to run away from him. 'It was, oddly enough, an idea
Milly seemed half to accept. "I don't know *what* I want to run away
from!"' (4, 3, 142). When she comes across Densher, she retreats
from any confrontation, so that just as Mrs Lowder calls her 'you
dear American thing' (5, 5, 190), Densher calls her the 'American
girl' (6, 5, 268), 'the little American girl who had been kind to him in
New York' (8, 1, 341). The diminutive repeats an earlier recalling of

his time in New York: 'Little Miss Theale's individual history was not stuff for his newspaper; besides which, moreover, he was seeing but too many little Miss Theales. They even went so far as to impose themselves as one of the groups of social phenomena that fell into the scheme of his public letters' (6, 1, 222–3; see also 6, 3, 247; 8, 3, 371; 9, 2, 399).

After Mrs Stringham has seen her on the edge of the precipice, Milly Theale suddenly asks her what Dr Finch in New York had said when she saw the doctor alone (it being Milly's guess that Mrs Stringham had done just that). But it is not clear at this stage of the book that Milly is unwell. Asked if she is, she answers, 'I don't know... but it might be well to find out.' Her concern, she says, is 'if I shall have much of it'. The word 'it' refers to 'Everything. Of everything I have':

> Anxiously, again, our friend cast about, 'You "have" everything; so when you say "much" of it...'
> 'I only mean,' the girl broke in, 'shall I have it for long? That is if I *have* got it.'   (3, 2, 93)

A moment later she adds, 'I don't think I've really *everything*' (3, 2, 94).

Possession and dispossession go together. Milly, soon to be betrayed, does not have 'uplifted and unlimited possession' as Mrs Stringham had thought; indeed, the question is what she possesses, and what 'it' is. Perhaps nothing. When Kate urges Densher to 'console' Milly, whatever that means, she adds 'she has nothing' (6, 3, 253). Sir Luke, examining Milly Theale for 'what she supposed, [found] something else', according to Mrs Stringham; when Mrs Lowder asks what, she answers 'God keep me from knowing' (7, 1, 296). It seems to be woman's desire that he has found in examining Milly – her desire as interpreted by the male, as noticed by Milly Theale, who says to him that 'when you talk of "life" I suppose you mean mainly gentlemen' (7, 2, 309). That desire turns Milly Theale towards life or death.

In *The American Scene*, the tragedy of the American woman is that when all the men have to do is to be business-men, she has to be everything else, to represent 'the social'. America shows 'a society of women "located" in a world of men' (1, 8, 52, compare this with 11, 2, 254). 'The men are not to be taken as contributing to [civilisation] but only the women' (4, 1, 123). In these circumstances, the American girl says

> what do I know...about manners or tone, about proportion or perspective, about modesty or mystery, about a condition of things that involves...other forms of existence than this poor little mine...? How can I do *all* the grace, *all* the interest, as I'm expected to? – yes all the interest that isn't the mere interest on the money.... Was there ever such a conspiracy, on the part of a whole social order, toward the exposure of incompetence?...Who, at any turn, for an hour, ever pityingly overshadows or dispossesses me? By what combination of other presencers ever am I disburdened, ever relegated and reduced, ever restored, in a word, to my right relation to the whole? All I want...is...that my parents and my brothers and my male cousins should consent to exist otherwise than occultly, undiscoverably, or, as I suppose you'd call it, irresponsibly.... Haven't I, however, as it is, been too long abandoned and too *much* betrayed?
>
> (*The American Scene*, 14, 2, 317–18)

The American girl longs for 'dispossession', talks of betrayal. She expresses Milly Theale's desire and, psychoanalytically, her abandonment. Virginia Fowler refers to the passage in *The American Scene* where masculine assumptions in 'young, fresh, frolicksome architecture' – that of the skyscraper and the hotel – destroy values associated with the woman, by effacing differences between inside and outside:

> Thus we have the law fulfilled that every part of every house shall be...visible, visitable, penetrable....Thus we see systematized the indefinite extension of all spaces and the definite merging of all functions; the enlargement of every opening, the exaggeration of every passage, the subsitution of gaping arches and far perspectives and resounding voids for enclosing walls, for practicable doors, for controllable windows, for all the rest of the essence of the room-character, that room-suggestion which is so indispensable not only to occupation and concentration, but to conversation itself, to the play of the social relation at any other pitch than the pitch of a shriek or a shout. [The visitor] sees only doorless apertures, vainly festooned, which decline to tell him where he is, which make him still a homeless wanderer, which show him other apertures, corridors, staircases, yawning, expanding, ascending, descending, and all as for the purpose of giving his presence 'away,' of reminding him that what he says must be said for the house. (4, 2, 125–6)

Fowler draws attention to the sexual imagery here and sees the architecture as an assault on the feminine and civilised in the name of what James calls 'publicity' – the opposite of privacy. In these images of an American home thoroughly penetrated, James evokes the tragedy of the American girl, given no separate space, or room for any separate desire.[8] Where there are no doors, no separate spaces, there is no uncanny, no ghost. The attempt to abolish or ignore the uncanny and the elimination of the feminine may be linked. American architecture as described in *The American Scene* is as different as possible from the old house in Albany with the 'melancholy' 'office' where Isabel Archer reads books, where the door onto the street has been bolted and the sidelights filled with green paper. 'She had no wish to look out, for this would have interfered with her theory that there was a strange, unseen place on the other side – a place which became to the child's imagination, according to its different moods, a region of delight or of terror' (*The Portrait of a Lady*, 3, 33).

The non-survival value of the 'American girl' represents a real issue to James and a mask for himself. In the Preface to *The Wings of the Dove*, he begins with the

> very young or very old motive... of a young person conscious of a great capacity for life, but early stricken and doomed, condemned to die under short respite, while also enamoured of the world.
>
> (*AN*, 16, 288)

At the same time, and in contrast, 'I had from far back mentally projected a certain sort of young American as more "the heir of all the ages" than any other young person whatever.' Putting these two things together would produce someone as 'the heir of all the ages only to know [the self] as that consciousness should deepen, balked of [the self's] inheritance' (*AN*, 16, 292). The American has so much but has no survival value. It becomes ever more important for James to see Mary Temple as dead. In the early stages of planning the novel, the Notebook entry (3 November 1894) refers only to 'some young creature (it seems to me preferably a woman, but of this I'm not sure)'. Then comes *The Wings of the Dove*, then the Preface, then the Autobiography's comments. And the novel at least does not succeed in laying the 'ghost' – perhaps it did not really mean to – by wrapping it 'in the beauty and dignity of art', as though art as described here was a device for eliminating the uncanny or the ghostly. The terms 'beauty and dignity' are certainly dangerously inappropriate to the novel form: they could never fit with any Bakhtinian prescription. They aestheticise, as much as the Preface sees Milly Theale's death as determinate, a premise of the novel, death as waste. The tone of the Preface resembles Pater's conclusion to *The Renaissance*:

> While all melts under our feet, we may well grasp at any exquisite passion, or any contribution to knowledge that seems by a lifted horizon to set the spirit free for a moment, or any stirring of the senses, strange dyes, strange colours, and curious odours, or work of the artist's hands, or the face of one's friend. Not to discriminate every moment some passionate attitude in those about us, and in the very brilliancy of their gifts some tragic dividing of forces on their ways, is, on this short day of frost and sun, to sleep before evening....
>
> Well! we are all *condamnés*, as Victor Hugo says: we are all under sentence of death... our one chance lies in expanding that interval, in getting as many pulsations as possible into the given time. Great passions may give us this quickened sense of life...[9]

Despite these Paterian stresses, it is noticeable that James refuses to allow the fulfilment of any passion except for Kate Croy and Densher, once. (Though they will never again be as they were, they have once been together, even if the circumstances are equivocal.) Perhaps, with Milly Theale, the text colludes with her lack of will power, making it a waste of time for Sir Luke Strett to speak as he does, for the text is already marked for death, down to its title: compare the equivocally-named *Daisy Miller: A Study* and *The Portrait of a Lady* with *The Wings of the Dove* (and if *The Ambassadors* is named in any sense for Holbein, all of the 'major phase' novels, including *The Ivory Tower*, memorialise products of art with diminished referentiality). 'Wings', in so far as they apply to Milly, reduce her to part-objects.

III JAMES AND THACKERAY

Milly Theale interprets London in terms of an earlier nineteenth-century literature. She is like James who, in *The Middle Years*, records his first visit to London in 1869 and notices 'the incomparable truth to type of the waiter, truth to history, to literature, to poetry, to Dickens, to Thackeray, positively to Smollett and to

Hogarth' (*Autobiography*, III, 549). Literature is, for James, the indispensable archive without which he cannot begin to work. It is not, for James, equivalent to the Flaubert whose texts suggest that there is nothing else to do but recycle the already said, the platitudinous. Rather that Dickens and Thackeray, the latter with words and pictures 'from his own expressive hand' (*Autobiography*, I, 24, 186), give the sense of a spontaneous art which the later writer feels embarrassed to match. James gives a conscious evaluation of the novelistic world of Dickens and Thackeray when recollecting in the *Autobiography* the arrival at the end of 1859 of the first *Cornhill Magazine*, Thackeray's journal (which later published *Daisy Miller, An International Episode* and *The Portrait of a Lady*):

> Thackeray...appeared to us to guarantee personally, intimately, with a present audibility that was as the accent of good company, the new relation with him and with others of company not much worse, as they then seemed, that such a medium could establish.... For these appearances, these strong time-marks in such stretches of production as that of Dickens, that of Thackeray, that of George Eliot, had in the first place simply a genial weight and force, a direct importance, and in the second a command of the permeable air and the collective sensibility, with which nothing since has begun to deserve comparison. They were enrichments of life, they were *large* arrivals, these particular renewals of supply – to which frankly, I am moved to add, the early *Cornhill* giving me a pretext, even the frequent examples of Anthony Trollope's fine middle period, looked at in the light of old affection and that of his great heavy shovelfuls of testimony to constituted English matters; a testimony of course looser and thinner than Balzac's to *his* range of facts, but charged with something of the big Balzac authority.... I witnessed...the never-to-be-equalled degree of difference made... by the prolonged 'coming-out' of *The Newcomes*, yellow number by number... (*Autobiography*, II, 1, 251–2)

The assessment of Thackeray is generous, perhaps higher than that of Dickens because of his part in James's development. James repeats George Eliot's view of Thackeray, seeing him as 'our most important novelist' and perhaps this estimate, while it does not do Thackeray harm, finds Dickens less interesting than he is, and suggests something contradictory in James. He could outdo Thackeray, and *The Wings of the Dove* is consistently more interesting than *The Newcomes*, to which it pays tribute, but there is an evasion of Dickens, and a transposition to Thackeray of much that Dickens represents, which, unconscious as it may be, gives a piquancy to James's sense of failure as recorded in his Preface ('one's plan, alas is one thing, and one's result another' – *AN*, 16, 296).

In the Preface to *The Tragic Muse*, James is more qualified about *The Newcomes*, and the critique implies what is conflictual within James's art:

> A picture without composition slights its most precious chance for beauty.... There may in its absence be life, incontestably, as *The New-comes* has life, as *Les Trois Mousquetaires*, as Tolstoy's *War and Peace* have it; but what do such large loose baggy monsters, with their queer elements of the accidental and the arbitrary, artistically *mean*? We have heard it maintained, we will remember, that such things are 'superior to art,' but we understand least of all what *that* may mean, and we look in vain for the artist, the divine exploratory genius, who will come to our aid and tell us. There is life and life, and as waste is only life sacrificed and thereby prevented from 'counting,' I delight in a deep-breathing economy and an organic form.   (*AN*, 5, 84)

The critique of 'huge baggy monsters' implies amorphousness, and in the *Autobiography*, James dicusses the London of the 1850s as amorphous too:

> a much more eccentrically and variously characterised place, than the present great accommodated and accommodating city.... It was extra-ordinarily the picture and the scene of Dickens, now so changed and superseded; it offered to my presumptuous vision still more the reflec-tion of Thackeray – and where is the *detail* of the reflection of Thack-eray now? – so that as I trod the vast length of Baker Street, the Thackerayan vista of other days, I throbbed with the pride of a vastly enlarged acquaintance.   (*Autobiography*, I, 22, 171–2)

Walter Benjamin quotes G. K. Chesterton saying that Dickens 'did not stamp those places [London streets] on his mind; he stamped his mind on those places' (Benjamin, *Baudelaire*, p. 70). London for James is uncanny, because of the ghosts left behind by Dickens and Thackeray; so is Boulogne on account of *The Newcomes*. (*Autobio-graphy*, I, 29, 225). James speaks the language of a 'deep-breathing economy and an organic form' in the Preface because the other forms – which enabled the creation of Dickensian and Thackerayan char-acters with their rich difference from each other and from James's London – are now impossible, in a loss James's art cannot make up.

The Preface to *The Tragic Muse* can be paired with the Preface to *The Spoils of Poynton*. Here

> life blunders and deviates, loses herself in the sand. The reason is of course that life has no direct sense whatever for the subject and is capable, luckily for us, of nothing but splendid waste. Hence the opportunity for the sublime economy of art, which rescues, which saves, and hoards and 'banks'...thus making up for us, desperate spendthrifts that we all naturally are, the most princely of incomes ... (*AN*, 7, 120)

One page further, James refers to 'clumsy Life again at her stupid work' (*AN*, 7, 121). It is a strange, excessively dismissive note. The contrast between life and art in these Prefaces is like the distinction between the earlier nineteenth-century novel and the art that James intended to lay Mary Temple in, ideal, sublimating, without 'waste'. In the Preface, he speaks for art as preventing life from going to waste in an undifferentiated mass, and the contrast is with the Dickensian and Thackerayan modes whose excess implies waste (as Dickens thematises waste in the dust-heaps of *Our Mutual Friend*). The language of art over life sounds like a refusal of life, a turning away from it, but the irony is that such an economy of art and James's economic metaphors repeat the obsessions with money running through *The Wings of the Dove*. As Milly Theale is told by Lord Mark, 'nobody here, you know, does anything for nothing' (4, 1, 114). Lord Mark could have stepped out of Thackeray, and *The Newcomes* is certainly about cynical obsessions with money-power, but that obsessionalism is not repeated in Thackeray's diffuse novel form. Rather, the Jamesian language is of Georges Bataille's 'restricted economy', the world without the gift, of a measured economy without excess, no expenditure without reserve. James plays on this restricted economy in his images in the Preface to *The Spoils of Poynton*, another novel about what is waste. The economy is denied when Milly Theale dies leaving her fortune to Densher, but it is still affirmed in the way the text regards Milly as redemptive, or, as Kate Croy puts it to Densher:

> 'she died for you then that you might understand her. . . . She did it *for* us. . . . I used to call her, in my stupidity – for want of anything better – a dove. Well she stretched out her wings and it was to *that* they reached. They cover us.' (10, 6, 508)

The language of redemption may be linked to the desire for possession, which word, contrasted with 'waste', echoes through the text. Before returning to James on waste, note the resonances of 'possession', which Merton Densher feels he needs – 'life was what he must somehow... annex and possess' (2, 1, 36), as does Kate Croy with regard to him:

> What she felt was that, whatever might happen, she must keep [Densher's looks], must make them most completely her possession and it was already strange enough that she reasoned, or at all events began to act, as if she might work them in with other and alien things, privately cherish them and yet, as regards the rigour of it, pay no price. (2, 1, 43)

Densher is motivated by 'pride of possession' (6, 1, 220) towards Kate (just as Mrs Lowder says about him, 'I want him... for myself' (7, 2, 303). In Venice, in the Piazza San Marco, Densher and Kate Croy, together for a moment, feel 'in possession':

> the splendid Square... furnished them, in their remoteness from earshot, with solitude and security. It was as if, being in possession, they could say what they liked; and it was also as if, in consequence of that, each had an apprehension of what the other wanted to say. It was most of all for them, moreover, as if this... begot in the heart of each a fear. There might have been a betrayal of that in the way Densher broke the silence... (8, 2, 355)

Being 'in possession' comes from the place, which seems to sustain them, giving to them confidence that they cannot be overlooked, that their subjectivity is unimpaired. Possession of subjectivity, however, depends on control of the other, and immediately the text aligns 'possession' with fear of 'betrayal'. Desire for the first, as always in James, produces the other. Densher must possess Kate Croy sexually and as a knowable object who is not opaque to him, as when he 'possesses himself of her arm' and feels that 'he was already in a sense possessed of what he wanted' and that 'what he was possessed of was real' (8, 2, 361). But since, as has been noticed repeatedly in this study, 'possession' has to do with the ghostly and is two-way (being possessed by ghosts), possession is also unreal. Milly Theale, whose 'uplifted and unlimited possession' (3, 1, 89) has been commented on, and who is also aware of the possibility of 'betrayals' (4, 3,

136), feels in the atmosphere of the doctor's the absence of possession:

> She struck herself as aware, aware as she had never been, of really not having had from the beginning anything firm. It would be strange for the firmness to come, after all, from her learning in these agreeable conditions that she was in some way doomed; but above all it would prove how little she had hitherto had to hold her up. If she was now to be held up by the mere process – since that was perhaps on the cards – of being let down, this would only testify in turn to her queer little history. (5, 3, 168)

The lack of 'firmness' links possession to dispossession, and evokes, almost, the necessity of betrayal, as though the best way to be held up is to be let down. And this, here, may be the meaning of 'queer': only a life which is not laid out with traditional narrative order – from the beginning – has survival value.

The sense of everything slipping away links with the text's anxiety about waste, which thematises it in Milly Theale's early death. Illness – beginning with Lionel Croy's hypochondria (1, 1, 3) – is an image for wasting (10, 2, 469). When Milly, her head filled with fictional references, first sees Kate Croy, she seems

> the wondrous London girl in person.... The only thing was that she was nicer.... She saw this striking young person from the first in a story, saw her, by a necessity of the imagination, for a heroine, felt it as the only character in which she wouldn't be wasted... (1, 2, 122–3)

Waste is Kate Croy's thought as she meditates on 'the failure of fortune and of honour' (1, 1, 1), a Thackerayan theme. She has reached twenty-five with the sense that 'the world was different – whether for worse or for better – from her rudimentary readings, and it gave her the feeling of a wasted past' (1, 2, 20). James colludes in this waste: he gives her *two* brothers, and both have died. But beyond this sense of social waste, the energies of Kate Croy and Morton Densher produce at the end Densher's 'wasted passion' – turning to 'mere cold thought' – Kate working unsuccessfully to forestall it (10, 2, 469). Here appears the impossibility of Kate Croy and Merton Densher ever confirming an identity together. Kate's anger at the beginning of the novel made her show herself 'in the glass over the mantel, a face positively pale with the irritation that had brought her to the point of going away without seeing [her father] (1, 1, 1). At the end there is an incremental development – or else an entropic movement – of the waste of passion: 'it had come to the point really that they [Kate and Densher] showed each other pale faces, and that all the unspoken between them looked out of their eyes in a dim terror of their further conflict' (10, 6, 506). The word 'pale' suggests the ghostly, and death, and the world of Holbein's 'The Ambassadors'. Looking – whether in the glass, in the Lacanian 'mirror-stage', where the subject receives its identity, or looking at the lover – produces an uncanny paleness. For what is to be seen is disconfirmatory, dispossessing. For Lacan:

> From the outset, we see, in the dialectic of the eye and the gaze, that there is no coincidence, but, on the contrary, a lure. When, in love, I solicit a look, what is profoundly unsatisfying and always missing is that – *You never look at me from the place where I see you.* Conversely, *what I look at is never what I wish to see.*[10]

The loss, or absence, of symmetry, the power of disconfirmation, Kate Croy touches on these in her last line: 'we shall never be again as we were'.

IV WRITING A NEW YORK HISTORY

Milly Theale finds more that is Thackerayan than Dickensian in what she sees, and James seems to concede more to Thackeray than to Dickens. Yet *The Wings of the Dove* is, I think, more Dickensian. Lionel Croy as the impoverished father in the first chapter is not like Colonel Newcome, who takes himself off to the almshouses to die after he has impoverished himself and his family; he is the more difficult and intractable Dickensian father, part John Dickens (the father who was sent to prison), part Mr Micawber (note the reference to Mrs Micawber), part William Dorrit, and, in his reference to 'the business world', part Harold Skimpole. These Dickensian ghosts haunt James's text and make Lionel Croy ghostly. The disgraced father is reduced to living in a boarding house (the situation suggests *Père Goriot*), repeatedly described as 'vulgar' – the repetition is Dickensian. Slippery and sticky, like the furniture, he is the latest commentator on James's 'awkward age' and its 'deplorably superficial morality' which he negotiates with an extraordinary mixture of self-interest and disingenuousness, calling it 'vulgarised and brutal-ised' (1, 1, 12), like an aesthete. Eve Kosofsky Sedgwick, whose work on James I discuss in Chapter 8, contends that the unnamed disgrace that Mr Croy has brought on his family is homosexuality, adding that 'Kate Croy's construction as a woman, her sexing and gendering, have her father's homosexual disgrace at their very core . . . they have installed . . . the irresolvable compound of a homophobic prohibition with a nascent homosexual identity, both in a gender not her own.'[11] In the years succeeding the Oscar Wilde scandal, the possibility of a homosexual scandal could not have been out of public discourse. None the less, Sedgwick's reading seems unnecessary, considering the line of disgraced fathers in Dickensian and Thackerayan texts. There is nothing sympathetic about Croy, and his behaviour in the first scene presents him as self-indulgent, hypochondriac, and sponging in a way which suggests that this is not newly learned. His faults seem to fit financial irregularity as much, or more than, sexual ones, and the hypocrisy of the English. And apart from his separation from business, nothing contestatory emerges about his masculinity, a con-trast to Wilde, save that the last time he is heard of, at Mrs Condrip's, he is in tears (10, 5, 492–3), in terror of something, like John Marcher in *The Beast in the Jungle*.

Sedgwick's reading of Lionel Croy does, however, direct attention to the father, and to the impact that the previous failure has had on the present generation, past, encrypted secrets being carried forward, disabling present knowledge. Kate Croy recalls that 'one cold black Sunday morning, when on account of an extraordinary fog, we hadn't gone to church' she was reading a history book by the lamp and heard from her sister of her father's disgrace. The investment in this past, precisely caught in its historical moment and yet vague, enshrouded in fog, is Dickensian, not Thackerayan in its psycho-analytic investments, in suggesting a history which is also unknow-able, though its secret weighs on the present and makes Kate Croy, the present subject, also unknown to herself. When, on the first page, waiting for her father, she looks in the glass over the mantel, she is trying to establish a subjectivity, trying to form a coherent image, but that attempt is confounded by its incorporation of something else that she cannot 'annex'. The secret has annexed her; she tells Densher her father's dishonour is part of her (2, 1, 47–9). If her face is 'positively pale' as she looks in the glass, its ghostliness fits with the London fog, and with her father's joke about effacing himself

(1, 1, 14). To distinguish between ghosts and real people requires being able to suggest that real people possess discernible identities. But identity cannot be established, and the ghostly seems all that there is.

People are possessed by something they cannot wholly know. The absence of an explanation about Mr Croy means that Kate Croy's existence, like that of Milly Theale, lacks 'anything firm'; narrative origins disappear. To make the scandal determinate and then to use it to read Kate Croy's desire in relation to both Milly and Densher, means that the text is committed to a knowable secret. Milly Theale thinks Kate Croy has a secret, which is then called 'some smothered [i.e., repressed] trouble', and this leads Susan Stringham to say 'we move in a labyrinth' (4, 3, 133), which suggests the no place and the no identity that is implied in the London fog. As Kate Croy is haunted by a secret, Milly Theale has two: her illness, whether she is ill or not, and with what, and her background, the 'general wreck' (5, 3, 172) that has left her an orphan with nothing more said about her loss of family except the reference to 'a high degree of speculation and dissipation' (4, 2, 124). Does that wreckage have any relation to Milly Theale's putative illness? Do past and present link? That is another kind of 'speculation'. Perhaps the past hangs over her life, infecting her health in a way that she does not know; perhaps her own subjectivity is something she cannot possess. In the two women, secrets meet secrets, but Kate's desire is knowledge – 'I'll be as silent as the tomb if I can only have the truth from you' (5, 3, 166) – willing mastery. She correspondingly denies explanations. When Merton Densher asks why Milly should deny herself the joy of meeting him, if she likes him so much, 'Kate cast about – it would take so long to explain. "And perhaps it's true that she *is* bad. She easily may be"' (6, 4, 251). Her reply is elliptical, a 'broken sentence', giving the subordinate rather than the important reason. Her refusal to explain – where even the excuse that it would take so long may not be her reason for silence – matches other textual silences.

An unpossessed subjectivity goes with another detail of the text: everyone's displacement. No-one has a space of their own. Kate Croy depends on her aunt; Lionel Croy has ugly rented rooms with an alienating view; Milly Theale is out of her home, moves through three countries and dies in rented rooms; Densher and Kate make love in cheap lodgings and have no place to meet; Densher, in the last but one chapter, moves from his club to meet Kate at Mrs Condrip's, where she is spending Christmas, and the book finishes with Kate turning to the door, walking out. She begins and finishes in rooms not her own, and as she is about to leave, on the first page, she is on the threshold on the last. Milly Theale comes with her secrets to this London to encounter other forms of secrets in Kate Croy, which the text only partially reveals. Dickens's plots – *Bleak House*, *Little Dorrit*, *A Tale of Two Cities* or *Great Expectations* – involve the secrets of the dead past, including the past of the parents, 'the dead generations'. This is not Thackerayan, but I think that James was aware of this distinction between Dickens and Thackeray, and it may be why Dickens is not one of the authors James accused of writing 'huge baggy monsters'. James's American girl, who has so little attachment to history, does not fit a Dickensian plot, and perhaps we come back from this point to the reason why for James she has so little survival value – because her destiny is to be thrown amongst those Europeans who have such a past. (So there are two books given over to the Europeans before there is any mention of the American: the European history is already set up, to catch the American.) The difference in *The Wings of the Dove* is that here the American is approaching the conditions of the European. She has her own unknowable past, her own 'New York history' (3, 1, 75). America is accorded a history to compete with the European. The survival-value of these different histories is tested in the scene at the National Gallery, in a meeting uncanny in its coincidence – again, a Jamesian and Dickensian theme, not a Thackerayan one.

Desire for autonomy marks each of the people at the National Gallery – Kate Croy, Merton Densher, Milly Theale. Neither of the women are or can be clear to themselves, while Densher's anxiety is less about knowing, as Kate desires to know; it is fear of loss of masculinity.[12] In Venice, he feels he is 'perpetually bent to [Kate's] will', he feels he has surrendered to 'her pure talent for life':

> The proof of a decent reaction in him against so much passivity was, with no great richness, that he at least knew – knew, that is, how he was, and how little he liked it as a thing accepted in mere helplessness.... His question connected itself, even while he stood, with his special smothered soreness, his sense almost of shame; and the soreness and the shame were less as he let himself, with the help of the conditions about him, regard it as serious.... His question, as we have called it, was the interesting question of whether he really had no

will left...whereas he had done absolutely everything that Kate
had wanted, she had done nothing whatsoever that he had.

(8, 1, 342–4)

Forced to keep silent, and not possessing Kate at all save on her
terms, which he cannot recognise as valid, he feels ashamed. His
masculinity – the same as his 'will', with the Shakespearian phallic
puns intended – is brought into question. Dickensian figures of both
the hero and the father, such as John Jarndyce (*Bleak House*), Arthur
Clennam (*Little Dorrit*) and Sydney Carton (*A Tale of Two Cities*)
are associated with a lack of will, which threatens to bring things to a
stasis, or to run them down altogether, and the Dickensian text
requires the woman to be redemptive. Book 8 of *The Wings of the
Dove*, with all the action taking place on one day, culminates with
Densher's commitment to betrayal: of Milly Theale, and then, by
demanding that Kate Croy comes to him at his rooms, of Kate's
'honour', that word which echoes from the first page. He says that
he will stay in Venice to trap Milly 'on my honour, if you'll come to
me. On *your* honour' (8, 3, 382).

He makes her honour-bound to come to him. But to do so would
be to lose both her honour and what she is trying to play for
(honourable marriage). He wants her as the woman over whose
honour he can have victory. At the end of the section, 'he saw himself
master in the conflict' (8, 3, 383), since she has submitted. His
victory is over her 'talent for life' – the will and the talent for life
stand opposed to each other in Densher's perception of things, and
the imposition of the will becomes more important. The last Book of
the text is Densher's, and since it gives his point of view, there is no
question of a simple condemnation of this man who now lives in a
reverie after the death of Milly Theale, not wanting to open her letter,
and in love with her memory. None the less he was complicit in a will
to destroy life. Since he is now a 'haunted man' (10, 2, 464), no ghost
can have been laid; the American girl has created a sense of the past
for the European, specifically English, male.

James speaks of 'capacity for life' in the Preface, and yet a drive
towards aestheticism, which he calls economy in art, separates him
from the novelists Dickens and Thackeray, whose excess and waste-
ful exuberance he substitutes for by a commitment to the beauty and
dignity associated with the death of Milly Theale. In so far as James
recalls Dickens and Thackeray, he articulates the easier comparison

between this text and Thackeray and *The Newcomes*, confronting Dickens openly more intermittently. Desiring not to waste, desiring to organise and imposing the will towards economy are aspects of the drive which takes him beyond Thackeray in the conditions of indifference and *ennui* of the 'awkward age'. Millie Theale sees what is wrong with the age in England when saying to Lord Mark, a figure that Thackeray would have identified with as Dickens's cultural formation meant that he never could, 'You're *blasé* but you're not enlightened. You're familiar with everything, but conscious really of nothing. What I mean is that you've no imagination' (4, 1, 115–16). Being *blasé* is the condition of the telegraphist in *In the Cage* (section 2): it is endemic to modernity, especially English modernity.

Densher has acquired an imagination by the end. James's attempt to write like Dickens means that the American gives to the European a new sense of the uncanny.

8

The Haunted Man:
The Beast in the Jungle

The Beast in the Jungle begins with John Marcher and May Bartram's second meeting one October (seasons in this text are springs or autumns) at a house called Weatherend, a name bringing narrative to an abrupt end before it starts.[1] He is thirty-five, she thirty, and she, not he, recollects their first meeting in Italy ten years before, when he said that his destiny was to be kept for something catastrophic. She promises to watch with him for the event. In the second part, the thing to happen is allegorised and made a reason for not marrying:

> But the devil in this was that the very basis itself put marrying out of the question. His conviction, his apprehension, his obsession, in short, was not a condition he could invite a woman to share; and that consequence of it was precisely what was the matter with him. Something or other lay in wait for him, amid the twists and the turns of the months and the years, like a crouching beast in the jungle. It signified little whether the crouching beast were destined to slay him or to be slain. The definite point was the inevitable springing of the creature; and the definite lesson from this was that a man of feeling didn't cause himself to be accompanied by a lady on a tiger-hunt. Such was the image under which he had ended by figuring his life. (2, 287)

He has an image for himself – a man of feeling – and for the disaster to overtake him – a beast which becomes a tiger – plus a rationale for not marrying, which is hardly enough, since the last thing he is doing in his life is hunting anything. Further, he thinks within an accepted gender-stereotyping, of marriage to the woman. The names, March(er) and May, contain their own uncanny, faintly alluded to in the phrase 'amid the twists and turns of the months' – twists which are tropes of language, which generate significance, turns like turns of the screw, postponing, pressurising, creating narrative anticipation as the months pass.

These things settled, the two become friends in London. The third part picks up a specific conversation, leading into a revelation that she has a disorder in her blood, which prompts the fear that she will die before the catastrophe occurs. The fourth part begins one April evening. He asks her what is the worst that can befall him, and she rises from her chair, coming close to him, 'as if still full of the unspoken':

> Her movement might have been for some finer emphasis of what she was at once hesitating and deciding to say. He had been standing by the chimney-piece, fireless and sparely adorned, a small, perfect old French clock and two morsels of rosy Dresden constituting all its furniture; and her hand grasped the shelf while she kept him waiting, grasped it a little as for support and encouragement. She only kept him waiting, however; that is he only waited. It had become suddenly, from her movement and attitude, beautiful and vivid to him that she had something more to give him; her wasted face delicately shone with it, and it glittered, almost as with the white lustre of silver, in her expression. She was right, incontestably, for what he saw in her face was the truth, and strangely, without consequence, while their talk of it as dreadful was still in the air, she appeared to present it as inordinately soft. This, prompting bewilderment, made him gape but the more gratefully for her revelation, so that they continued for some minutes silent, her face shining at him, her contact imponderably pressing, and his state all kind, but all expectant. The end, none the less, was that what he had expected failed to sound.   (4, 301–2)

What had he expected? The moment of the beast coming at him in the form of a crisis of his relationship with her? So he interprets it at the end (6, 311). Instead, she becomes ill at that moment, and the fifth part gives his last conversation with her, when she says that the 'it' has indeed touched him (5, 303). She dies and is buried in a London suburb. In the last section, he travels, returning a year later to the cemetery. He feels that his fate is settled, and this being so everything has lost its distinction, so that he is a mere tourist in the places where he visits. Back in the cemetery, the mourning face of another man suddenly awakens him to the absence in him of a sense of 'deep ravage' (6, 311). His fate is to have had nothing happen, to have done nothing but wait:

> This the companion of his vigil had at a given moment perceived, and she had then offered him the chance to baffle his doom. One's doom, however, was never baffled, and on the day she had told him that his own had come down she had seen him but stupidly stare at the escape she had offered him.
>
> The escape would have been to love her.   (6, 311)

As the narrative closes, he has the feeling of the beast springing out of the jungle and he falls on his face on the tomb. It is as though he has been caught by two things, both being the beast in the jungle. He has done nothing, his fate has been to be nothing, and he has lost the opportunity to escape that fate by loving the woman for herself:

> He saw the Jungle of his life and saw the lurking Beast; then, while he looked, perceived it, as by a stir of the air, rise, huge and hideous, for the leap that was to settle him. His eyes darkened – it was close; and, instinctively turning, in his hallucination, to avoid it, he flung himself, on his face, on the tomb.   (6, 312)

The hysterical reaction makes this a ghost-narrative: like the governess he sees something cancelling out the field of vision. He has had a sense that the beast has sprung (6, 311), but the spring is also a fall: after that spring, there is no more future, as the narrative has not begun which would give one. He fears the future, which ends further postponement, but the real which has overtaken him is that he could not begin, so could have no future.[2]

II   THE NAME OF THE BEAST

Leon Edel reads *The Beast in the Jungle* as though it was James's working over a supposed non-relationship with Constance Fenimore Woolson. Fred Kaplan's biography also refers to Woolson, but connects the narrative to James's putative homosexuality, following Eve Kosofsky Sedgwick's 1986 reading of the text.[3] Kaplan writes, 'Perhaps [James] had seen in Gosse's letter to Symonds, or perhaps Gosse had mentioned to him his reference to his struggles with "the wild beast" of homosexual desire that "is not dead, but tamer: I withstand him and the tricks of his claws"' (Kaplan, p. 456). This letter that Kaplan (p. 402) quotes was from 1890. Kaplan says John Marcher's experience follows James, who

> ponder[ed] what he had missed. Marcher, who is not an artist, cannot claim the relevance of an incompatibility between art and marriage – that rationalization must have seemed slim, even to James. It was not devotion to art alone that kept him from loving women. It was also deep fear of the experience itself, primarily based on his indirectly articulated panic about what the experience would entail for him   (Kaplan, p. 457)

This uses Sedgwick's phrase 'homosexual panic', and modulates from discussion of Marcher to James. References to the 'queer' in this text – 'the rest of the world thought him queer, but she, she only, knew how, and above all why, queer' (2, 288); or 'his queer consciousness' (3, 296) – now co-opt James for 'queer theory'. Sedgwick has extended her reading of James to *The Wings of the Dove*, and to the Prefaces, where she looks for anal imagery to help in a reading which will not 'make [James] sound as if he *isn't* gay'.[4] Her influence has been felt in readings of *The Author of Beltraffio* and *The Pupil*, and more loosely throughout other James texts.[5] It turns on her *Between Men: English Literature and Male Homosocial Desire* (1985), which reads the patriarchy of Western culture as 'homosocial' in its exclusion of women, policed by homophobia and the institutionalisation of 'homosexual panic'. Homosocial relations between men are always likely to be in a continuum with homosexuality, which inscribes male–male relations with paranoia. The argument seems opposed to the contrasting enabling conditions of women's associations together (the argument is silent about lesbianism and women's desire), and puts all male–male relationships into complicity in patriarchy, from which homosexuality can hardly be separated.[6] In *Epistemology of the Closet*, Sedgwick argues that homosexuality

> has been an exceedingly potent and embattled locus of power over the entire range of male bonds, and especially over those that define themselves, not *as* homosexual, but *as against* the homosexual. Because the paths of male entitlement, especially in the nineteenth century, required certain intense male bonds that were not readily

distinguishable from the most reprobated bonds, an endemic and irradicable state of what I am calling male homosexual panic became the normal condition of male heterosexual entitlement.

(Sedgwick, p. 185)

'Homosexual panic' comes from her summary of Freud on Schreber's paranoia that 'paranoia in men results from the repression of their homosexual desire' (Sedgwick p. 187),[7] and since it originates from that, this panic interpellates all males, constructing them with anxiety. This primacy of 'queerness' over the 'straight' is, of course, at the heart of queer theory. The bachelor, as a nineteenth-century type, she associates with Thackeray (*sic*) and with James, as a desexualised, Victorian response to fears caused by homosexual panic. This point leads her to Edel's linking of *The Beast in the Jungle* with James and Constance Fenimore Woolson, only with a stronger implication, that 'James felt that he had with her...something sexually to prove.' His mistake was 'moving blindly from a sense of the good, the desirability, of love and sexuality to the automatic imposition on himself of a specifically *hetero*sexual compulsion' (p. 196), not 'resist[ing] actively' heterosexual compulsions within culture. May Bartram loves John Marcher; he does not reciprocate until at the end; he reflects that 'the escape would have been to love her; then, *then* he would have lived' (6, 311). The certainty introduced in the last paragraph of the text she reads as panic. The unspeakable 'secret of the gods' (3, 296) that Marcher possesses is homosexuality; he ends 'not the finally self-knowing man who is capable of heterosexual love, but the irredeemably self-ignorant man who embodies and enforces heterosexual compulsion' (Sedgwick, p. 210). The argument is harsher on Marcher than those accounts which notice his egotism: he should have been aware of himself in homosexual terms, which would have been affirmative, rather than keeping him irredeemably self-ignorant. And what forces him towards this psychic move of affirming heterosexuality in a state where the homosexual is panicked into the reverse is his reaction to another man mourning, who invokes in Marcher both desire and 'the denial of that desire' (p. 211).

Sedgwick's reading concentrates on the cemetery-scene, which gives the ironic point to the text. She also opts to read the silence of the text about the secret in a determinate way: a textual silence is explicable by reference to homosexuality: reading can know what is at issue with the characters (and with James). But a silence to do with homosexuality is entirely comprehensible and no mystery at all in the context of this text, which, written in 1902, seven years after the Wilde trial, and depicting a narrative that extends over half a lifetime at least, must be presumed to date back in its imaginary time-references to around 1870. The feeling that 'something or other lay in wait for him' loses its point, however, when it can be rendered in such one-to-one terms. Are we to assume that over the course of years, if the mystery was homosexuality, it would have received *no* articulation at all between May Bartram and John Marcher? (May Bartram describes herself as more 'free and easy' than she was ten years ago (1, 283): she can ask a straight question about love, which she could not then, so she fits with the rise of the 'new woman'.) If 'her involvement with him occurs originally on the ground of her understanding that he is imprisoned by homosexual panic; and her own interest in his closet is not at all in helping him fortify it, but in helping him dissolve it' (Sedgwick, p. 206), could she not have been frank? But if the answer is no, that no articulation would have been possible then, which may be the case, even though it denies the status within culture of *women*'s desire for each other (like Alice James with Katherine Loring), then Sedgwick's reading, like calling James 'gay', is antihistorical, reading May Bartram as though she were a twentieth-century feminist: as the reference to the closet seems also antihistorical, as though there was an open space for the nineteenth-century homosexual to occupy, as though all desire was not then closeted.

In one paragraph, Sedgwick comes down hard on May Bartram, implying she is more attracted towards Marcher because of his sexual crisis, while in the next paragraph she suggests that May Bartram has the advantage and therefore can help him (pp. 209–10). This second paragraph suggests Sedgwick's own investment in writing about male homosexuality – speaking for it and for male sexuality: 'the fact that male heterosexual entitlement in (at least modern Anglo-American) culture depends on a perfected but always friable self-ignorance in men as to the significance of their desire for other men means that it is always open to women to know something that it is much more dangerous for any nonhomosexual-identified man to know' (p. 210). Yet it remains that May Bartram does seem to offer herself to Marcher and if at some level she does know his secret, this seems strange, since Sedgwick says that she has been 'fostering his homosexual potential as a route back to his truer perception of herself' (p. 210) as a woman investing creatively in him.

But the notion of the secret needs inspecting. Marcher has told May Bartram, in the context of a presumably erotically tinged boat trip to Sorrento (1, 280–1), that he had 'from his earliest time, as the deepest thing within [him] the sense of being kept for something rare and strange, possibly prodigious and terrible, that was sooner or later to happen to [him] that [he] had in [his] bones the foreboding and conviction of, and that would perhaps overwhelm [him]' (1, 282). This is not the matter for a secret; that is elsewhere:

> It had never entered into his plan that anyone should 'know', and mainly for the reason that it was not in him to tell anyone. That would have been impossible, since nothing but the amusement of a cold world would have waited on it.   (2, 285)

The secret is caused by his sense of difference from the world: 'He had disturbed nobody with the queerness of having to know a haunted man, though he had moments of rather special temptation on hearing people say they were "unsettled". If they were as unsettled as he was – he who had never been settled for an hour in his life – they would know what it meant. Yet it wasn't, all the same, for him to make them, and he listened to them civilly enough. This was why he had such good – though possibly such rather colourless – manners; this was why, above all, he could regard himself, in a greedy world, as decently – as in fact even a little sublimely unselfish' (2, 286). It is a separation from other people which she knows about, being 'in the secret of the difference between the forms he went through...and the detachment that reigned beneath them and that made of all behaviour...a long act of dissimulation' (2, 288). As Sedgwick reads it – 'there are at least two secrets: Marcher feels that he knows but has never told anyone (secret number one) that he is reserved for some very particular, uniquely rending fate in the future, whose nature is (secret number two) unknown to himself' (Sedgwick, pp. 204–5). But the second of these is not a secret, unless anything unknown can be said to be that. Sedgwick sees it as homosexual panic – i.e., fear of toppling into homosexual desire. Finally, in the course of this discussion, Sedgwick quotes the words, that he ' "has but one desire left": that *it* "be decently proportional to the posture he had kept, all his life, in the threatened presence of it" ' (p. 205). But this misreads James's text:

It wouldn't have been failure to be bankrupt, dishonoured, pilloried, hanged; it was failure not to be anything. And so, in the dark valley into which his path had taken its unlooked-for twist, he wondered not a little as he groped. He didn't care what awful crash might overtake him, with what ignominy or what monstrosity he might yet be associated – since he wasn't, after all, too utterly old to suffer – if it would only be decently proportionate to the posture he had kept, in the promised presence of it. He had but one desire left – that he shouldn't have been 'sold.'   (3, 296)

The statement suggests that Marcher wants the disaster to befall him – but also, as Freud says about the organism and the death-drive, in *Beyond the Pleasure Principle* (chapter 5), he wants to 'follow his own path' to disaster. He is prepared to become a Lionel Croy ('bankrupt, dishonoured') or even an Oscar Wilde ('pilloried'). For nothing to happen would make nonsense out of his separation from the others, negating his own sense of being special – which allows him to have the secret, as I have described it, in the first place. When the text reads at the end 'he had been the man of his time, *the* man, to whom nothing had happened' (6, 311) – an ironic distinction for anyone – he knows he has been 'sold'. He has thought of himself as singular; his fate as he thinks it, is that he has had the singular fate of having nothing happen to him, which of course is not singular, since it is also the fate of May Bartram, and of other James figures, such as Lambert Strether or Kate Croy waiting. The fate of nothing happening makes him like the rest; perhaps it describes a modern condition.

The feeling Marcher has that something might happen is a desire, inseparable from the death-drive. What he calls an 'obsession' (1, 284), making him a 'maniac' (2, 288), and what enables him to have colourless manners in public – because his emotional investments are elsewhere – is his fascination with the idea of something entirely crushing falling upon him. Sedgwick's account leaves this out: her Marcher is passive, victim of a 'totalizing, basilisk fascination with and terror of homosexual possibility' (Sedgwick, p. 206), unable to think through to alternatives, whereas the rhetoric of obsession gives him two sides: a self-protective aspect that guards his own subjectivity, using May Bartram for that effect, and an impulse towards destroying that ego, since it 'signified little whether the crouching beast were destined to slay him or to be slain' (2, 287). These two sides of his subjectivity do not know each other, though they help explain why he is a haunted man. One side is Freud's pleasure principle, guaranteeing homeostasis; the other one is beyond the pleasure principle, if anything is 'beyond' that, the death-drive.

Indeed, the sense at the end that 'he had never thought of her (ah, how it hugely glared at him!) but in the chill of his egotism and the light of her use' (6, 311) suggests not so much how the woman can see things the man cannot, but that May Bartram's own subjectivity has been created by Marcher; her own desire has been blocked off by his words. (This is repeated in the narrative structure of the text where the events are told from his point of view.) She remembers him, though to him her face is 'a reminder, yet not quite a remembrance' (1, 277); nor does he recall their conversation. She has been constituted a subject of his discourse by these words and her only release at the end is death. His narcissism, which casts her as his victim and his audience, relates to his sense at the beginning that he is 'lost in the crowd' (1, 277). This is an urban text, even if it opens at a country house. In the conditions of late nineteenth-century urbanism and commodity culture, creating the subject with 'poetry and history... press[ing] on him' (1, 277), the modern subject's memory is deficient, so it is not coincidental that the text begins with an opening deliberately arbitrary ('What determined the speech that startled him in the course of their encounter scarcely matters...') and that there are no narrative beginnings, apart from drifting as a tourist in Italy seven or ten years ago. (He again becomes a tourist after her death.) He must 'invent' romantic origins (1, 280), the point being that his life is to show no signs of anything having happened, that being the representative fate of 'the man of his time'. The obsessionality with an image he has created, the beast which 'glares' at him, links him with Hawthorne's obsessives, Ethan Brand, Wakefield or the Minister with the Black Veil, men who create fictions and allegories, to give themselves narrative beginnings, and, characteristically, to coerce women.

Though Sedgwick's reading has become largely hegemonic, and has intersected with studies of masculinity[8] and of James's relationship to Wilde, to change ways of seeing James's texts, I do not see that she illuminates *The Beast in the Jungle*, except perversely, by writing another text which the critic wishes James had written. Her reading has licensed a sense of James that examines his texts as though they had a missing determinate content of homosexual or homoerotic desire now suppliable. She makes homosexuality a matter which could have entered late nineteenth-century English public discourse in a way which could have been affirmatory, so that at the end of the text it is not possible for her to read as though Marcher ever could have desired May Bartram: the homosexual is homosexual, and cannot relate to a woman. (And if he does, he drives her towards her death, as James, on this reading, might have done with Constance Woolson.)

III   DESIRING TRAUMA

In giving a critique of Sedgwick's reading, I have hinted at my own, in discussing Marcher's obsessiveness, which goes further than the earlier Jamesian treatments of male hysteria. This text is not new in James: there have been anticipations of the material before, as with Lambert Strether feeling a 'waft from the jungle' (*The Ambassadors*, 5, 2, 154), or with the hesitancy of Douglas in *The Turn of the Screw*. James's nightmare of the Galerie d'Apollon is also relevant for the idea of confronting a destiny. The distinction in Marcher is his awareness of the uncanny (as opposed to the crowd that listens to ghost-stories at Weatherend [1, 278]), but that binarism goes through all James.

As calmly as with the Preface to *The Turn of the Screw*, as though 'facing the uncanny'. the Preface to *The Beast in the Jungle* disallows any autobiographical reading, saying that to discover the determinants of the narrative, 'I remount the stream of time, all inquiringly, but come back empty-handed' (*AN*, 14, 246). This reverses the sense of *The Aspern Papers*' 'visitable past' and repeats the ignorance instantiated in the tale's opening, its lack of beginning, its amnesia, the narrative being 'a sequel of something of which [Marcher] had lost the beginning' (1, 278).[9] Yet, as if affirming that the origin of any text is textual, or in an evasion of the past, James also refers to 'ten lines of an old note-book'. The *Notebook* editors refer to an entry of 5 February 1895, evoking 'the idea of *Too late* – of some friendship or passion or bond – some affection long desired and waited for, that is formed too late? I mean too late in life altogether.... It's a passion that *might* have been' (*Notebooks*, 1, 112). This, which only repeats the problem of the impossibility of getting back to an origin, and which has resonances with *The Ambassadors* – crosses with another note (27 August 1901) for 'a very tiny *fantasie*' 'of a man haunted by the fear, more and more, throughout life, that *something will happen to him*: he doesn't quite know what' (*Notebooks*, 199). The first entry puts everything in the past, but in the second the 'haunted man' is held, not by the past – the 'haunted man' of Dickens's Christmas Book – but by the future. In this version, James thinks of some love-interest, as 'pretty', part of a narrative plotting intended to catch the reader, generated by a 'second consciousness', who is not haunted. The discovery, generated by her rhetoric, that the woman loved him, makes a neat resolution – both something and nothing has happened to him. But a reading of *The Beast in the Jungle* that marks the irony that May Bartram loved Marcher and he has lost her and nothing has happened, this being his discovery in the last pages, mistakes that and the presence of the second consciousness for the primary plot. And the notebook entry gives no sense of what James's title implies.

The text shows Marcher's reason for not marrying May Bartram to be a rationalisation. It is not less than that when he feels at the end that he should have married her, a feeling which is beside the point, since the rationalisation shows he did think about it in her lifetime and rejected the possibility, so that she does not enter into his desire in that way. You rationalise when there is something you do not want to do, but this rationalisation invents a reason for something needing no explaining: marriage would have been dutiful, not from desire. Given his time again, he would do exactly the same; Marcher does what he wants to do. Something is going to happen to him, and he feels that that gives a reason for not doing anything, which is as much the expression of a desire as the other desire is – i.e., that he wants the catastrophe (which he also gets). The text highlights the absence of passion in Marcher – which links him to Isabel Archer (not just by the similarity of the name) – and makes him the man of his time, to whom nothing on earth was to have happened.

The question is: why such indifference, such lack of affect? Why the melancholia until the last 'hallucination' with which the text finishes – a marker of schizophrenia, perhaps? It is not that there is a buried homosexual content in Marcher – that would imply the power of positive desire. Sexuality in this text seems to be conveyed by a contrast in the crowd of people searching out possessions at Weatherend, with their 'excited sense of smell' and 'sounds of ecstasy' and 'silences of even deeper import' and acquisitiveness 'like a dog sniffing at a cupboard'. These are the people without distinction, and the instinctualism conveyed in the sense of smell may recall the audience in the opening scene of *Nana* smelling what she possesses as she walks on stage, but even here it is not sexually directed, being turned onto things, spoils: suggesting the power of empire.

Perhaps being 'the man of his time, *the* man, to whom nothing on earth was to have happened' links to a crisis in James's productivity, when after *The Tragic Muse* (1890) he produced no more novels till the time of the Wilde trial (though he wrote plays).[10] The novels after that show more complexity, even building into their titles resistance to total interpretation. Todorov points out that during this moment of change, 1892–1904, James wrote almost half of his 112 tales,[11] arguing that the new developments in these tales – illustrating these with *The Figure in the Carpet* (1896)[12] – are

> based on the quest for an absolute and absent cause.... The cause is absolute: everything in the story owes its presence, in the last analysis, to it. But it is absent and we set off in quest of it. And it is not only absent, but for most of the time unknown as well.... The secret of James's tales is, therefore, precisely this existence of an absent, overwhelming force which puts the whole present machinery of the narrative into motion.... The absence of the cause is present in the text...the cause is that which, by its absence, gives rise to the text. The essential element is absent; absence is an essential element. (Todorov, pp. 74–5)

Todorov's point applies to the *The Turn of the Screw* where Douglas tells a story, and the narrator comments on his 'long silence', and on his past repression – his 'thickness of ice' (Introduction, p. 146). But nothing in the governess's narrative explains Douglas's repression, or indifference, even if he takes the ghosts and the hauntings as indisputably real; nor is any explanation given about his death. Douglas is like Marcher, only in *The Turn of the Screw* the story deflects attention from Douglas's own state. *The Beast in the Jungle* gives us Douglas without that narrative, shorn of explanatory power. Douglas and Marcher are both figures of indifference. Barthes, in *Camera Lucida* sees indifference as a modern form of hysteria, and hysteria as produced by history. But in *The Turn of the Screw*, history does not impinge on Douglas, and in *The Beast in the Jungle*, history is in the future. If hysterics suffer from reminiscences, that applies to Douglas, perhaps, whose reminiscences – not his own, but part of his culture's – are kept in a drawer at home, but it does not fit

Marcher, whose memory of the past before the opening is blocked, as though an unsymbolisable trauma has held him, and he can only hope to have reminiscences after a trauma in a future anterior state.

IV UNREPRESENTABLE NARRATIVES

For Todorov and *The Beast in the Jungle*, 'the search for the secret and for truth is never anything but a search, a search without any content whatsoever' (Todorov, p. 101). The tale is 'about' its own premise: there is no possibility of a beginning without severance; hence its strangeness in opening, and tilt towards a blank future. The tale ending with the view that nothing has happened to him suggests the futility of narrativising: if anything has happened, it is outside representation. Todorov thinks Marcher's cure would be to love May Bartram, which would stop the search for absence. But it would *not* stop it, since he only 'loves' her after her death, which introduces a supplementary absence. He says to the dying May, 'I liked it [the menace] better present, as you say, than I can like it absent with *your* absence.' Two absences make up 'the absence of everything' (5, 304). The originary absence is followed by the absence of a relationship between the two: this narrative cannot get started, which makes the name Marcher ironic (no march of events). To work like that, the narrative must begin with a severance from the real, a refusal of relatedness. The point of severance remains to scar the text with the impossibility of its own elliptical way of being.

Todorov's argument works against a more determinate one, that a political unconscious is signified within silences and gaps. Fredric Jameson's *The Political Unsconscious* (1981) made texts allegories of politics and of history. Jameson argued that history, which for him is the real, 'is *not* a text . . . but . . . as an absent cause, it is inaccessible to us except in textual form, and that our approach to it and to the Real itself passes through its prior textualization'.[13] For Todorov, the initial absence does not refer outside itself to an absent but real cause, nor does it ask to be read symptomatically. In *this* absence, history has not taken a hold. *The Turn of the Screw* begins 'The story had held us . . .', and the auditors start already gripped. Todorov's argument implies either that no prior text or discourse has put its imprint or its hand upon the figures of the text, or that Marcher has been completely traumatised, beyond remembering. The present (the end of the nineteenth century) takes no hold of Marcher. Yet he is not free, and May Bartram even takes the form of the sphinx (4, 297), monstrous, a supplementary beast at that moment to him, outside male interpretation, resistant to it, and challenging the other in relation to both past and future from an unidentifiable source. Woman's desire is anti-Oedipus, but this point, which would help glimpse what the narrative might contain if it started, cannot become a narrative, for Marcher is an already severed Oedipus, shorn from the knowledge of his history which he cannot narrativise. No crisis appears to propel narrative into existence (the contrast with Oedipus).

Todorov's 'absence' links with James's discussion of the romance in the Preface to *The American*. James defining the 'real' anticipates Jameson (who derives it from Lacan). For James 'the real represents, to my perception the things we cannot possibly *not* know, sooner or later, in one way or another' (*AN*, 2, 31). Throughout James, people – Lambert Strether, Isabel Archer, Maggie Verver – become aware, late, of things though what they become aware of, as with Strether, is not necessarily 'the truth'. In contrast, 'the romantic stands ... for the things that, with all the facilities in the world ... we never *can* directly know; the things that can reach us only through the beautiful circuit and subterfuge of our thought and our desire' (*AN*, 2, 31–2). Thought circulates round what cannot be known directly and desire works by subterfuge, or by displacement. Otherwise, the act of willing to know constructs the situation, as maybe with the governess's pursuit of truth in *The Turn of the Screw*.

Writing romance demands liberation from a 'related' state, sacrifice of 'the "related" sides of situations' (*AN*, 2, 33). This implies loss of relativity (the situation is treated as an absolute), loss of narrative (the power to relate), loss of beginnings, since starting means breaking with a previous relation, and loss of power to link episode to episode, since 'relations stop nowhere' and the 'artist' must draw 'by a geometry of his own, the circle within which they shall happily *appear* to do so' (*AN*, 1, 5). Here, James gives 'the artist', accorded the reified status of possessing single identity and singleness of mind (like Oedipus), the task of delimiting the circle and so controlling it, but in John Marcher he shows the impossibility of this. Marcher cannot close his circle, because he does not possess an identity known even to himself. Romance, which needs not define the circle, de-legitimates beginnings: the opening has cut the rope that links the balloon of experience to the earth. Like *The Beast in the Jungle*, it is based on severance. Beginning with an *absent* cause, it affirms that there can be no beginning. The impossibility exists in the serial nature of *The Turn of the Screw*, where narrative is only enabled by taking place within the context of a house-party, where tale follows tale but with no origin, and the governess's attempt to nail 'the author of our woe' is foiled. *The Sacred Fount*, which shows an attempt to generate narrative, is set at a house-party. *The Beast in the Jungle* opens with a house-party, where John Marcher and May Bartram re-coincide, but its premise is a void. In these narratives, the realist/romance distinction disappears. The realist text only begins by becoming romance, or allegory, i.e., other-speaking – by effacing its relations to the real, severing its relationship to causes, making these absent. Jameson would agree since texts for him must be allegories of the real, but here the real, as what is at the beginning, as the primal scene, has been put out of sight, replaced within the symbolic order by the image of the beast, and at the end, in an 'hallucination', it is the beast that leaps, so whatever he sees is still kept within the symbolic, not quite the outbreak of the real through the holes of the symbolic order.

In Jameson, the absent cause is still present, to be deduced from a symptomatic reading of the text. In historicising terms, this allows the reader to deduce a contemporary crisis for James in his perception of English life, perhaps seeing it as the void, and attended by several traps in ways of writing about masculinity in the 1890s, which we assume he faced, but such a reading cannot be commanding without it becoming a will to truth, a will to interpret. We cannot 'directly know' – and the point holds with James's autobiographical writings, as well as with the texts which Edel, Sedgwick and Kaplan opt to read autobiographically. In Todorov the absent cause is indecipherable.

But there is a history in the title, which gives another text, another narrative, extraneous to a tale originally called *John Marcher*. Toni Morrison, discussing white American literature and its suppressed subtext – the presence of the Afro-American – says 'Never are we invited to a reading of *The Beast in the Jungle* in which that figuration is followed to what seems to me its logical conclusion.'[14] For her, the title means that the text's unconscious is explorable through the discourse of race, as though the figure of 'the beast in the jungle' evokes the non-European (Marcher at the end travels in Asia, specifically in India) or implies the black American, with the potential to appal the American white. The image of the 'beast in the jungle' as the aestheticised rendering of a threat from black culture would create paranoia in any imperial consciousness. Morrison points to a different form of 'otherness' which threatens the stability of the text, and another politics from Sedgwick's.

The text makes itself an allegory of the impossibility of giving a coherent narration, because it comprises a closed circle between Marcher and May Bartram. Marcher's solution thinks he missed a relationship with her, which keeps the circle closed, but the 'beast' is an other. The past has not been available to Marcher, who fears the future and what that will say about a buried history, how it will reveal what has been buried outside consciousness (the issue relates back to Valerio's absent-mindedness, before the statue of Juno is uncovered, in *The Last of the Valerii*).

Taking the strongest reading of the title, *The Beast in the Jungle*, and recalling its American authorship, it becomes not quite an English text (though it would be hard to see Marcher as American). It might be compared with W. E. B. Du Bois writing in the same year of its publication, 1903, at the opening of a new century, that 'the problem of the Twentieth Century is the problem of the color-line'[15] – a line both visible and invisible. Marcher, living at the centre of the British Empire, never has to face that 'problem' as English life, in James's time, lacked that shadow, and the modernism it inflected. James, however, in part, faced it in visiting America in 1904. Whereas Amerigo, in *The Golden Bowl*, undergoes a crisis with white America, the last text I discuss, *The Jolly Corner*, another ghost-narrative, is more ambiguous about what is to be unfolded within the American uncanny. Going to America searches out the 'beast'.

9

What Does the American Want? *The Golden Bowl*

The plot of *The Golden Bowl* is spare. As James recognises, referring in the Preface to its 'more or less bleeding participants' (*AN*, 18, 328), it is not easy to find a reading for it which does not imply a sense of loss running right through despite the visible signs of material wealth. One of its minor characters, the New Yorker Fanny Assingham, who married an Englishman, Bob Assingham, years ago – around the time of *An International Episode*[1] – refers to 'the beautiful symmetry of my plan'. That symmetry and that plan, however, are as nothing to James's set-up. The tightness of design would indeed make a Lambert Strether say: 'It's a plot.'

Two Americans – Adam Verver, the millionaire, and his daughter Maggie – have acquired an impoverished Italian Prince, Amerigo, whom Maggie is to marry, a marriage engineered by Mrs Assingham as part of her plan. Maggie's schoolgirl friend, Charlotte Stant, American but brought up in Florence, has recently broken off a relationship with Amerigo, on account of their mutual poverty, and only Mrs Assingham knew about it. Amerigo re-meets Charlotte Stant, who is back in London from America and is husband-seeking because of her impoverishment, at the house of Mrs Assingham in Cadogan Place. After Maggie and Amerigo marry, and two years later, with the 'Principino' born, Maggie suggests to her widowed father that he should marry Charlotte, which he does. Father and daughter are much together at Eaton Square, and Amerigo and

Charlotte resume their relationship and soon afterwards, following a weekend house-party at Matcham, commit adultery in Gloucester.

In the second half of the novel, Maggie intuits the situation. Her procedure is not to publicise it, which would end two marriages, but to challenge her husband, to get him to agree to confide no longer in Charlotte, to tell nothing to her father and get Charlotte to believe that she needs to return to America and to 'American City' with Verver, as Maggie is in danger of breaking up her marriage by coming between her and Mr Verver. Maggie and her father separate, Charlotte loses the Prince and returns to America, and the novel ends with reunion between the Prince and Maggie, on Maggie's terms. Virtually no-one else appears in the novel apart from the four characters (the two couples), the Assinghams, and the antique-dealer, who sells Maggie the golden bowl.

The symmetry involves two husband and wife sets, who are also father and son-in-law; father and daughter; step-mother and daughter; step-mother and son-in-law. Fanny Assingham has a large role to play in bringing about both the marriage and the re-meeting of Charlotte and the Prince. Since this is a novel with an 'international' theme, the symmetry also follows this pattern: Maggie, an American, marries a European, and her father marries a quasi-European American (Charlotte Stant). Father and daughter, two Americans, are in a close relationship, which has frequently been read as quasi-incestuous. The relationship of the Prince to Charlotte, adulterous and a case of virtual incest, since she is his step-mother-in-law, is between the European and the American quasi-European. The only true marriages seem to be American to European (Maggie to the Prince, and also Fanny to Bob Assingham), only these being, as it were, nationally exogamous. Everything else, the quasi-incestuous father–daughter relationship and the adulterous relationship, is endogamous, including the less than ideal marriage of Verver and Charlotte. The situation makes Maggie as pure American better than Charlotte as mother, and it highlights her as the saver of marriages. Adultery is impurity (adulterating), which in this case is doubly incestuous (because it is son with step-mother-in-law; European with quasi-European). Only exogamous marriage is pure. Yet even this symmetry is complicated, since Amerigo's 'was the name, four hundred years ago, or whenever, of the pushing man who followed, across the sea, in the wake of Columbus, and succeeded, where Columbus had failed, in becoming godfather, or name-father, to the new Continent' (1, 4, 59). Amerigo's name has associations of mythic origins, of patriarchal, naming powers, of primal violence. It associates Machiavellianism with colonisation, makes Italy part of the prehistory of America, and is said to be the reason why Maggie was attracted to Amerigo. The marriage is not truly endogamous, but rather an appropriation of the mythical origin by the later American, and, while it evokes the reversibility of conquest, it suggests that the marriage is in pursuit of creating a purer America.

Further, discussing the novel's symmetry in relation to endogamy and exogamy draws attention to its preoccupation with blood. In terms of Foucault's *History of Sexuality*, the unconscious of this novel – its subterranean fascination with incest and the incest taboo, and of purity of blood which licenses racism – would fit with those obsessions which were coming into discourse at the end of the nineteenth century.[2] Amerigo's brother has married a Jewish wife (1, 1, 14); Fanny Assingham has something Oriental, perhaps Jewish, about her (1, 2, 26); Mr Gutermann-Seuss, who sells to Mr Verver, is Jewish and his extended family (his 'tribe') is commented on (1, 12, 158); and the antique-dealer who sells the golden bowl, who denies being Italian and waives the question whether he is English, is also called, by both the Prince and Charlotte, 'the little swindling Jew' (1, 22, 264). Charlotte refers to the Prince's ineptitude in reading Bradshaw, and says it takes 'Anglo-Saxon blood' to do it, to which he replies, 'Blood? ... You've that of every race' (1, 22, 266). If Charlotte is like Fanny Assingham, of mixed blood, this contrasts with Amerigo, whose genealogy can be checked on by the Americans, and it suggests that the text has its own obsessions with whiteness, with purity, which relate back to the acute concentrations on symmetry.

The text refers to three empires – the Roman, a model for future imperialism, the British and the American, the last informal but no less real. At the beginning of the novel, Adam Verver staying at Portland Place has 'pitched a tent suggesting that of Alexander furnished with the spoils of Darius' (1, 1, 15) – as one imperialist taking over from another empire. The word 'spoils' picks up from the references to the wealth seen by the Prince in Bond Street – 'objects massive and lumpish, in silver and gold [the golden bowl is just hinted at] in the forms to which precious stones contributed or in leather, steel, brass, applied to a hundred uses and abuses, were as tumbled together, as if, in the insolence of the Empire, they had been the loot of far-off victories' (1, 1, 3). The British and the Americans work together in the despoiling of other and earlier empires. 'Loot' and 'spoils' both suggest the waste of Veblen's 'conspicuous consumption' (*The Theory of the Leisure Class*, 1899). Between 1870 and 1900, white Americans settled more land in the United States than they had done in the past 300 years combined; they defeated the Sioux Amerindians in 1890 and the Apaches in the Southwest; occupied Hawaii in 1897, Puerto Rico, Cuba and the Philippines in 1898, and increased their sphere of influence in Latin America and East Asia.[3]

Verver and Maggie represent the power of American hegemony. Adam Verver's name replays issues within the allegorical name of the Westerner Christopher Newman in *The American* (1879). Materially successful, Mrs Tristram, a fellow-American, calls him 'the great Western Barbarian, stepping forth in his innocence and might, gazing down awhile at this poor effete Old World' (3, 68). James makes Newman's masculinity complex, both an occasion for satire, and the cause of his vulnerability and a source of masochism.[4] In the same way, his name oxymoronically affirms and denies a history for America. Verver also recalls the American banker 'Daniel Tracy Touchett, a native of Rutland in the State of Vermont' who came to England with an American bank (*The Portrait of a Lady*, 5, 43) when Ralph, born around 1835, was 'a very small boy'. Junius Spencer Morgan (1813–90) arrived in London in 1854 to work for Peabody's bank; his country property, Dover House, at Roehampton, suggests a model for Gardencourt. Or perhaps Mr Touchett comes from George Peabody, creator of financial links between London and New York before the Civil War.[5] As Isabel Archer is endowed with a fortune by father and son together, so Verver buys Amerigo, appropriating him for America. Verver could also be put alongside Pierpont Morgan (1837–1913), Spencer Morgan's son, the millionaire and art-collector, epitome of the Morgan era (1890–1913) of big business and 'robber barons' – Vanderbilt, E. H. Harriman and James J. Hill (railroads), Cyrus McCormick (agricultural reapers), Rockefeller (oil), James B. Duke (tobacco), Gustavus Swift and Philip Armour (meat packing) and Carnegie (steel). Verver recalls Veblen's 'conspicious consumption' and 'conspicuous leisure', since 'rich Americans spent more money on art during the thirty years 1880 to 1910 than had ever been spent by a similar group in the world's history'.[6] Most of what they acquired was European.

While Amerigo is sexually imperial and commodity-conscious in looking at Charlotte Stant's body on her first appearance (1, 3, 36–7), as though the blood of the old imperialists remained in him, Verver never changes his imperialist attitudes, in which his daughter is collusive. Aged forty-seven, he marries Charlotte Stant, and this new marriage is sexually empty (1, 18, 225). James writes about his courtship of Charlotte: 'Nothing perhaps might affect us as queerer, had we time to look into it, than this application of the same measure of value to such different pieces of property as old Persian carpets, say, and new human acquisitions; all the more indeed that the amiable man was not without an inkling, on his own side, that he was, as a taster of life, economically constructed' (1, 11, 145). This is evasive, as 'had we time to look into it' indicates, as though the text is refusing to go below the surface. The same possible refusal appears in the last chapter, where it is said that behind the formal arrangements, 'a view more penetrating' can see a design at work which is to control people:

> [Maggie] had passed her arm into his, and the other objects in the room, the other pictures, the sofas, the chairs, the tables, the cabinets, the 'important' pieces, supreme in their way, stood out, round them, consciously, for recognition and applause. Their eyes moved together from piece to piece, taking in the whole nobleness – quite as if for him to measure the wisdom of old ideas. The two noble persons seated, in conversation, at tea, fell thus into the splendid effect and the general harmony; Mrs Verver and the Prince fairly 'placed' themselves, however unwittingly, as high expressions of the kind of human furniture required, aesthetically, by such a scene. The fusion of their presence with the decorative elements, their contribution to the triumph of selection, was complete and admirable, though, to a lingering view, a view more penetrating than the occasion really demanded, they also might have figured as concrete attestations of a rare power of purchase. There was much indeed in the tone in which Adam Verver spoke again, and who shall say where his thought stopped? '*Le compte y est.* You've got some good things.'
> Maggie met it afresh – 'Ah, don't they look well?' (2, 42, 561)

An interest in property and the aesthetic prevents awkward questions being asked about control, the commodification of people and the denial of their sexuality. Yet, to press them, Mr Verver's conquistador-like approach to art explicitly entails rejection of what the first Mrs Verver has stood for. He speculates on what would have happened had she not died. Referring to Keats's sonnet, 'On First Looking into Chapman's Homer' (1, 7, 104), he asks, 'Would she have prevented him from ever scaling his vertiginous Peak? – or would she, otherwise, have been able to accompany him to that eminence, where he might have pointed out to her, as Cortez to *his* companions, the revelation vouchsafed? No companion of Cortez had presumably been a real lady' (1, 7, 106). Leaving aside the ambiguity in the word 'real', this suggests that Verver's world has been exclusionary of women; homosocially formed; the psychic or sexual damage this implies that Maggie has felt waits to be read adequately, but the text suggests it and I shall return to it.

In this last tableau, Maggie and her father settle for a symmetry that comes from the rare power of purchase, so can it be said that the novel, with its own highly symmetrical plan, is for or against symmetry? If it goes into a series of geometric patterns, is the geometry the sign of abjection, and so of repression, as Victor Burgin argues that it is in architecture?[7] Here the point about the text's ambiguity about, if not refusal of, racial difference would be important: anti-semitism would be a classic example of the anxiety that surfaces in the text for purity. But it needs to be added that the symmetry is problematic anyway. The first part of the novel is called 'The Prince', the second, 'The Princess'. True Machiavellianism belongs to the woman. There is no symmetry between the two parts. The power-basis is in the second half, not the first.

It seems that symmetry is destroyed by its own intensity as symmetry which destabilises it, and by something else, which may or may not be different from what is in the structure of symmetry itself. Whatever it is will never be known, since the golden bowl, which appears as a destabilising agency whenever a character uses it, and not just as a commodity among the other commodities that are collected by the Ververs, is smashed. The 'something else' aligns this with a ghost novel, since when Maggie watches the four (Mr Verver, Mrs Assingham, the Prince and Mrs Verver) playing bridge at Fawns, the country house in Kent which belongs to Mr Verver, she reflects upon the knowledge they possess behind their appearance. She thinks of

> The horror of finding evil seated, all at its ease, where she had only dreamed of good; the horror of the thing hideously *behind*, behind so much trusted, so much pretended, nobleness, cleverness, tenderness. It

was the first sharp falsity she had known in her life, to touch at all, or be touched by; it had met her like some bad-faced stranger surprised in one of the thick-carpeted corridors of a house of quiet on a Sunday afternoon; and yes, yes, amazingly she had been able to look at terror and disgust only to know that she must put away from her the bitter-sweet of their freshness. (2, 36, 471)

This recalls 'the interest *behind* the interest' (James, on what obsesses Hawthorne (*LC* II, 471)), and the governess meeting the ghosts in *The Turn of the Screw*. But rather than the stranger surprising the primary character, the stranger is surprised, or, as in James's dream of the Galerie d'Apollon, or with *The Jolly Corner*, the ghost is haunted. Maggie's feeling that terror and disgust (unlike conventional, romantic, 'nobleness, cleverness, tenderness') have 'freshness' invokes another Keats sonnet, 'On Sitting Down to Read *King Lear* Once Again', where romance is replaced by 'the bitter-sweet of this Shake-spearian fruit'. The fruit of tragedy and the fruit of the tree in the garden come together in a suggestion of a fascination with disgust, which is what Maggie learns in contrast to her father: as it were, his knowledge stops short with the earlier Keats sonnet.

Such knowledge as Maggie acquires is uncanny, and the text plays with different forms of oddness within the familiar:

> Charlotte was in pain, Charlotte was in torment, but he himself [Amerigo] had given her reason enough for that; and, in respect to the rest of the whole matter of her obligation to follow her husband, that personage [Adam Verver] and she, Maggie, had so shuffled away every link between consequence and cause, that the intention remained, like some famous poetic line in a dead language, subject to varieties of interpretation. (2, 41, 550)

The uninterpretable line does not fit the narrative of cause and effect; it stands out by its oddness, and haunts by its disjunction (it is still alive or it is living on, and it is still haunting when the language is dead). Anticipating the 'stranger', the most obvious image of strangeness, however, is that of the pagoda in the centre of the garden. Maggie, at this stage of the novel, beginning the second book, devoted to her consciousness, has just intuited something about the Prince and Charlotte:

> This situation had been occupying, for months and months, the very centre of the garden of her life, but it had reared itself there like some

strange, tall tower of ivory, or perhaps rather some wonderful, beautiful but outlandish pagoda, a structure plated with hard, bright porcel-
ain, coloured and figured and adorned, at the overhanging eaves with
silver bells that tinkled, ever so charmingly, when stirred by chance
airs. She had walked round and round it – that was what she felt; she
had carried on her existence in the place left her for circulation, a space
that sometimes seemed ample and sometimes narrow; looking up, all
the while, at the fair structure that spread itself so amply and rose so
high, but never making out, as yet, where she might have entered
had she wished. She had not wished till now – such was the odd
case; and what was doubtless equally odd, besides, was that, though
her raised eyes seemed to distinguish places that must serve, from
within, and especially from aloft, as apertures and outlooks, no
door appeared to give access from her convenient garden level. The
great decorated surface had remained consistently impenetrable and
inscrutable.   (2, 25, 299–300)

The stranger met with is within the 'house of quiet', a place that itself
cannot quite be interpreted, except that it has overtones of death,
despite its thick carpets, which increase the sense of silence. The
uninterpretable line lodges within a dead language and the Oriental
pagoda – which suggests cultural if not racial difference – and which
cannot be entered, is housed within Maggie's own sphere, the garden
of her life.[8] What is strange is within herself, but not for that reason
accessible. These examples are all resistant to symmetry and declare
the breakdown of the distinction between inside and outside, just as
the crack is within the gilt of the golden bowl.

II THE OTHER HOUSE

Some of the terms in the pagoda image reappear in the Preface to *The
Portrait of a Lady*, written a few years later than *The Golden Bowl*:

The house of fiction has in short not one window but a million – a
number of possible windows not to be reckoned, rather; every one of
which has been pierced, or is still pierceable, in its vast front, by the
need of the individual vision and by the pressure of the individual will.
These apertures, of dissimilar shape and size, hang so, all together,
over the human scene that we might have expected of them a greater
sameness of report than we find. They are but windows at the best,
mere holes in a dead wall, disconnected, perched aloft; they are not
hinged doors opening straight upon life. But they have this mark of

their own that at each of them stands a figure with a pair of eyes, or at least with a field-glass, which forms, again and again, for observation, a unique instrument, insuring to the person making use of it an impression distinct from any other. He and his neighbours are watching the same show, but one seeing more where the other sees less, one seeing black where the other sees white, one seeing big where the other sees small, one seeing coarse where the other sees fine. And so on, and so on; there is fortunately no saying on what, for the particular pair of eyes, the window may *not* open; 'fortunately' by reason, precisely, of this incalculability of range. The spreading field, the human scene, is the 'choice of subject'; the pierced aperture, either broad or balconied or slit-like and low-browed, is the 'literary form'; but they are, singly or together, as nothing without the posed presence of the watcher – without, in other words, the consciousness of the artist. Tell me what the artist is, and I will tell you of what he has *been* conscious, Thereby I shall express to you at once his boundless freedom and his 'moral' reference.   (*AN*, 3, 46–7)

The pagoda and the fictional house of fiction are the same in that neither have doors.[9] At least doors are not mentioned in the 'house of fiction'. James used the formulation 'had we but time to look into it' with regard to the 'queerness' of Adam Verver; but that evasion screens another point if there are no doors to look into the things that might be examined. The people in the house force windows through 'dead wall' in order to see: Maggie in the garden can see the whole pagoda, and is dimly aware that she is being watched. The relations here suggest the governess seeing the ghost on the tower; or Maggie is like Isabel Archer, caught between four walls, in 'the house of darkness, the house of dumbness, the house of suffocation. Osmond's beautiful mind gave it neither light nor air; Osmond's beautiful mind indeed seemed to peep down from a small high window and mock at her' (*The Portrait of a Lady*, 42, 360). The window from which Osmond looks is inside the house: Isabel is immured in architecture, but there is a house within the house.

At the time of the pagoda image, Maggie feels she is being seen, and she cannot enter into the tower. Put together, the images of the pagoda and the house of fiction convey a sense of something maimed, incomplete. James's house of fiction is marked by insufficiency, as such phrases as 'at the best', 'mere holes', 'dead wall', 'disconnected' suggest; the windows are all aloft so that the people looking out – even through 'low-browed' windows – are cut off from ground level (no hope for popular culture then). The people in the house are as it were in a prison without windows; they must force access out by making windows. (There is no question of the house being looked at from the outside.) But with such partial vision permitted, it is unsurprising that the common image to be seen in James is of the significant detail being overlooked, the obvious thing, like Poe's purloined letter, not being noticed.

The Preface to *The Portrait of a Lady* gives the 'house of fiction', and this is ghosted in the novel itself by the villa where Osmond lives:

> a long, rather blank-looking structure, with the far-projecting roof.... The house had a front upon a little grassy, empty, rural piazza which occupied a part of the hill-top; and this front, pierced with a few windows in irregular relations...this antique, solid, weather-worn, yet imposing front had a somewhat incommunicative character. It was the mask, not the face of the house. It had heavy lids, but no eyes; the house, in reality looked another way – looked off behind...

The narrative describes people inside the room giving onto the piazza:

> The windows of the ground-floor, as you saw them from the piazza, were, in their noble proportions, extremely architectural; but their function seemed less to offer communication with the world than to defy the world to look in. They were massively cross-barred and placed at such a height that curiosity, even on tiptoe, expired before it reached them. In an apartment lighted by a row of three of these jealous apertures.... (*The Portrait of a Lady*, 1, 22, 195–6)

Architecture here serves as an alibi for paranoia. The writing here – as architecture does – gives things only to take them away. The house has a front, but it is not the front; it has no eyes, but it does have windows; it has windows, but no-one can see out of them, either from within or from without. There is the appearance of a face (the roof provides eye-lids) but it is like an allegorical death-mask, or the blank wall of Moby-Dick's forehead.[10] Windows imply communication, but these windows actively refuse communication, and refuse the notion that anything be represented through them.

The 'house of fiction' and Maggie's pagoda stand in some relationship to this house, and in the case of the Preface, they diminish the usefulness of windows. The elements of only partially-enabled looking that appear with the 'house of fiction' recur in the novel when Isabel Archer feels that marriage has been a form of estrangement:

She had suddenly found the infinite vista of a multiplied life to be a dark, narrow alley with a dead wall at the end. Instead of leading to the high places of happiness, from which the world would seem to lie below one, so that one could look down with a sense of exaltation and advantage, and judge and choose and pity, it led rather downward and earthward, into realms of restriction and depression...

(*The Portrait of a Lady*, 42, 356)

Maggie has resemblances to Isabel, except that she does not view herself as trapped. She thinks of herself as having the freedom to walk in a garden, though this has at its centre something she cannot possess, a dead wall, however brightly decorated, that she cannot see into though she can see it as something that vaguely menaces her. It is too literal to say that the Prince and Charlotte are inside: the point about the pagoda is that it is other, and further that it is in turn haunted by something other. If there are no doors, the question remains how the people who may be in there got there. Maggie has the feeling that she has knocked at the wall, in a way, and waited for something to happen, and 'something *had* happened; it was as if a sound, at her touch after a little, had come back to her from within; a sound suggesting that her approach had been noted' (2, 25, 300). There is a recall of the shopkeeper tapping the bowl with his key to get the finest, sweetest sound from it (1, 6, 87–8), but the detail is also Kafkaesque; the passive tense and the word 'noted' implies surveillance and bureaucracy together, possibly approving, possibly disapproving. Neither has much to do, in context, with the Prince and Charlotte, but it is ambiguous whether there is anybody inside this structure, which gives it a ghostly quality. As architecture, the 'house of fiction' is inadequate; it could be prisonous, only valuable when a strenuous consciousness looks out. The pagoda as architecture suggests the power of an alienating structure, mocking the security of the 'blooming' garden, which is also a form of comforting architecture (a *hortus conclusus*). It makes the garden poisonous, like that of Rappacini's daughter in Hawthorne's tale. Maggie in the garden is in her own prison though what tells her that is the inability to get into the tower or pagoda or mosque – she compares the structure to all these, in an ascending order of exclusion, concluding with the total barring of all women. However 'visible and admirable doubtless, from any part of the social field' – perfect as architecture – the structure may be, it remains alienating, like architecture itself. Pagoda and garden redefine the nature of the prison;

just as much as the house of fiction has oddly prisonous qualities itself.

Gabriel Pearson links the pagoda-image with the child trying to get into the garden in *Alice in Wonderland*.[11] Perhaps the pagoda implies the sexuality that Maggie is excluded from. Maggie in the garden is Maggie with her de-sexualised father (2, 25, 300), and the Prince, near the end of the first book, has got himself to the state of thinking about Maggie and her father as 'good children...and the children of good children' [the American Puritans, presumably] (1, 20, 245). The European thinks of the Americans as outside sexuality, 'know-ledge [not being] one of their needs' (1, 20, 245). The line compares with Charlotte saying that 'Maggie thinks more, on the whole, of fathers than of husbands' (1, 14, 188), for knowledge is, of course, sexual. Mrs Assingham has already said 'there are things...that no one could tell Maggie...she'd be so frightened. She'd be, in her strange little way, so hurt. She wasn't born to know evil. She must never know it' (1, 4, 58–9). Maggie is made, by this evasiveness, to sound like Hilda in *The Marble Faun*, pure nineteenth-century American womanhood. In the same way, Amerigo's pairing of Maggie and her father suggests the irony of Adam Verver's name: innocence, childlikeness. The price of all this is implied by the pagoda. Sexuality, if this is one of the meanings of the ivory tower/pagoda, is classically, and psychoanalytically, associated with the interdictions imposed by patriarchy, by the realm of the father (Maggie thinks of the 'polished old ivory of her father's inattackable surface', 5, 39, 517): hence the image of the mosque. Its unknowability, its uncertainty is the point behind the reference to the space the pagoda leaves her for 'circulation', 'a space that sometimes seemed ample, and sometimes narrow'. (Alice's changes in size are analogous, but she only enters the garden by growing small, more childlike.) The first half of the book has shown the 'fair structure' of a classically adulterous sexuality spreading itself amply and rising so high, and now at the opening of the novel's second half, Maggie feels that it has both excluded her, noted her and even marginalised her, as though – to change paradigms abruptly – the pagoda were Bentham's or Foucault's panopticon tower.

What disturbs is the sense that at the same time the pagoda, intimating a knowing sexuality, must also be – or lead to – the Jamesian house of fiction – the place that generates fiction, because it is only from there that 'consciousness' can look out. The house of

fiction is that impossible place to get into, and once in it, allows no
way out, but it suggests that the absorbed, silent, and intent and
uncommunicating watchers at each of the windows are all ghosts, all
possessed by nothing but their consciousness. Putting the 'house of
fiction' and the pagoda together suggests the imprisonment of the
subjects who are inside the house, and the imprisonment of those
who are outside, but yet the necessity to be of the house. It is always
the 'other house' in James, always the other possibility that fascinates.[12]

III JAMES AND ARCHITECTURE

The novel's opening also relates to the discovery of something other,
and so is symmetrical with the opening of the second book, with its
new awareness of the pagoda. It begins 'The Prince had always liked
his London when it had come to him' (1, 1, 3), which suggests a
confident relationship, positively sexual, between the knower and a
feminine reality, but on this occasion it is apparent that he has no
mood of confidence. He strays into Bond Street, to look at the
commodities there, not realising that he is looking at himself, since
he has also been turned into a commodity, and he moves in stops and
starts. It is as though he is looking for something that may not be
there:

> The young man's movements, however, betrayed no consistency of
> attention – not even, for that matter, when one of his arrests had
> proceeded from possibilities in faces shaded, as they passed him on
> the pavement .... (1, 1, 3)

The end of the paragraph makes clear that there will be no sexual
pursuit: 'he was too restless ... for any concentration' (1, 1, 4), and in
this mood he thinks to himself of Adam Verver and of Maggie's
conversations with him, she and her words appearing in his consciousness. In this discussion, where American imperialism is represented as romanticism and innocence, the Prince comments on his
double consciousness (to recall the term used about Lambert
Strether):

> 'There are two parts of me ... one is made up of the history, the doings,
> the marriages, the crimes, the follies, the boundless *bêtises* of other

people – especially of their infamous waste of money that might have come to me. Those things are written – literally in rows of volumes, in libraries; are as public as they're abominable. Everybody can get at them. . . . But there's another part, very much smaller doubtless, which, such as it is, represents my single self, the unknown, unimportant... personal quantity. About this you've found out nothing.' (1, 1, 7)

Amerigo's familial and national history imposes a burden of guilt, of unhappy consciousness, for 'the happiest reigns, we are taught, you know, are the reigns without history' (he has a preference for no memory, no history and no narrative), but Maggie as the American has replied to this, 'Oh, I'm not afraid of history' (1, 1, 8), which marks her attitudes as unaware of anything uncanny or queer, unaware of anything in the past that might be a nightmare or a source of hysteria. She has no sense of anything that cannot be entered, sacked and carried off as trophies for American City. For her and her father, collecting is a substitute for knowing, as it is also a means of establishing an identity.[13] She is a Miranda from *The Tempest*, looking at the Machiavellian princes, who are still planning to kill, even on the island, but she sees only 'the world, the beautiful world – or everything in it that is beautiful' (1, 1, 9). As Miranda's father, Prospero has an arsenal of tricks to control both the island and his enemies. So this Miranda is associated with 'vast modern machineries' (1, 1, 12) that her father controls. Amerigo's idea is that this modernity with its 'science' will give him 'some new history that should, so far as possible, contradict, and even if need be flatly dishonour, the old' (1, 1, 13). The European might by 1900 regard a history of their trying to colonise or influence America as 'futility': what he cannot see is that Maggie's modernity, expressed in her appropriations, which, cheerful or not, persist to the last page, and her lack of fear of history, represents a new form of imperialism characterised by the power that military technology confers, to dominate:

> This [the memory of futility] was a memory in fact simply to screen out – much as, just in front of him while he walked, the iron shutter of a shop, closing early to the stale summer day, rattled down at the turn of some crank. There was machinery again, just as the plate glass, all about him was money, was power, the power of the rich peoples. (1, 1, 14)

In this writing with its apparently casual associations, James associates repression with the machinery of modernism (a machinery associated with imperialism). The plate glass is the opposite of the pagoda, or of the golden bowl; it suggests the absence of the uncanny and the power of architecture to deliver a world entirely transparent, though 'a view more penetrating', as James puts it, would see that transparency is only to aid purchase by making the spoils more visible; transparency does not produce openness. Yet the Prince, though attracted to his future, still feels 'oppression' (1, 1, 14), has still a 'crisis' which keeps him pausing on corners and crossings (a man to double business bound), held by a 'consciousness, sharp as to its source while vague as to its end...an appeal to do something or other, before it was too late, for himself' (1, 1, 15). He is aware that he does not know the Americans, nor America:

> He remembered to have read, as a boy, a wonderful tale by Allan Poe, his prospective wife's countryman – which was a thing to show, by the way, what imagination Americans *could* have: the story of the ship-wrecked Gordon Pym, who, drifting in a small boat further toward the North Pole – or was it the South – than anyone had ever done, found at a given moment before him a thickness of white air that was like a dazzling curtain of light, concealing, as darkness conceals, yet of the colour of milk or of snow. (1, 1, 17)

The romantic imagination celebrated with Edgar Allan Poe is the antithesis of that romanticism of Verver and his daughter, expressed in Keats's 'On First Looking into Chapman's Homer'. Keats sublimates imperial conquest by suggesting that the realms of gold that Cortez sought for are found simply and are fulfilled in a pure and fine artistic consciousness; Poe, however, allows for no such sublimation. For Amerigo to read Poe is like trying to read these Americans for their desire, and becoming aware that it may be impossible to read them completely, since the narrative involves a foiled attempt to know (to attain the South Pole), and the thickness of white air – the opposite of plate glass – that the explorer faces is his equivalent of the pagoda. It is the mystery, the other, whose proximity and difference mocks attempts to produce any symmetrical design.[14]

Yet in Poe's narrative, Arthur Gordon Pym is American, and the text registers a crisis of whiteness. Pym has just escaped from the island of Tsalal, where the natives have a taboo on whiteness; this makes the American – specifically the South's – desire for a single, homogeneous, white society 'other'. As the little boat speeds south into the whiteness in the last chapter, the madness of the American aim becomes overpowering, and it is seen to be death-dealing. The text critiques everything that Adam Verver and his daughter aspire towards in their absoption of everything into their system. They see nothing but the material, but, it is hinted, this pursuit of whiteness is a form of death. Verver, with his white waistcoat, faced with 'the many-coloured human appeal', prefers 'the blessed impersonal whiteness for which his vision sometimes ached' (1, 7, 93). The phrasing echoes Poe, but also Shelley's *Adonais*; Verver wants the white radiance of eternity.

Amerigo reflects that the Americans are not likely to find out much about him, or his history, apart from what they can establish through public records and public history. He reflects that he is never to be 'tried or tested' by them so that they would never know, nor would he, 'how many pounds, shillings and pence he had to give' (1, 1, 18). No-one has ever yet found out, not what the woman wants, but what this father and daughter want. 'Lost there in the white mist was the seriousness in *them* that made them take him' (1, 1, 18). They want something; as pure white Americans they are looking out of the mist, which means that with all their money they are marked by lack. But they could not put the point that way, since they are not bothered with Amerigo's unique qualities, and when, at Fawns, Mr Verver reflects on the subtle but real shift that has occurred since Maggie married, his image shows he has no way of assessing Amerigo:

> It was as if his son-in-law's presence ... had somehow filled the scene and blocked the future – very richly and handsomely, when all was said, not at all inconveniently ... their decent little old-time union, Maggie's and his own, had resembled a good deal some pleasant public square, in the heart of an old city, into which a great Palladian church, say – something with a grand architectural front – had suddenly been dropped; so that the rest of the place, the space in front, the way round outside, to the east end, the margin of street and passage, the quantity of overarching heaven, had been temporarily compromised. Not even then, of a truth, in a manner disconcerting – given, that is, for the critical, or at least the intelligent eye, the great style of the façade and its high place in its class. ... The Palladian church was always there, but the *piazza* took care of itself. The sun stared down in his fulness, the air circulated, and the public not less; the limit stood off, the way round was easy, the east end was as fine, in its fashion, as the west, and there were also side doors for entrance, between the two – large, monumental, ornamental, in *their* style – as for all proper great churches. (1, 7, 99–100)

The pagoda image replays this later: the Italian Palladian church looks familiar, because Italy can be appropriated, but the pagoda is more of a challenge to the imperialist. Architecture is a way of imaging the male; there is perhaps no architecture that could be used in the representation of the female, and it serves as a domestication of the situation, (piazza and church are both architectural, both ways of setting up symmetry), familiarising by its regularity, and providing doors for entry, making access proper, signalled by the architectural style. As you go round the church, you know what features to expect at each of the four, symmetrical, points of the compass. This contrasts with the pagoda, for a doorless pagoda disorients, means that you can go right round the building without knowing you have fully circled it. The jauntiness of the prose follows the ease of Verver's thoughts; it would not be beyond his means to transpose a literal Palladian church to American City. But the image he has happened on is no way to know the other, or to come near to Amerigo's doubts.

IV SYMMETRY

I return to the beginning of the novel. In order to adjust to these Americans, the Prince decides to visit Mrs Assingham; the second chapter shows him in conversation with her, and the narrative turns, with a change of tense out of the pluperfect, into the realisation that Mrs Assingham has given to his 'nervous unrest' (1, 2, 24) no relief, because she is also not at ease, nervous. The opening action of the novel, its cessation of reminiscence, comes when two nervous people talk to each other, and what is on Mrs Assingham's mind, she says, 'isn't anything that properly concerns you' (1, 2, 28). The Prince asks the question, 'What do you mean by "properly"?' (1, 2, 28), and the question works right through the text, touching on Mrs Assingham's symmetry, and the sense of the transgressive together. The nervousness is caused by the return of Charlotte Stant, the point that she is just arriving, and that she is a 'handsome, clever, odd girl' (1, 2, 33 – the phrase is repeated at the beginning of the next chapter).

'Odd' – which suggests that which cannot be collected (or else which must be) – makes the difference to the symmetry of plans, and it figures what is not proper. 'Odd' was twice used in relation to the pagoda, and it characterises the behaviour of the Prince in his unrest, and Mrs Assingham's loss of ease, making the novel an encounter with the odd, like the 'queer'. The nervous impulses which bring the Prince and Charlotte back into contact with each other proclaim that both are members of that 'house' which is picturable either as the house of fiction or as the pagoda; they belong to a sexuality that excludes Maggie. Once Charlotte Stant and the Prince have re-met, the sequence follows whereby they go ostensibly to buy a present for Maggie, and see the golden bowl of which the dealer says 'I think I must have been keeping it, madam, for you' (1, 6, 86). The golden bowl haunts the situation, seeming to be ideal – yet 'it seemed indeed to warn off the prudent admirer' (1, 6, 84). It is the impossible gift, beautiful yet containing a crack, which means that it could never be given to anyone without some deception being involved, dangerous because it is 'exquisite' as the Prince tells Charlotte (since he can see for himself that it has a flaw). It is like Wilkie Collins's Moonstone, beautiful but flawed, feminine and feminising. Charlotte says that Amerigo thinks it is dangerous because he is superstitious, but he refuses that narrative; instead, he simply owns to being superstitious, and to seeing the crack as an omen (1, 6, 89). When the bowl is dashed against the floor by Fanny Assingham, it breaks not into two, as would seem dictated by the crack and the symmetry, but into the odd number three.

The golden bowl's exterior suggests the ghostly power of repression, which can be covered over, but which remains none the less. In the second book there comes a moment when Maggie has the sense that she might break out and say something in public about the adultery, which would destroy all the polish and decorum. The commentary that follows seems reminiscent of George Eliot (I am thinking of the use of 'we'):

> There reigned for her, absolutely, during these vertiginous moments, that fascination of the monstrous, that temptation of the horribly possible, which we so often trace by its breaking out suddenly, lest it should go further, in unexplained retreats and reactions. (2, 36, 468)

The choice is either breakage, which marks the prior existence of a suicidal emotion, or 'retreats and reactions' – i.e., responses of personal repression, which presumably cannot be 'traced' and because they cannot, the prior mood of 'the fascination of the monstrous' cannot be traced or tracked either (recalling Strether's 'all one's energy goes into facing it, to tracking [the uncanny]' [*The Ambassadors*, 4, 2, 118]). But the sentence is curious, and unlike George Eliot. The breaking out suddenly takes the form not of a smash-up, which would be expected, but rather of an unexplained retreat. Yet in French, the trace and the retreat would both take the form of Derrida's word *retrait*: retreat contains its own trace/tracing, just as the golden bowl when smashed exhibits that all along it has had the trace in it – the crack – that makes 'breaking out' so inevitable, not a matter of Fanny Assingham's dramatic action, but already inherent in the bowl. Tracing (marking the crack, or the cracking itself) disturbs narrative continuity by a suggestion of prolepsis. Narratively, it exists to be broken: on its first appearance, the antique dealer even tells Charlotte how to break it, like a George Eliot 'delicate vessel'. A plot where there is breakage, like the smashing of the golden bowl, has some intelligibility, but the writing also points towards another narrative – like this one – where nothing breaks, but where all is repressed, even though the crack in the bowl seems to anticipate the need for an outbreak and seems to point to the prior or ongoing fascination of the monstrous. Yet this fascination is absent: it is traced not by an action but by a retreat. But a retreat from what? Not from any action that can be discerned, but a retreat from the trace, from the crack, from that which speaks of difference. The action here is superficially the slightest, but it engages with that which is most uncanny, the originary mark of otherness or difference.

The history of the bowl is not known; it comes from a 'lost art' and a 'lost time' and was executed by 'some very fine old worker and by some beautiful old process' (1, 6, 85). It implies the history Maggie says she is not afraid of. She might have learned from *The Portrait of a Lady*, for the bowl replays the incident of Madame Merle's cracked cup that Osmond fiddles with. The cup may imply Isabel, or Pansy, or Madame Merle, all treated with contempt by Osmond because they are female, works of art which fail to be perfect. Certainly, Madame Merle, expert in the art of not being natural (not going without her clothes, as she puts it to Isabel in a famous exchange [chapter 19]), only succeeds at the end in being like the cup:

> So Madame Merle went on, with much of the brilliancy of a woman who had long been a mistress of the art of conversation. But there were phases and gradations in her speech, not one of which was lost upon Isabel's ear, though her eyes were absent from her companion's face.

> She had not proceeded far before Isabel noticed a sudden break in her voice, a lapse in her continuity, which was in itself a complete drama. (52, 458)

Madame Merle has become like her cracked cup. But the bowl is different, for it has an originary crack, the elements that make it up – the glass and the gold – belonging to the same moment of narrative, cracking and gilding going together, denying any pure origin, making it antithetical to Maggie's values, which accept no entropy, saying of the items she and her father have collected, 'we've never lost anything yet' and 'there's nothing, however tiny...that we've missed' (1, 1, 11). The spirit of the book-keeping business dealer is apparent, thinking in terms of beginnings and endings, desiring Amerigo as the source of that which will seamlessly join the past to the present. If she allowed herself to be afraid of history, she would have no such faith in the completely recallable, or the non-entropic. Maggie's desire is for ' "the golden bowl – as it *was* to have been." And Maggie dwelt musingly on this obscured figure. "The bowl with all happiness in it. The bowl without the crack" ' (2, 35, 456). But *how* the bowl was to have been is obscured, left figurative only, behind the real bowl, the only one there was, the cracked one. She wants an artwork with no doubleness in it, that gives her the appearance that the narrative of perfect symmetry (the marriage between herself and Amerigo) can be based on something ideal.

It is, indeed, a yearning for a pure origin, which the golden bowl, already cracked, deconstructs: indeed, to continue with Derrida's terms, it is the desire for a differentiated world which is not marked by *différance* – *différance* with an 'a', invisible when the word is spoken, but present in writing, in the 'trace', which means that *différance*, like a crack, a gap, is inscribed in every system of thought though forgotten by those which think that there can be a natural state of affairs, other than one which is textual, represented in writing. A bowl without a crack would be only a 'figure' – it could only exist as a representation chosen for its ideological value. The marriage Maggie aims for is kitsch, or possessive, or both. Critics have read Maggie's 'blameless egoism' (2, 32, 405) – the context of this is when she feels that she is 'using' Mrs Assingham 'to the topmost notch' – in contrasted ways. Dorothea Krook (*The Ordeal of Consciousness in Henry James*, 1962) sees her as redemptive, saving a social situation. Mark Seltzer, in *Henry James and the Art of Power* (1984), sees her as destructive, and her love a coercive policing of desire, inflicting cruelty in which her father is collusive – 'holding in one of his pocketed hands the end of a long silken halter looped round [Charlotte's] beautiful neck' (2, 38, 508) – compelling the attention of her husband and all in the name of love, itself the emotion which she does not question (2, 30, 384). Imperialism cannot afford not to be pious. At no stage is there self-criticism of herself and her father, with the suggestion that this might have contributed to the adultery. Never does she criticise her own and her father's lack of knowledge. She never asks where Amerigo's own interest lies. When she intuits the truth, her instinct is towards creating terror (2, 30, 384). Jonathan Freedman says that Maggie ends up as 'a more powerful Osmond'.[15] If this overstates, it still seems right, and fits with Osmond's imperial ambitions. Discovering that she has been betrayed, she becomes the aesthete disposing of different lives as she chooses. To function as an Osmond, observing the forms and conventions, coercive and impervious to other points of view, she has the advantage of her cultural and national imperialism, and the unknowing this grants. The process whereby an Isabel (Maggie) becomes an Osmond (Maggie again) enables the discovery of an affinity between the two partners in *The Portrait of a Lady*, despite their differences. Marriage consecrates both affinities and differences. Having been made to look at herself by the pagoda, having been made other, and seen herself as that, she partially settles for a normalising tendency – inseparable from a desire for symmetry – where she sees human relations, as Leo Bersani suggests, as James in this novel does, 'entirely in terms of their compositional appeal'[16] – as Osmond does.

The case against Maggie is persuasive, even if it does not change the minds of those who read the text in terms of her power to bring about a sublimation of the situation. She buys the golden bowl and puts it, like the purloined letter, on the chimney piece, prominent and accusing like the scarlet letter, and as though she was a patriarchal Puritan conscience. For her it 'represents' (2, 33, 421) the state between her husband and Charlotte, having 'almost miraculously' (2, 33, 422) passed on the truth to her, in a way which requires her, for to see it is proof, not to see the gaps in its evidence. Under the influence of the bowl, she too now has passed into the sphere of what it represents – a troubled art, an unhappiness based on sexuality, on something 'strange' (2, 33, 421) which the bowl 'strangely – too strangely almost to believe at this time of day' (2, 33, 417) reveals. It takes Mrs Assingham to dash the bowl to the ground, 'Whatever you meant by it – and I don't want to know *now* – has ceased to exist' (2, 33, 430). At that very moment, as though like a genie released from the bottle (Matthiessen's comparison),[17] Amerigo appears and his voice breaks in on the two women together. Some moment of reversal has happened, some possible turning of the tables, something of repression has been lifted, something could be out in the open. The text, however, turns towards an exorcism of what the bowl represents. The Prince hears Maggie out in her story of the bowl and says that 'the coincidence [of her going to the shop where Charlotte and he had been] is extraordinary – the sort of thing that happens mainly in novels and plays' (2, 34, 442). And Maggie's own development is away from what is strange and haunted; she needs 'conscious repossession' (2, 25, 305) of her intuitions; she works by enjoying 'the perpetual throb of this sense of possession' (2, 35, 449) in contrast to Charlotte, who says, 'I risk the cracks' (1, 22, 264), thereby displaying her 'odd'ness.

Maggie fixes and centres the truth, as though this were a detective novel (2, 34, 437).[18] The effect of pinning the truth on Amerigo confirms her centred position – 'something in the tone of [his comment, in reaction to her] gave it a sense, or an ambiguity, almost foolish – leaving Maggie to feel, as in a flash, how such a consequence, a foredoomed infelicity, partaking of the ridiculous even in one of the cleverest, might be the very essence of the penalty of wrong-doing' (2, 34, 439). The fixed terms ('wrongdoing') confirm the status of the fixed subject who is at the centre of the text. Whatever she knows about Amerigo, she has not lost her sense of herself. Yet the context of her feeling that foolishness is of the essence of wrongdoing itself destabilises Maggie's centring of herself in judgement. She has become sure, she says to the Prince, 'of your having, and of your having for a long time had, *two* relations with Charlotte'. He is puzzled by 'two', so she answers, after the parenthesis already quoted, 'Oh, you may have had fifty – had the same relation with her fifty times! It's the number of *kinds* of relation with her that I speak – a number that doesn't matter, really, so long as there wasn't only one kind, as father and I supposed. One kind... was there before us; we took that fully for granted, as you saw, and accepted it. We never thought of there being another, kept out of our sight...'.

Maggie, who says 'we', meaning her father and herself, not her husband and herself, shows that she is in more than two kinds of relationships herself, and as 'relations stop no-where', Maggie's number of the kinds of possible relationships between Charlotte and the Prince – two – could easily be doubled: they are Italians, former friends, adventurers, former lovers, connected by the golden bowl, mother and son by marriage, and lovers. Maggie thinks in twos, which implies symmetry and the absence of the odd, but even the word 'two' produces an 'ambiguity' – which suggests that relationships can only be kept going by repetition. Symmetry and relationships are not static. Maggie distinguishes number of relationships from kind, but no two relationships in a number sequence are the same, any more than any two kinds are necessarily different. It is an example of the uncanny, the odd, appearing as the comic in her speech and in his reaction, which she tries to fix. She drives out the uncanny by instituting herself instead of the pagoda at the centre.

V THE FOLD

At the end, in the last paragraph, Amerigo embraces her, 'his whole act enclosing her' – centring her, and giving her the sense of being ringed, held in by something complete. He completes 'the vicious circle' that Maggie started (1, 24, 289). James writes, 'He tried, too clearly, to please her – to meet her in her own way; but with the result only that, close to her, her face kept before him, his hands holding her shoulders, his whole act enclosing her, he presently echoed: "'See'? I see nothing but *you*." And the truth of it had, with this force, after a moment, so strangely lighted his eyes that as for pity and dread of them she buried her own in his breast (2, 42, 567). 'I see only you' makes Amerigo the subservient observer.[19] Yet she cannot look at his eyes. Perhaps the light in them suggests a horror at the implications of seeing nothing but her. 'Strangely' suggests that she has not banished the unknown in him, but that something else shows itself in a sudden breaking out in the eyes. 'Pity and dread' imply that Aristotelian tragedy must follow (this gives the ending a likeness to the last lines of *The Bostonians* – with different gender-relations), or else that these qualities are what she as the spectator must read in his submission, his renunciation, if she could look. She has what she wants in having him, but there is so much else there that she sinks her head on him in an act of repression, like the governess clutching Miles.

The portrait of an imperialist, Verver, is succeeded by the portrait of the daughter, made like one of Cortez's companions. From the stance of not knowing, she gathers sexual knowledge, and 'knowledge, knowledge, was a fascination as well as a fear' (2, 32, 402). In making knowledge a fascination – like the 'fascination of the monstrous' – James de-stabilises this female subject who wants to centre herself and to control other destinies. She wishes to attack Charlotte, and she does so by ensuring, to her mind at least, that Charlotte tacitly knows how she is being treated, and she also wishes to destroy herself:

> Our young woman was to have passed, in all her adventures, no stranger moment, for she not only saw her companion [Charlotte] fairly agree to take her then for the poor little person she was finding it so easily to appear, but fell, in a secret, responsive ecstasy, to wondering if there were not some supreme abjection with which she might be inspired. Vague, but increasingly brighter, this possibility glimmered on her. It at last hung there adequately plain to Charlotte that she had presented herself once more to (as they say) grovel... (2, 39, 527–8)

She desires her own annihilation through a martyrdom which will be a source of ecstasy, as though she were a Teresa of Avila, only the figure wielding the spear to pierce her will be Charlotte Stant. The echoes of the gender-politics of *The Bostonians* is suggestive; she will not be rendered abject by a man, but by a woman. Her masochistic grovelling is performance, but perhaps there is nothing but performance anyway, and its symbiosis with sadism, and lack of self-criticism implies that the imperialist's attitude to her body is one of rejection, where it takes the form of despising her own mirror-image, as a 'poor little person'. The person who finds ecstasy in abjection touches on Julia Kristeva's analysis: it suggests that the subject has no borders, and revolts from them and establishes them at the same time. The Prince at the end encloses her, but that is precisely the source of a further self-hatred and self-repression.

The loss of borders, or of the circle, the sense of being thoroughly penetrated, or, what is the same thing, thoroughly haunted, appears in James's most baroque image, of the company at Fawns together. The situation, of Maggie acting the part of the unknowing wife, and

Charlotte that of the wife who must re-possess her husband, and Amerigo not speaking to Charlotte, and Adam Verver remaining apparently innocent and unknowing, is recorded through the consciousness of Maggie, thinking how the unbearable social situation is saved by the frequent arrival of visitors:

> Beautiful and wonderful for her, even, at times, was the effect of these interventions – their effect above all in bringing home to each the possible heroism of perfunctory things. They learned fairly to live in the perfunctory; they remained in it as many hours of the day as might be; it took on finally the likeness of some spacious central chamber in a haunted house, a great overarched and overglazed rotunda, where gaiety might reign, but the doors of which opened into sinister circular passages. Here they turned up for each other, as they said, with the blank faces that denied any uneasiness felt in the approach; here they closed numerous doors carefully behind them – all save the door that connected the place, as by a straight tented corridor, with the outer world, and, encouraging thus the irruptions of society, imitated the aperture through which the bedizened performers of the circus are poured into the ring. (2, 38, 509)

The overglazed rotunda invokes the golden bowl, with the fundamental flaw or crack being masked by the gilt of art, and it stands in complex relationship to the Palladian church around which, in Verver's thinking, the air 'circulated', and the pagoda, which allows space for 'circulation'. In the central chamber, haunting is disavowed, and what takes place in the circular passages – the space for 'circulation' – is repressed from knowledge because the doors are shut, adding to and doubling the 'blank faces' of the people entering. (The phrase recalls the 'dead wall' of the 'house of fiction', and Osmond's villa, the 'mask, not the face of a house'.) The haunted house becomes like the pagoda. Coming into this chamber is like entry into a room within rooms, but it is no place for sociality. Within this haunted house, the corridors are offstage, and the circular centre room is the place for agreed action, which is no action (only 'retreats and reactions'). As ever, a James novel turns upon action out of sight, unknown.

Architecture delimits a space exclusionary of the uncanny, but the architectural round chamber and square church, doubling each other, create other spaces which Gilles Deleuze, reading Baroque architecture, defines through the 'fold', pleats of matter which sever 'the façade from the inside...the interior from the exterior'.[20] The fold disjoins spaces and introduces the uncanny, so that symmetry is not all there is. Poe's thickness of white air, an indeterminate space, like Deleuze's fold, between the inside and the outside, also implies the heterotopic, which the actors coming into the central chamber avoid.

The central space engenders formality and repression. Entry into it is not entry upon action, nor is it arriving at a centre, since centre and action are always deferred. The outsiders pour in like circus performers. They intrude, yet are unreal because they are the performers. The ring seems complete, but is not because its sides are pierced by doors. They have come past folds, shadowy, haunted, to find no wholeness in the circle, only cracks, preventing closure or resolution, however much these are desired for symmetry.

10

The Jolly Corner: A Tale of New York

I

The Jolly Corner[1] starts with Spencer Brydon speaking after a few weeks' return to New York, and it defines him as self-absorbed and 'obsessive':

> 'Everyone asks me what I "think" of everything,' said Spencer Brydon, 'and I make answer as I can – begging or dodging the question, putting them off with any nonsense. It wouldn't matter to them really,' he went on, 'for, even were it possible to meet in that stand-and-deliver way a demand on so big a subject, my "thoughts" would still be almost altogether about something that concerns only myself.' (1, 313)

The rest of the paragraph and the next pages fill in details about this 56-year-old returnee to New York. He is like Mr Longdon in *The Awkward Age*, returning to the metropolis, and Strether, who has made the opposite journey to his, and like James, who had returned to New York in 1904, four years earlier, aged 61. The occasion seems to be his birthday. The paragraph which brings the reader back to the remark, and to the date of the opening, appears at 'It was a few days after this' (1, 320). 'This' refers to an incident beginning with the paragraph that starts 'She had come with him one day' (1, 316), and it refers to Brydon and a friend from his youth in New York, Miss Staverton (he left New York aged 23), going to see two houses he owns in New York, one which is being developed, the other, the house on the 'jolly corner', his childhood dwelling. By the time the reader returns to the point of the beginning, the narrative is ready to advance from the standpoint of his birthday. In the same way, *The Golden Bowl* spends an opening chapter and a half on past reminiscence before settling to the present moment, which begins with the news of the arrival of Charlotte Stant. The reminiscence focuses on the Prince's non-specific sense of unease, which both launches the drama by making something happen, and does so further by making him receptive to the disaster that is about to strike.

Brydon's first speech denies any ability to say what he thinks about anything because he says his thoughts are only about something that concerns himself. That this is a specific point, not just a way of saying that thoughts are always private, is unconfirmed until the later paragraph which gives the continuance of his utterance, now presented in reported speech – 'he was wholly taken up with one subject of thought. It was mere vain egoism, and it was moreover, if she liked, a morbid obsession.' If the subject is birthdays, then, assuming that the imaginary date for this story is around 1905, James envisages a hero born in about 1850 and a house built in about 1836, around the time that Dr Sloper moves into his house on Washington Square. Brydon refers to the house being seventy years old, and to his grandfather being the first person to die in it (1, 318).) He lived till the age of 23 in this house, situated on the eastward corner of a street with a 'conservative Avenue' – presumably Fifth Avenue – to its east. The westward end of this street is said to be 'disfigured' – a resonant word for the tale. This house has not been altered: he was born in it (hence the significance of the birthday) and his family lived there before him. The other house is already being renovated and both have proved hugely profitable in rents.

James, born at No. 21 Washington Place, had lived in this area as a child; firstly between 1847 and 1848 at 11 Fifth Avenue, and then, till 1855, near Union Square, at 58 West Fourteenth Street, near Sixth Avenue. He left for his second big European tour in 1872 and made a final test of New York for living at the beginning of 1875 (111 East Twenty-fifth Street, between Lexington and Fourth Avenue, and near Madison Square), before moving to Paris. He returned to America in 1882–3, but then stayed away until 1904–5. Critics have taken *The Jolly Corner* as autobiographical reflection[2] and like much of the work of the 'major phase' it is, if it is not assumed that the autobiographical subject is determinate. Brydon's opening words give the clue. To read something as autobiography assumes that we know what the writer's concerns should be, what he or she should be interested in. Spencer Brydon is not interested in 'everything' – which means the new and modern New York. His interests are oblique to that, because the subject is not predictable, because not known, even to itself.

New York was now modern. The first houses to use electric lighting had done so in 1883; now New York city, with a reputed 17,000 street lights, far more than any European equivalent, was wholly lit by 'the white electric lustre which it would have taken curtains to keep out' (2, 325). Besides being electrified and illuminated, the busiest port in the world, the centre for finance capital, a manufacturing centre (producing half of America's ready-to-wear clothes), and the most cosmopolitan city in America, on account of the immigration, New York had amalgamated its five boroughs in 1898 and become the world's most populous city after London, with 3,437,000 inhabitants. The 'El' of *The Bostonians* had opened in 1867, but by 1890, the city had 94 miles of elevated railways, 265 miles of horse railways and 137 miles of horse omnibus lines, and the narrator refers to Miss Staverton 'making use of the street-cars when need be, the terrible things that people scrambled for as the panic-stricken at sea scramble for the boats' (1, 315). New York's subway began operations on 27 October 1904, when James was in America. Steel-frame construction allowed for skyscrapers; by 1895, there was the concept of New York having a distinctive, vertical 'skyline'. The regularisings of its streets that had begun at the beginning of the nineteenth century makes Brydon refer to 'the dreadfully multiplied numberings which seemed...to reduce the whole place to some vast ledger-page, overgrown, fantastic, of ruled and criss-crossed lines and figures' (1, 315), but as the Baroque details in this description imply, it still has pockets which make up different forms of space. Such a one is Miss Staverton's existence in Irving Place, a name with its own ghost, Washington Irving. Miss Staverton dusts her relics in her house, as a relic herself, in a fold of the city, while it changes around her. The other relic is the house on the jolly corner.[3]

Remembering Deleuze on the fold, and Derrida, who says that 'everything begins, then, with citation, in the creases (*faux plis*) of a certain veil',[4] it is suggestive to start with the initial quotation from Brydon, reflecting that a corner between two walls is a fold (a *pli*), which suggests doubleness, so that everything begins not with the singular word, but in repeating or doubling something that has already gone before. As a title, *The Jolly Corner* suggests language as the fold, involving creases, alternative spaces or pockets, so that while there is the attempt to familiarise by the use of the ultimate term in bourgeois (Dickensian) cheerfulness, 'jolly', the question is what will come out of this particular fold. Spencer Brydon shows in the quotation his own doubleness – he does not know what he thinks; his thoughts are about himself, and that self turns out to be plural. At the same time, the question people ask him is what he thinks about modern New York, or 'everything'. He cannot answer the question about himself, for while unable to come to terms with the 'bignesses' of New York (1, 313) – which must mean, amongst other things, its skyscrapers, he is helping another bigness to rise from the ruins of an earlier house. He is a figure of contradiction. George Santayana, as a critic of America's 'genteel tradition', defines that term by referring to contradictions visible in American architecture:

> The truth is that the one-half of the American mind, that not occupied intensely in practical affairs, has remained, I will not say high-and-dry, but slightly becalmed; it has floated gently in the backwater, while, alongside, in invention and industry and social organization the other half of the mind was leaping down a sort of Niagara Rapids. The division may be found symbolized in American architecture: a neat reproduction of the colonial mansion – with some modern comforts introduced surreptitiously – stands beside the sky-scraper. The American Will inhabits the sky-scraper; the American Intellect inhabits the colonial mansion. The one is the sphere of the American man; the other, at least predominantly, of the American woman. The one is all aggressive enterprise; the other is all genteel tradition.[5]

With only a few differences, this could be a description of the splits in *The Jolly Corner* between the man and the woman, and in the man himself.

The difficulties in reading the late James, the James of the 'major phase', are real, because it attempts to turn language into a series of folds or corners, or to realise its existence as such, and to locate a doubleness or uncanniness inside narrative prose; to find the presence of something haunting, something different, that can only be tracked through pushing grammar to its limits, and turning it round on itself. Brydon brackets off his whole life in Europe; his actual existence there he regards as nothing in comparison with the notion that he might have been in America and have been changed the way that

America has been changed. The idea is impossible in realist terms as he has not been in New York. The alternative life grasps James: supposing Strether had read the books he brought back with him from Paris? Another form of 'double consciousness' opens up with the possibility that since these books *have* existed in his 'subconsciousness' (*The Ambassadors*, 2, 2, 62), he has been plural, not a single identity. The children in *The Turn of the Screw*, by being jointly haunted, pluralised identity, made one identity to be split between two, or identity to be a repression of plurality. When the beast springs in *The Ambassadors*, it is when two people, ghostly revenants, arrive in one boat. In realist terms, there is always something else in James that cannot be seen. As the narrator in *The Sacred Fount* says to Ford Obert, 'I feel ... altogether destitute of a material clue. If I had a material clue I should feel ashamed: the fact would be deterrent. I start, for my part, at any rate, quite in the dark – or in a darkness lighted, at best, by what you have called the torch of analogy' (*The Sacred Fount*, 4, 40). Analogy – in that novel, the dominant analogy is that of the vampire, the person who feeds on another – becomes the way to understand reality, doubling reality, creating folds where before there was flatness. Analogy is the art of figuring, and the word 'figure' appears in the text, suggesting also the ghost; analogy can only be figurative, textual, and the structure of the prose, refusing the plainness of a narration which will give surface details, creates analogies which double the apparent flatness of the story, and so mimes Spencer Brydon's own actions. Over the first few pages, in the interval between the first description of his conversation on his birthday, and the second description, its continuation, there is a process whereby a ghost is tracked across the prose, or a fold opens up which may conceal another presence, a foreign body. Similarly, *The Birthplace* (1903) focuses on Morris Gedge's obsession with the dead writer who lived at the 'birthplace' of the title that he and his wife are caretakers of for the public, and his speeches to tourists seem to attempt to create the writer once again in the birthplace. Analogously, the obsession here is to find a reality, a 'presence', haunting but real, in the house on the jolly corner in New York.

The prose generates its own ghosts, moves to create something, through such details as the repeated 'surprise' of the first paragraph, or the phrase 'uncanny phenomena' in the second (meaning the ugly things he had known in his youth), through the word 'monstrous', repeated on several occasions, and then, in describing Alice Staverton, the word 'presences':

> They had communities of knowledge, 'their' knowledge (this discriminating possessive was always on her lips) of presences of the other age [New York thirty years back], presences all overlaid, in his case, by the experience of a man and the freedom of a wanderer, overlaid by pleasure, by infidelity, by passages of life that were strange and dim to her, just by 'Europe' in short, but still unobscured, still exposed and cherished, under that pure visitation of the spirit from which she had never been diverted. (1, 316)

The next paragraph, where he takes Miss Staverton to see the house which is being developed, concludes with a reference to her words which act like 'a small silver ring' (a bell) sounding over 'the queerest and deepest of his own lately most disguised and muffled vibrations' (1, 316), and then the sense of something other but not definable that is also present appears in the following paragraph:

> It had begun to be present to him after the first fortnight, it had broken out with the oddest abruptness, this particular wanton wonderment: it met him there – and this was the image under which he judged the matter, or at least, not a little, thrilled and flushed with it – very much as he might have been met by some strange figure, some unexpected occupant, at a turn of one of the dim passages of an empty house.
>
> (1, 316)

It is not yet *his* empty house that is under comparison, but the image – the strange figure, both human and a rhetorical figure – that expresses the uncanniness which appears in James's prose is like Maggie Verver's sense of meeting a stranger in a 'house of quiet', and it also recalls Peter Quint, especially as the passage here continues 'the *quaint* analogy quite hauntingly remained with him' (my emphasis). The sense of a ghost possibly hovering in the text has been established, and it persists through the accounts of the past of the house. Inside it, visiting it after seeing the house under development, there is 'nothing but Mrs Muldoon's broomstick, in a corner, to tempt the burglar' (1, 317) – Mrs Muldoon being the woman who comes in to clean; the corner – the familiar corner, which unconsciously now has associations of witches – is that in which he puts his stick when he comes to haunt the house himself (2, 324). But Mrs Muldoon will not come after dark in the 'ayvil hours' (1, 317).

The discussion ensuing between Miss Staverton and Brydon focuses on his desire not to change this house in any way. As he has two houses, his life is split between a nostalgic desire and a modernising one, epitomised in his ability to handle builders' questions on the other site. He speaks about values other than the financial, and Miss Staverton replies by referring to the unconscious duplicity of his answer, the answer which shows his belief as empty, like the house: 'In short you're to make so good a thing of your skyscraper that, living in luxury on *those* ill-gotten gains, you can afford for a while to be sentimental here' (1, 318). He has given himself away as a moderniser and developer. Unlike Miss Staverton's home, this house is unfurnished: it is only an altar to the dead, a mausoleum; he is not living on it, which makes his desire to hold onto it at all costs sentimental. Yet the deconstruction she has performed of his attachment to the house does not settle everything. In a city where, he says, 'there are no reasons but of dollars', not even 'the ghost of one' (1, 319), the question is why he should wish to keep it on. It is evident, by the end, that he will not; it too will succumb to the developers.

The man who lets dollars talk is, however, the man whose sense of himself is as an obsessive. The text returns to its beginning, and to his self-critique. The ghost has been produced through the folds of the prose, and that multiplication of analogies produces the question he asks openly on his birthday – what would he have been if he had stayed on in New York, and not gone to Europe, an Oedipus acting in the teeth of 'his father's curse'? (1, 320). If he had stayed in the house, what would he have become? He thinks he would have become 'huge and offensive' (this implies a negative view of the New York skyscraper) as a man with power, a billionaire (1, 321). His view is that of the alienated Europeanised figure, but Miss Staverton replies she would have liked him.

II BUILDING AMERICA

Billionaires and skyscrapers go together: billionaires required them and their builders became billionaires. Bryson on leaving New York would not have known any skyscrapers, even though one of the first requirements for them, the elevator, had been pioneered on Broadway before the war, in 1857, by Elijah Otis. Alice Staverton suggests that had he stayed he might have anticipated the inventor of the skyscraper, have started 'some new variety of awful architectural hare and run till it burrowed in a gold-mine' (1, 316). By 1875, when James left, New York had 10-storey office buildings, but the name 'skyscraper', creating them as the markers of a new, different New York, came in the late 1880s, certainly by 1891.[6] When he revisited New York, skyscrapers were over 20 storeys high. Daniel Hudson Burnham's Flatiron building (1901–3) bounded by Broadway, Fifth Avenue and East 23rd Street, had 21 storeys; the Times Building on Broadway and 42nd Street, finished in 1905, had 25. New York also had millionaires, the title being first given to Pierre Lorillard, a snuff manufacturer, when he died in 1843. In 1848, John Jacob Astor left $20 million, and the scale of riches increased exponentially, when Commodore Cornelius Vanderbilt, in 1877, left $105 million. His son, William Henry, doubled this amount before dying in 1888. The skyscraper sets up the model of money and the power of money; it celebrates 'bignesses' – different kinds of them.

This other person, this pure American, who would have been at home in this New York, an American unadulterated with anything European, this *alter ego* (1, 321) unknown like an important letter which has been burned, unopened (1, 320), Brydon wants to know, and wants to create. James talks about Americans having a 'superstitious overvaluation of Europe', and the American who, by becoming European, has denied his past, as Oedipus does, must find out what it would have meant to have remained in America. To evaluate America, in contrast to being in Europe with its dependence on tradition and history, is not a matter of looking at a static and timeless object and weighing that up. Alice Staverton can imagine him, for she has stayed in New York, and she speaks about the dreams she has had of the 'other' Brydon. He asks, from the standpoint of a Europeanised American asking about an American, 'what's the wretch like?' (1, 322). The word suggests his alienation, and suggests that his subjectivity depends on being able to split off the American self – which gives orders to the developers – from his European self. He cannot see that the European self is the one that gives the orders: that there is no difference, or if there is a difference, it depends on finding an American ghost (in other words, an American past, a history, like the one desired in the Preface to *The Aspern Papers*).

In the second part Brydon gives way to his 'obsession' (1, 322) and goes to the house in 'the lampless hour', avoiding New York's electrification. He concentrates his prowling towards the back of the house, the part not illuminated by street-lights, and creeps into nooks and corners, trying to hunt down this other self, as in the dream in the Galerie d'Apollon, and unlike John Marcher, seeing himself as dominant – the hunter, not the hunted, 'turning on the uncanny' (*The Ambassadors*, 4, 2, 118). In so acting, like the representation of James in his nightmare turning on the figure on the other side of the door, there is the problem of how to read these texts. Is turning on the uncanny the action of *ressentiment*, of envy, a display made by Nietzsche's reactive type? Or is it a Nietzschean drive towards spontaneity? Was it such a will to spontaneity that activated James even on his deathbed when he dictated letters as though he were Napoleon, the man who really *did* possess the Louvre and the Galerie d'Apollon – and so linked art to empire? Nietzsche, it is important to realise, saw Napoleon as a non-reactive, spontaneous, natural figure.[7]

The house is uncanny; the modern America Brydon is helping to bring into being on the site of the other house will not be a place for ghosts, for it will yield no folds or doublenesses. The point comes out near the end of the second part when towards the dawn he looks out of a high window – like the house of fiction, which is what the house on the jolly corner is – and feels – like the consciousnesses at the windows – 'the failure of response of the outer world':

> It seemed to him he had waited an age for some stir of the great grim hush; the life of the town was itself under a spell – so unnaturally, up and down the whole prospect and known and rather ugly objects, the blankness and the silence lasted. Had they ever, he asked himself, the hard-faced houses, which had begun to look livid in the dim dawn, had they ever spoken so little to any need of his spirit? Great builded voids, great crowded stillnesses put on, often in the heart of cities, for the small hours, a sort of sinister mask, and it was of this large collective negation that Brydon presently became conscious... (2, 332)

The ugliness of the city he has known from his youth. These buildings negate Brydon's existence by their blankness. 'Hard-faced' evokes the dollar motive in New York as well as the unyieldingness of the houses, and 'mask' recalls Osmond's villa in Florence. Describing buildings as having faces (façades) makes architecture prosopopoeia, suggesting the need that Brydon has to see the face of his opponent, the self he is haunting, the desire to give a face to the city. He is the reverse of the haunted Count Valerio of *The Last of the Valerii*. James discusses the city with no face when commenting in *The American Scene* on the absence of mural tablets in New York:

> Where, in fact, is the point of inserting a mural tablet, at any legible height, in a building certain to be destroyed to make room for a skyscraper? And from where, on the other hand, in a façade of fifty floors, does one 'see' the pious plate recording the honour attached to one of the apartments look down on a responsive people? We have but to ask the question to recognise our necessary failure to answer it as a supremely characteristic local note – a note in the light of which the great city is projected into its future as, practically, a huge, continuous, fifty-floored conspiracy against the very idea of the ancient graces, those that strike us as having flourished just in proportion as the parts of life and the signs of character have *not* been lumped together, not been indistinguishably sunk in the common fund of mere economic convenience. (*The American Scene*, 2, 71)

The lack of relation between modern urbanism and humanism is the point. Recalling Brydon's inability to come to terms with 'bignesses' it may be said that James is facing what the architectural theorist and architect Rem Koolhaas in the 1990s calls 'bigness' – the phenomenon of modern urbanism that displaces any form of humanism, in so far as architecture is premised on humanist principles.[8] Modernist architecture works on analogies between the inside and outside of buildings, ensuring that these have a significant relationship, so that it feeds into the humanism of thinking of a building as 'honest', not lying, not telling false stories. The bigness of skyscrapers means the disappearance of the relationship which architecture tries to establish between the form and the function ('form follows function' had been Louis Sullivan's phrase in 1896, in his essay 'The Tall Building Artistically Considered').[9] For the building can no longer have one function.

The American Scene is fascinated by the number of windows in skyscrapers (windows as a marker of modernity in producing, or framing, the subject, bringing it into view). The presence of windows which allow for vision from without implies the absence of ghosts (the house on the jolly corner has shutters):

> Window upon window, at any cost, is a condition never to be reconciled with any grace of building, and the logic of the matter here happens to put on a particularly fatal front. If quiet interspaces, always

half the architectural battle, exist no more in such a structural scheme than quiet tones, blest breathing-spaces occur, for the most part, in New York conversation, so the reason is, demonstrably, that the building can't afford them.... The building can only afford lights, each light having a superlative value as an aid to the transaction of business and the conclusion of sharp bargains. Doesn't it take in fact acres of window-glass to help even an expert New Yorker to get the better of another expert one, or to see that the other expert one doesn't get the better of *him*?   (2, 74)

Objecting to windows is equivalent to objecting that the building affords no 'interspaces', corners, folds, or places of difference: the windows in the skyscraper are the antithesis of those in the house of fiction. Brydon, who discusses with Alice Staverton the 'old silver-plated knobs of the several mahogany doors, which suggested the pressure of the palms of the dead' (1, 318), has also fantasised about 'opening a door behind which he would have made sure of finding nothing, a door into a room shuttered and void, and yet so coming, with a great suppressed start, on some quite erect confronting presence, something planted in the middle of the place and facing him through the dusk' (1, 316). The text makes play of the keys he needs to get in the front door, and when he is haunting the house at night, he reflects on how the house needs doors. 'The house, as the case stood, admirably lent itself; he might wonder at the taste, the native architecture of the particular time, which could rejoice so in the multiplication of doors – the opposite extreme to the modern, the actual almost complete proscription of them...' (2, 330). Doors separate the house into spaces, different pockets, so that the house is not homogeneous, but separate jolly corners. In the notebooks, James plays with the idea of the door which is locked up or walled up, but with occasional knockings coming from it. In the first subject for a ghost story, written on 2 January 1879:

> The occupant of the house, or room... has long been familiar with the sound, and regarding it as ghostly, has ceased to heed it particularly.... But this person may be imagined to have some great and constant trouble, and it may be observed by another person, relating the story, that the knocking increases with each fresh manifestation of the trouble. He breaks open the door and the trouble ceases – as if the spirit had desired to be admitted, that it might interpose, redeem and protect.

In the second passage (16 May 1899):

> Note the idea of the knock at door (*petite fantasie*) that comes to young man (3 loud taps, etc.) *everywhere* – in all rooms and places he successively occupies – going from one to the other. *I* tell it – am with him: (*he* has told *me*); share a little (through joking him always) his wonder, worry, suspense. I've my idea of what it means. His fate, etc. 'Sometime there *will* be something there – some one.' I am *with* him once when it happens. I am with him the 1st time – I mean the 1st time *I* know about it. (He doesn't notice – I do; then he explains: 'Oh, I thought it was only –' He opens; there *is* someone – natural and ordinary. It is my *entrée en matière*.) The denouement is all. What *does* come – at last? What is there? This is to be ciphered out.   (*Notebooks*, 10, 183)

In contrast to these persistent ideas of what is on the other side of the door, an architecture which does not use doors evokes total openness, or flatness. Perhaps different architectures produce different forms of psychic behaviour. Around 1904, Henry Adams described the modernity of New York as hysteria-inducing, because of the production of power on a scale never seen before:

> As he came up the bay again, ... he [Adams] found the approach more striking than ever – wonderful – unlike anything man had ever seen – and like nothing he had ever much cared to see. The outline of the city became frantic in its effort to explain something that defied meaning. Power seemed to have outgrown its servitude and to have asserted its freedom. The cylinder had exploded and thrown great masses of stone and steam against the sky. The city had the air and movement of hysteria, and the citizens were crying, in every accent of anger and alarm, that the new forces must at any cost be brought under control.[10]

Architecture with doors, as with the Galerie d'Apollon, produces a different behaviour, more Gothic, and associated with hauntings, fear and paranoia. The young man of James's second notebook entry suggests, in his 'wonder, worry and suspense' (the last word generates 'Spencer'), the existence of psychic hauntings which carry through to John Marcher as much as to Spencer Brydon, save that these two are not young men. Perhaps they suggest that the young man in the narrative described in the notebook, attended by a presumably older narator, displaces certain homoerotic feelings in James; perhaps these feelings of homoeroticism themselves are uncanny, as well as uncertain in outcome (the notebook entry gives no clue as to what the knocks will produce). In both Adams and James, architecture is productive of character; the house on the jolly corner produces obsessional behaviours that could not, perhaps, be known within the totalising powers of the skyscraper. The first house produces fears associated with the past, with history, with repression (uncoincidentally, the setting for the room with the door closed is at the top of the house, for it implies what is hidden away from public view). The ghost there represents his attitude to history, to the past, reflecting the point that he wishes to keep one house, and wants to build up memories there at the moment of impossibility, since the house is bare. His obsessional, repetitive behaviour is a reminder again that hysterics suffer mainly from reminiscences, and it is interesting that he tries to free himself from near-hysteria by deliberately not opening the shut door – as he had in time past been able to burn a letter unopened. He does so in the name of 'discretion' (2, 330), and by saying that he 'renounces' (331). It is a rhetorical way of saving his sense of his own subjectivity, declaring his ability to control a situation.

But he has panicked. He moves away to the other side of the fourth floor where he is, and looks out of the window, isolated so much that he even desires to see a policeman below – till he feels, in the dawn, that he must go. But he has not the nerve to see whether the door that was open, and that closed, is open again, and his panic shows in his near suicide, by throwing himself out of the window (333). Themes related to Alice James and Constance Fenimore Woolson return in their melancholia and hysteria: fears of what James called 'the Medusa face of life' which John Marcher faces when he throws himself on the tomb. Brydon's fear of being doubled by another in the house, fear of being repeated, brings home a basic originary emptiness to him, as Freud argues that the phenomenon of the double (the ghost), denying the notion of originality and uniqueness, presages death.[11] At the same moment, he is determined to let the developers in, to annihilate the past and his own history. (Pulling the house down, like breaking the golden bowl, will release the ghost-energies of the house into New York city.) Arrived at the bottom of the stairs, at the entrance hall, and feeling safe, he finds that the doors of the vestibule have been thrown back, throwing open another space, whereas he had carefully shut the doors. 'The penumbra, sense and dark, was the virtual screen of a figure which stood in it as still as some image erect in a niche [a corner, a fold] or as some black-vizored sentinel guarding a treasure' (334). The figure is ambiguous, to be read in different ways. He is the American businessman seen as though dollars were now 'treasures', in a portrait by some master which has come to life from its 'frame' (335). This figure 'advance[s] as for aggression'. It suggests the power that Henry Adams noted in New York – the power of someone with 'a million a year' (3, 340). Yet the ruined eyes and missing fingers, which make it an Oedipus, blind and the figure of loss, imply an alternative view, as well as a history of male sexuality, in some ways defeated. He contrasts with John Marcher, who was a dispossessed Oedipus, where even May Bartram had the potential to be the Sybil. But then this American ghost, so different from Marcher, is not only one of the gilded age robber-barons, but also, in another anamorphosis, 'a black stranger' (3, 339). In America, the black is also dispossessed, like Oedipus.

Writing about the other self, the alternative self as black, links *The Jolly Corner* to *The Beast in the Jungle*. Between the two tales had come James's encounter with 'the inconceivable alien' at Ellis Island (*The American Scene*, 2, 66), and the black, encountered at Washington and at Richmond:

> I had found my own [ease] threatened, I remember – my ease of contemplation of the subject, which was all there could be question of – during some ten minutes spent, a few days before, in consideration of an African type or two encountered in Washington. I was waiting, in a cab, at the railway station, for the delivery of my luggage after my arrival, while a group of tatterdemalion darkies lounged and sunned themselves within range. To take in with any attention two or three of these figures had surely been to feel oneself introduced at a bound to the formidable question, which rose suddenly like some beast that had sprung from the jungle. These were its far outposts; they represented the Southern black as we knew him not, and had not, in the memory of man known him, in the North... (*The American Scene*, 12, 276)

The beast in the jungle *is* a question. Characters like Gloriani in *The Ambassadors* can partake of the beast's nature, by being tigerish, as the black seems also metonymic for the beast's presence, but as there is not yet a narrative beginning for *The Beast in the Jungle* (as if America – James's displaced subject – has not yet provided one, so that America must be re-imagined, re-invented, in a 'family romance'), so there is not yet a question definable as such which would allow for narrative as a reply. None the less the restless analyst, like the restless mover through the house in *The Jolly Corner*, is dispossessed of his 'ease' by the otherness that shows up the inadequacy of his existing origins, as a white American, brought up in that America without a shadow. Origins change as soon as they are looked at: in *The American Scene*, one place of beginnings – a house in Boston James once lived in – is there one month, a 'gaping void' the next time he looks (*The American Scene*, 7, 1, 170). The mutilated figure in *The Jolly Corner* allegorises such a maimed opening, and if the Europeanised Brydon cannot accept him, Alice Staverton in her dream (how few dreams there are in James!) can. His 'poor right hand' recalls what James wrote about seeing his no longer present birthplace in Washington Place: 'the effect for me...was of having been amputated of half my history' (*The American Scene*, 2, 71). Amputation – whether the father's, Henry James senior's literal one, or the son's figurative one, or as with this figure of aggressive modernity – allegorises loss, a disfiguring, like that enacted in the New York street. A ghost evokes incompleteness, non-reality, and a ghost without fingers is a double form of absence, which solicits questions of the history of loss – it evokes what Milly Theale also had, a 'New York history', as the black in Richmond also challenges a normative history. And the ghost challenges notions of a whole identity. In this tale, are there two ghosts or one? There can be no answer here. Just as pulling the house down, the birthplace, so full of ghosts and of otherness, is an amputation, so also is the wish – also associated with modernity – to isolate and fix an identity itself.[12] When Bryson sees the ghost, 'the bared identity was too hideous as *his*' and 'such an identity fitted his at *no* point, made its alternative monstrous' (2, 335). Its alternative is himself: if the ghost mirrors him, he becomes 'monstrous', which is his reason for abject repudiation: it offends the narcissism on which his subjectivity depends. Alice Staverton reconciles him to the ghost's humanness ('he has been unhappy, he has been ravaged' [3, 339] and 'Brydon winced – whether for his proved identity, or for his lost fingers' [340]). But it is less the question whether the identity is his or not, than that lost fingers define the subject as always maimed, and identity when reduced from its plural possibilities to the singular, as amputated. Yet the amputated, deprived life, different from what the skyscraper stands for in ideology, is how Freud envisages thinking and being in the conditions of modernity, when at the end of *Beyond the Pleasure Principle* – asserting his own lack of knowledge – he quotes:

> Was man nicht erfliegen kann, muss man erhinken.

and

> Die Schrift sagt, es ist keine Sünde zu hinken.

(What we cannot reach flying we must reach limping. . . . The Book tells us it is no sin to limp.)

Limping, or chasing, in a nightmare the ghost – James's art contains the possibilities of both.

Notes

CHAPTER 1: INTRODUCTION: READING THE *AMERICAN SCENE*

1. On James's writings on Hawthorne, on Story, and on biography as 'portraiture', see Charles Caramello, *Henry James, Gertrude Stein and the Biographical Act* (Chapel Hill: University of North Carolina, 1996).

2. One positive account is Sara Blair, *Henry James and the Writing of Race and Nation* (Cambridge: Cambridge University Press, 1996). There is now a huge bibliography on the politics of *The American Scene*, and its relationship to James's autobiography, and his Americanness. See, for example, Ross Posnock, *The Trial of Curiosity: Henry James, William James and the Challenge of Modernity* (Oxford: Oxford University Press, 1991), which uses *The American Scene*, arguing for James's advanced intellectual positions, relating to European thinkers of urban modernity. For guides to James, see Daniel Mark Fogel (ed.), *A Companion to Henry James Studies* (Westport: Greenwood Press, 1993), and Jonathan Freedman (ed.), *The Cambridge Companion to Henry James* (Cambridge: Cambridge University Press, 1998).

3. For Howells and James, see John W. Crowley, '*The Portrait of a Lady* and *The Rise of Silas Lapham*: The Company they Kept', in Donald Pizer (ed.), *The Cambridge Companion to American Realism and Naturalism* (Cambridge: Cambridge University Press, 1995), pp. 117–37.

4. Quoted in F. W. Dupee (ed.), *The Question of Henry James: A Collection of Critical Essays* (New York: Octagon, 1945), p. 143.

5. Fredric Jameson, *The Political Unconscious: Narrative as a Socially Symbolic Act* (London: Methuen, 1981), p. 222.

6. F. R. Leavis, *The Great Tradition* (1948; Harmondsworth: Penguin, 1962), p. 188.

7. Letter of 18 November 1903, *Letters of Henry Adams*, ed. Worthington Chauncey Ford, 2 vols (Boston: Houghton Mifflin, 1938), vol. II, p. 414.

8. Quoted in Thaddeo K. Babiiha, *The James–Hawthorne Relation: Bibliographical Essays* (Boston: G. K. Hall, 1980), p. 13. See Edel, V, 312.

9. See Hugh Stevens, 'Homoeroticism, Identity and Agency in James's Late Tales', in Gert Buekens (ed.), *Enacting History in Henry James*:

Narrative, Power and Ethics (Cambridge: Cambridge University Press, 1997), pp. 145–6, on the word 'queer'.

10. H. G. Wells, 'Of Art, Of Literature, Of Mr Henry James', in *Henry James and H. G. Wells: A Record of their Friendship, their Debate on the Art of Fiction and their Quarrel*, ed. Leon Edel and Gordon N. Ray (1958; Westport: Greenwood Press, 1985), p. 248.

11. Mark Seltzer, *Henry James and the Art of Power* (Ithaca: Cornell University Press, 1984), p. 100.

12. Seltzer's debate with Rowe appears on pp. 158–61. Rowe's most developed account of James to date appears in *The Theoretical Dimensions of Henry James* (Madison: University of Wisconsin Press, 1984), subsequent to this discussion, and now in *The Other Henry James* (Durham, N.C: Duke University Press, 1998).

13. See also the criticism of Jean-Christophe Agnew, 'The Consuming Vision of Henry James', in *The Culture of Consumption: Critical Essays in American History, 1880–1980*, ed. Richard W. Fox and T. J. J. Lears (New York: Pantheon, 1983), pp. 78, 98–9, which sees James as appropriating commodity culture, as the critic in the Preface to *What Maisie Knew* makes the criticised thing 'his own' (*AN*, 8, 155).

14. M. Christine Boyer, *Manhattan Manners: Architecture and Style, 1850–1900* (New York: Rizzoli, 1985), pp. 226–7.

15. Fredric Jameson, *Postmodernism, Or the Cultural Logic of Late Capitalism* (London: Verso, 1991), pp. 38–44.

16. For Pullman, see Carl S. Smith, *Urban Disorder and the Shape of Belief: The Great Chicago Fire, the Haymarket Bomb and the Model Town of Pullman* (Chicago: University of Chicago Press, 1995), pp 177–270.

17. On the representations of the black in James, see Kenneth W. Warren, *Black and White Strangers: Race and American Literary Realism* (Chicago: University of Chicago Press, 1993), pp. 109–30. See also Beverly Haviland, *Henry James's Last Romance: Making Sense of the Past and The American Scene* (Cambridge: Cambridge University Press, 1997), pp. 108–34.

18. Du Bois (born Massachusetts) was teaching at Atlanta. William James sent James a copy of his book in 1903, before James left for America. See R. W. B. Lewis, *The Jameses* (London: André Deutsch, 1991), p. 538. William James recommends chapter 7, which is written as in a train journey going south through Georgia from Atlanta (but a train where 'Jim Crow' segregation is practised), and comments on the suppression of native Americans; and also chapter 11, which is an account of the death of Du Bois's child. It is evident that Du Bois's itinerary in his

chapter 7 prompts James's chapters 12–14, perhaps to an extent that James was not wholly aware of.

19. W. E. B. Du Bois, *The Souls of Black Folk*, ed. Donald B. Gibson (Harmondsworth: Penguin, 1996), pp. 1, 2.

20. Quoted in F. O. Matthiessen, *The James Family* (New York: Alfred A. Knopf, 1948), pp. 341–2.

21. Roland Barthes, *Camera Lucida: Reflections on Photography*, trans. Richard Howard (London: Fontana, 1982), pp. 26–7.

CHAPTER 2: 'THE INTEREST BEHIND THE INTEREST': *THE LAST OF THE VALERII* AND *THE AMBASSADORS*

1. 'The uncanny is something which is secretly familiar, which has undergone repression and then returned from it' – Sigmund Freud, 'The Uncanny' (1919), *The Penguin Freud*, vol. 14 (Harmondsworth: Penguin, 1985), p. 368.

2. Quoted in Nathalia Wright, *American Novelists in Italy: The Discoverers: Allston to James* (Philadelphia: University of Pennsylvania Press, 1965), p. 200.

3. On Balzac and James, see Peter Brooks, *The Melodramatic Imagination: Balzac, Henry James, Melodrama and the Mode of Excess* (New Haven: Yale University Press, 1976). James wrote on Balzac in 1875: *French Poets and Novelists*; in 1902: 'Honoré de Balzac', in *Notes on Novelists*; and in 1905: 'The Lesson of Balzac'. He reviewed Balzac's *Letters* in 1877.

4. He wrote on *Felix Holt* in the *Nation* in 1866, 'The Novels of George Eliot' in 1866 in *Atlantic Monthly*, reviews of *The Spanish Gypsy* in The *Nation* and *North American Review*, *Middlemarch* in 1873 in *Galaxy*, and *The Legend of Jubal* in 1874 in *North American Review*. '*Daniel Deronda*: A Conversation' appeared in December 1876 in the *Atlantic Monthly* (and James reviewed for the *Nation* the first part of that novel, which was serialised between February and September). In 1878, he reviewed *The Lifted Veil* and *Brother Jacob* for the *Nation*. Lastly, after George Eliot's death in 1880, he reviewed J. W. Cross's *Life of George Eliot* in 1885, for the *Atlantic Monthly*.

5. See Richard Freadman, *Eliot, James and the Fictional Self* (London: Macmillan, 1986), pp. 33–4.

6. Vivien Jones points out in *James the Critic* (London: Macmillan, 1985), p. 130, that James originally wrote 'the only reason for the existence of

the novel is that it *does* compete with life' and changed this in 1888. She sees 'The Art of Fiction' as a 'radical break' with 'naive contemporary discussions of realism' and with the nineteenth-century 'mimetic tradition', leading to James's modernism, which she sees as his relativism, his interest in 'the limitations of knowledge and of narrative' that are suggested by the novel being an *impression* of life (pp. 129, 132).

7. Quoted in Peter Keating, *The Haunted Study: A Social History of the English Novel, 1875–1914* (London: Secker and Warburg, 1989), p. 243. The chapter 'An End to Reticence' (pp. 241–84) discusses the Vizetelly trial; see also pp. 112–14 for discussion of 'The Art of Fiction'.

8. Terry Castle, *The Apparational Lesbian: Feminine Homosexuality and Modern Culture* (New York: Columbia University Press, 1993), pp. 150–85.

9. On *Nana*, see Peter Brooks, *Body Work: Objects of Desire in Modern Narrative* (Cambridge, Mass.: Harvard University Press, 1993), pp. 123–61.

10. James compares Charlotte M. Yonge's *The Daisy Chain* and Susan Bogert Warner's *The Wide Wide World*. See Ann Douglas, *The Feminization of American Culture* (1977; New York: Anchor, 1988).

11. Emile Zola, *Nana*, trans. George Holden (Harmondsworth: Penguin, 1982), ch. 8, pp. 336–7. Further references in the text.

12. Nathaniel Hawthorne, *The House of Seven Gables*, ed. Seymour L. Gross (New York: Norton, 1967), p. 1.

13. On the distinction, see such studies as Richard Chase, *The American Novel and Its Tradition* (New York: Doubleday, 1957); Michael Davitt Bell, *The Development of American Romance: The Sacrifice of Relation* (Chicago: University of Chicago Press, 1980); Nina Baym, *Novels, Readers and Reviewers: Responses to Fiction in Antebellum America* (Ithaca: Cornell University Press, 1984), pp. 224–48.

14. Karl Marx, 'The Eighteenth Brumaire of Louis Bonaparte', in *Surveys from Exile* (Harmondsworth: Penguin, 1973), p. 146.

15. Nathaniel Hawthorne, *The Marble Faun*, ed. Malcolm Bradbury (London: Everyman, 1995), pp. 33, 241.

16. David Quint, *Epic and Empire: Politics and Generic Form from Virgil to Milton* (Princeton: Princeton University Press, 1993), compares the epic and the romance on these grounds.

17. Walter Benjamin, *Charles Baudelaire: A Lyric Poet in the Era of High Capitalism* (London: New Left Books, 1973), p. 81. Further references in the text are to this edition.

18. This, which suggests the figure of prosopopoeia, Paul de Man's subject in his essay 'Autobiography as Defacement' (*The Rhetoric of Romanticism*, New York: Columbia University Press, 1984), is the clue to J. Hillis Miller's interpretation of the tale in his *Versions of Pygmalion* (Cambridge, Mass.: Harvard University Press, 1990), pp. 211–44.

19. Nathaniel Hawthorne, *The Scarlet Letter*, ed. Susan Cockcroft (Cambridge: Cambridge University Press, 1997), pp. 88–9.

20. Hillis Miller, *Versions of Pygmalion*, pp. 236–7.

21. Alan W. Bellringer discusses the chronology of the novel in his *The Ambassadors* (London: George Allen and Unwin, 1984), p. 96.

22. See the reading of the passage by David Lodge, 'Strether by the River', in *Language of Fiction* (London: Routledge, 1966), pp. 189–213.

23. David McWhirter, *Desire and Love in Henry James: A Study of the Late Novels* (Cambridge: Cambridge University Press, 1989), p. 70.

24. See the discussion of the passage by T. J. Lustig, *Henry James and the Ghostly* (Cambridge: Cambridge University Press, 1994), p. 195. Lustig refers to the analysis of Ruth Bernard Yeazell, in *Language and Knowledge in the Late Novels of Henry James* (Chicago: University of Chicago Press, 1976), pp. 32–3, for the Freudian sense that in the appearance of these two lovers there is the 'inevitable surfacing of suppressed facts'. See Lustig, pp. 195 and 278. On the enchantment and the charming, see D. W. Jefferson, *Henry James and the Modern Reader* (London: Oliver and Boyd, 1964), p. 192, who discusses the novel in terms of Strether entering into the world of Medieval Romance.

25. Richard Hathaway, 'Ghosts at the Windows: Shadow and Corona in *The Ambassadors*', *HJR*, 18 (1997), 81–96, p. 91.

26. See Aristotle's *Poetics*, in T. S. Dorsch, *Aristotle, Horace, Longinus: Classical Literary Criticism* (Harmondsworth: Penguin, 1965), Section 6, p. 40.

27. Letter to Jocelyn Persse, quoted in S. P. Rosenbaum (ed.), *The Ambassadors* (New York: Norton Critical Edition, 1964), p. 408. On Strether and autobiography, see William R. Goetz, *Henry James and the Darkest Abyss of Romance* (Baton Rouge: Louisiana State University Press, 1986), pp. 182–205.

28. Letter to Howard Sturgis, August 1914, in Percy Lubbock's edition of James's letters (1920), vol. II, p. 398. For James on the war, see Roslyn Jolly, *Henry James: History, Narrative, Fiction* (Oxford: Clarendon Press, 1993), pp. 206–23. The letter is cited on p. 211.

29. Lubbock, vol. II, p. 462 (cited in Jolly, p. 211).

30. The break-down in ability to tell a story is the theme of Walter Benjamin, 'The Storyteller', in *Illuminations*, trans. Harry Zohn (London: Jonathan Cape, 1970), where it is related to the experiences of the First World War soldier.

31. For James on *Louis Lambert*, see his review of Balzac's correspondence, in the magazine *Galaxy* (1877), reprinted in *French Poets and Novelists* (1878). See *LC* I, 76–7.

32. *Louis Lambert*, reprinted in *Séraphita*, trans. Clara Bell (Cambridge: Dedalus Books, 1989), p. 190. Further references in the text.

33. See Derrida's discussion of Nietzsche, *Spurs: Nietzsche's Styles*, trans. Barbara Harlow (Chicago: University of Chicago Press, 1979). The parasol makes Mme de Vionnet the affirmative woman Derrida claims that Nietzsche speaks of.

34. Evelyne Ender, *Sexing the Mind: Nineteenth-Century Fictions of Hysteria* (Ithaca: Cornell University Press, 1995), p. 79n, discusses James on George Sand, and quotes the passage (published in *French Poets and Novelists*, 1878): 'She [Sand] was more masculine than any man she might have married; and what powerfully masculine person – even leaving genius aside – is content at five-and-twenty with submissiveness and renunciation?' (*LC* I, 716). Ender sees this 'in line with [James's] later preoccupation with "living"' (as exemplified in the famous scene between Little Bilham and Strether in *The Amassadors*: 'Live all you can; it's a mistake not to'), and adds 'Are we meant to understand that living is masculine while renunciation would then be feminine?' The answer would be 'yes', with Strether as the model of renunciation.

35. Adeline Tintner, *Henry James and the Lust of the Eyes* (Baton Rouge: Louisiana State University Press, 1993), pp. 87–94, discusses the identifications and titling of the painting made in 1900 by Mary F. S. Bell in her book *Holbein's Ambassadors*, and links it to a *carpe diem* theme within *The Ambassadors*. R. W. Smallman, 'The Sacred Rage: The Time Theme in *The Ambassadors*', *Modern Fiction Studies*, 3, 1 (Spring 1975), 41–56 (the whole issue is given over to James), suggests that the object made in Woollett is watches, or clocks. It fits with the Woollett prosaicness. Maud Ellmann also links James to Holbein via Lacan in her essay on *The Ambassadors* in Ian F. A. Bell (ed.), *Henry James: Fiction as History* (New York: Barnes and Noble, 1984), pp. 98–113. On Holbein's painting, see Stephen Greenblatt, *Renaissance Self-Fashioning: From More to Shakespeare* (Chicago: University of Chicago Press, 1980), pp. 17–21. See also the discussion by Slavoj Zizek, *Looking Awry: An Introduction to Jacques Lacan Through Popular Culture* (Cambridge, Mass.: MIT, 1991), pp. 90–1.

36. Barbara Freedman, *Staging the Gaze: Postmodernism, Psychoanalysis and Shakespearian Comedy* (Ithaca: Cornell University Press, 1991), p. 17.

CHAPTER 3:   HISTORIES OF SEXUALITY IN
THE PORTRAIT OF A LADY AND *THE BOSTONIANS*

1. George Eliot, *Daniel Deronda*, ed. Barbara Hardy (Harmondsworth: Penguin, 1967), pp. 159–60.

2. *The Portrait of a Lady* was serialised between 1880 and 1881 and appeared in book form in November 1881; it was revised in 1908 for volumes 3 and 4 of the New York edition. The Norton edition (1995) indicates differences between the two versions. See Philip Horne, *Henry James and Revision: The New York Edition* (Oxford: Clarendon, 1990), pp. 184–227. *The Bostonians*, serialised in the *Century*, February 1885– February 1886, was not reissued.

3. The statement, by Raymond Fulgence, is quoted by Mark S. Micale, *Approaching Hysteria: Disease and Its Interpretations* (Princeton: Princeton University Press, 1995), p. 3.

4. See, generally, Elaine Showalter, *The Female Malady: Women, Madness and English Culture, 1830–1980* (London: Virago, 1987); Katrein Libbrecht, *Hysterical Psychosis: An Historical Survey* (New Brunswick: Transaction Publishers, 1995). In James studies, hysteria has been studied in relation to *The Bostonians*: see Claire Kahane, *Passions of the Voice: Hysteria, Narrative and the Figure of the Speaking Woman, 1850–1915* (Baltimore: Johns Hopkins, 1995), and Evelyne Ender, *Sexing the Mind: Nineteenth-Century Fictions of Hysteria* (Ithaca: Cornell University Press, 1995), which also contains discussion of George Eliot. On hysteria in Flaubert, see Janet Beizer, *Ventriloquized Bodies: Narratives of Hysteria in Nineteenth-Century France* (Ithaca: Cornell University Press, 1993). On male hysteria, see Jan Goldstein, 'The Uses of Male Hysteria: Medical and Literary Discourse in Nineteenth-Century France', *Representations*, 34 (1991), 134–65.

5. *Middlemarch*, ed. W. J. Harvey (Harmondsworth: Penguin, 1965), ch. 7, p. 87. Further references in the text.

6. Walter Benjamin, *Charles Baudelaire: A Lyric Poet in an Era of High Capitalism* (London: Verso, 1973), p. 87. Further references as 'Benjamin' in the text.

7. Freud, *Case Studies I: 'Dora' and 'Little Hans'*, Penguin Freud, vol. 8 (Harmondsworth: Penguin, 1977), p. 59.

8. See Kim Townsend, *Manhood at Harvard: William James and Others* (New York: W. W. Norton, 1995).

9. Quoted in William Greenslade, *Degeneration, Culture and the Novel, 1880–1940* (Cambridge: Cambridge University Press, 1994), p. 212.

10. Max Nordau (1849–1923) published *Entartung* in 1892 in Berlin (*Degeneration*, 1895), dedicated to Lombroso. John Stokes, *In the Nineties* (London: Harvester Wheatsheaf, 1989), says that it 'sought to demonstrate a universal thesis that modern artists were driven by pathological needs to portray in their work only the ugly and vicious aspects of life, an abnormal impulse which they then attempted to conceal with the fraudulent "Aesthetic" tenet that art had nothing to do with ethics' (p. 12).

11. Quoted, John Stokes, *In the Nineties*, pp. 26, 27. See also Greenslade, pp. 217–22.

12. Compare this with James's comments on William Wetmore Story, that though 'he loved the nude, as the artist, in any field, essentially and logically must', he preferred drapery – i.e. ornament, so that 'he was not with the last intensity a sculptor' (*Story*, II, 83). As if agreeing with the implications of this point, though long before it was made, Miriam in *The Marble Faun* (14, 98) rejects nudes and believes that 'sculpture [as the art of the nude] has no longer a right to claim any place among living arts'.

13. Katrein Libbrecht (p. 19) refers to Wilhelm Griesinger (1817–68), who discusses melancholia as a form of hysteria.

14. Marius Bewley, *The Complex Fate* (London: Chatto and Windus, 1952), pp. 11–30.

15. Nathaniel Hawthorne, *The Blithedale Romance*, ed. Seymour Gross and Rosalie Murphy (New York: W. W. Norton, 1978).

16. Quoted in Alfred Habegger, *Henry James and the 'Woman Business'* (Cambridge: Cambridge University Press, 1989), p. 93.

17. *Daisy Miller: A Study* appeared first in serial form in the *Cornhill* (1878). It was revised for the New York edition of 1909 (vol. XVIII). Though many prefer the earlier version – see Daniel Mark Fogel, *Daisy Miller: A Dark Comedy of Manners* (Boston: Twayne, 1990), pp. 87–94 – the New York edition is well written about by Philip Horne, pp. 228–64.

18. William Dean Howells, *The Rise of Silas Lapham*, ed. Don L. Cook (New York: W. W. Norton, 1982), ch. 1, p. 19.

19. Letter quoted in *Madame Bovary*, trans. Paul de Man (New York: W. W. Norton, 1965), pp. 309–10. See, for comments on Flaubert, as I have

discussed him, Beizer, pp. 90–2, 151, 161–2. Further on Flaubert, see Dominick La Capra's *Madame Bovary on Trial* (Ithaca: Cornell University Press, 1982), and Ross Chambers, *The Writing of Melancholy: Modes of Opposition in Early French Modernism* (Chicago: University of Chicago Press, 1993).

20. See Beizer, p. 136; Julia Kristeva, *Powers of Horror: An Essay on Abjection*, trans. Leon Roudiez (New York: Columbia University Press, 1981).

21. See, for the hysterical implications of this, Charles Bernheimer, *Flaubert and Kafka: Studies in Psychopoetic Structure* (New Haven: Yale University Press, 1982), pp. 57–65.

22. Quoted in *Madame Bovary*, trans. Paul de Man, pp. 339–41.

23. Sigmund Freud, *Studies in Hysteria*, *The Penguin Freud*, vol. 3 (Harmondsworth: Penguin, 1974), p. 58.

24. Jacques Lacan, 'The Agency of the Letter in the Unconscious, or, Reason since Freud', in *Ecrits: A Selection*, trans. Alan Sheridan (London: Tavistock, 1977), pp. 165, 166.

25. *Madame Bovary*, 3, 6, trans. cit., p. 211.

26. Gard, p. 374. James's essay of 1902 appeared as an Introduction to a translation of *Madame Bovary*.

27. 'The place struck [Ransom] with a kind of Roman vastness; the doors which opened out of the upper balconies, high aloft, and which were constantly swinging to and fro with the passage of spectators and ushers, reminded him of the *vomitoria* he had read about in descriptions of the Colosseum' (ch. 41, p. 371). While *vomitoria* means entrances, its use in Ransom's disdainful thinking is surely suggestive of disgust, or revulsion, against the people as the 'raving rabble' (42, 385).

CHAPTER 4: MONOMANIA AND THE AMERICAN PAST: *THE ASPERN PAPERS*

1. On the revisions between *The Aspern Papers*, 1888, and the New York edition, see Philip Horne, *Henry James and Revision: The New York Edition* (Oxford: Clarendon, 1990) and Ellen Brown, 'Revising Henry James: Reading the Spaces of *The Aspern Papers*', *American Literature*, 63 (1991), 263–70. Another version of this chapter appears as 'Henry James's American Byron', *HJR* (Winter 1999), pp. 43–50. I am grateful to the editors for permission to use this material here.

2. On the relationships, see Bernard Richards, 'How Many Children had Juliana Bordereau?', *HJR*, 12 (1991), 120–8.

3. On Teresa Guiccioli (died Florence, 1873), see Iris Origo, *The Last Attachment* (London: Jonathan Cape, 1949); on Claire Clairmont, see Robert Gittings and Jo Marton, *Claire Clairmont and the Shelleys* (Oxford: Oxford University Press, 1992); pp. 235–7 deals with Silsbee, who met Claire Clairmont in 1872. See also *The Journals of Claire Clairmont*, ed. Marion Kingston Stocking (Cambridge, Mass.: Harvard University Press, 1968).

4. Shelley seems to have written the 'Constantia' poems for her in 1817: see Neville Rogers (ed.), *Complete Poetical Works of Percy Bysshe Shelley, 1814–1817* (Oxford: Oxford University Press, 1975), p. 403.

5. See Preface to *Roderick Hudson*: 'Really, universally, relations stop nowhere, and the exquisite problem of the artist is eternally but to draw, by a geometry of his own, the circle within which they shall happily *appear* to do so' (*AN*, 1, 5).

6. Sigmund Freud, 'Family Romances', *The Penguin Freud*, vol. 7 (Harmondsworth: Penguin, 1977), pp. 221–5.

7. Quoted in Edgar Preston Richardson, *Washington Allston: A Study of the Romantic Artist in America* (Chicago: University of Chicago Press, 1948), pp. 2–3.

8. R. W. Emerson, *Journals and Miscellaneous Notebooks*, ed. William Gilman et al., 4 vols (Cambridge, Mass.: Harvard University Press, 1964), IV, I, 159.

9. See Evelyn Barish, *Emerson: The Roots of Prophecy* (Princeton: Princeton University Press, 1989), p. 94.

10. Quoted in Tony Tanner, *Venice Desired* (Oxford: Blackwell, 1992), p. 24.

11. John Ruskin, *Praeterita* (London: Rupert Hart-Davis, 1949), p. 268.

12. See Tanner, *Venice Desired*, pp. 24, 66.

13. See Adeline Tintner, *The Book World of Henry James: Appropriating the Classics* (Ann Arbor: UMI Research Press, 1987), pp. 95–102.

14. On the reception of Shakespeare's Sonnets in the Romantic period, and Byron's homosexuality, see Louis Crompton, *Byron and Greek Love: Homophobia in Nineteenth-Century England* (Berkeley: University of California Press, 1985), pp. 189–90. See also Jerome Christiansen, *Lord Byron's Strength: Romantic Writing and Commercial Society* (Baltimore: Johns Hopkins University Press, 1993), pp. 54–65. Andrew

Elfenbein, *Byron and the Victorians* (Cambridge: Cambridge University Press, 1995), pp. 208–13, discusses Byron's homosexuality as an open secret and refers to Wilde's awareness of Byron's homosexuality (pp. 236–46). James, by the time of writing the Preface to *The Aspern Papers* could hardly have been ignorant of this.

15. Quoted in Christopher Craft, 'Descend and Touch and Enter: Tennyson's Strange Manner of Address', *Genders*, 1 (Spring 1988), 83–101 (p. 85). See Richard Dellamora, *Masculine Desire: The Sexual Politics of Victorian Aestheticism* (Chapel Hill: University of North Carolina Press, 1990), pp. 16–41.

16. For Hawthorne in the text, see Richard Brodhead, *The School of Hawthorne* (Oxford: Oxford University Press, 1986), pp. 106–7. For Hawthorne as Aspern, see Gary Scharnhorst, 'James, "The Aspern Papers" and the Ethics of Literary Biography', *Modern Fiction Studies*, 36 (1990), 211–17.

17. Quoted in Robert Weisbuch, *Atlantic Double-Cross: American Literature and British Influence in the Age of Emerson* (Chicago: University of Chicago Press, 1986), p. 12.

18. Quoted in Richardson, *Washington Allston*, p. 14, note.

19. The 1888 version ends, 'When I look at it my chagrin at the loss of the letters becomes almost intolerable.'

20. J. Hillis Miller, 'History, Narrative and Responsibility: Speech Acts in Henry James's "The Aspern Papers"', *Textual Practice*, 9 (1995), 243–67.

21. No. 709 in *Emily Dickinson: The Complete Poems*, ed. Thomas H. Johnson (London: Faber, 1970), pp. 348–9.

22. Both Rappaccini, in 'Rappaccini's Daughter', and the narrator create gardens of flowers. In 'Rappaccini's Daughter', the flowers are ambiguous, like the daughter Beatrice: no fixed value can be assigned to either flowers or women. Tina Bordereau, virtually created as a woman through the gift of flowers given to her by the narrator, causes in the narrator a doubt of whether he has made love to her or not, which his hysterical disavowals cannot dissipate. The ambiguity of the flowers contrasts with the narrator's desire for fixed truth, the truth about the life, the wish to disambiguate Aspern's poetry, to not recognise its bisexuality/bitextuality. For suggestive connections between flowers, women and homosexuality, see Claudette Sartiliot, *Herbarium Verbarium: The Discourse of Flowers* (Lincoln: University of Nebraska Press, 1993).

23. Mary Shelley, *Frankenstein*, in *Three Gothic Novels*, ed. Peter Fairclough (Harmondsworth: Penguin, 1968), 4, 314.

24. On monomania, see Jan Goldstein, *Console and Classify: The French Psychiatric Profession in the Nineteenth Century* (1987), pp. 152–96; on its relation to hysteria, see pp. 322–4. Also Simon During, 'The Strange Case of Monomania: Patriarchy in Literature, Murder in *Middlemarch*, Drowning in *Daniel Deronda*', *Representations*, 23 (1988), 86–104.

25. See Goldstein, *Console and Classify*, p. 157.

26. Freud and Brueuer, *Studies on Hysteria*, *The Penguin Freud*, vol. 3 (Harmondsworth: Penguin, 1974), p. 58.

27. Dellamora, *Masculine Desire*, pp. 86–93, discusses Whitman's status in England.

CHAPTER 5:   ALLEGORICAL AUTOBIOGRAPHY: *THE TURN OF THE SCREW*

1. *The Turn of the Screw* appeared in *Colliers* from January to April 1898 as something seasonable (a Christmas narrative). The Norton Critical Edition, edited by Robert Kimbrough (New York: W. W. Norton, 1966), reprints some older criticism of the tale. Another anthology of criticism, printed alongside the New York edition of the text, edited by Peter G. Beidler (Case Studies in Contemporary Criticisms, New York: Bedford Books, St Martin's Press, 1995), reprints useful criticism, but includes only part of Shoshana Felman's study (see note 4) – in my view, the most important single study of the text. See also Terry Heller, *The Turn of the Screw: Bewildered Vision* (Boston: Twayne, 1989). One of the most complete analyses of the text, in a study which can be recommended not least for its bibliography, is T. J. Lustig, *Henry James and the Ghostly* (Cambridge: Cambridge University Press, 1994). For Delaroche's picture, see Stephen Bann, *Paul Delaroche: History Revisited* (London: Reaktion Books, 1997), pp. 94–106 (and see pp. 25–6 for James on Delaroche).

2. The tale's title appears again at 22, 240, where the governess reflects that her ordeal requires 'only another turn of the screw of ordinary human virtue'. The phrase appeared earlier in *What Maisie Knew* (12, 97), where Mrs Wix says that 'it would take another turn of the screw to make her desert her darling'. Since the 'screw' here implies constraint and effort (if it does not actually refer to thumb-screws and hence to torture), perhaps the governess uses the term to imply the torture – the effort – of being virtuous. She makes virtue painful, part of her passion for possession.

3. Sigmund Freud, 'Beyond the Pleasure Principle', *The Penguin Freud*, vol. 11 (Harmondsworth: Penguin, 1977), pp. 283–7. The child compensates

himself for, and masters, loss (of the other) by staging the disappearance and return of the substitute object in a pattern of repetition, which cannot, however, overcome the primary absence.

4. Shoshana Felman, 'Henry James and the Risks of Practice (Turning the Screw of Interpretation)', in *Writing and Madness: Literature, Philosophy, Psychoanalysis* (Ithaca, NY: Cornell University Press, 1985), pp. 141–247, especially pp. 205–20. Felman's essay first appeared in 1982.

5. Ibid., p. 172. Felman continues that 'the narrative emerges … not only authorless and nameless, but also unentitled to its own authority over itself, having no capacity to denominate, no right to *name itself*'.

6. Ibid., p. 211, note.

7. The argument of Ned Lukacher, *Primal Scenes: Literature, Philosophy, Psychoanalysis* (Ithaca, NY: Cornell University Press, 1986), pp. 115–35.

8. Cf. Jacques Lacan, 'You never look at me from the place where I see you. Consequently, what I look at is never what I wish to see' (*The Four Fundamental Concepts of Psychoanalysis*, trans. Alan Sheridan (Harmondsworth: Penguin, 1977), pp. 102–3). I discuss this passage further in Chapter 7, p. 157, below.

9. See Linda S. Kauffman, 'The Author of our Woe: Virtue Recorded in "The Turn of the Screw"', *Nineteenth-Century Fiction*, 36 (1981–2), 176–92. This account hazards the view that the narrator is a woman in love with Douglas.

10. Sigmund Freud, 'The Uncanny', in *The Penguin Freud*, vol. 14: *Art and Literature* (Harmondsworth: Penguin, 1985), p. 368. Cf. Douglas, who says that the governess's tale is 'beyond anything … for general uncanny ugliness, and horror and pain' (Introduction, 146).

11. The case formed the context for Genet's play *The Maids*. See Elisabeth Roudinesco, *Jacques Lacan*, trans. Barbara Bray (New York: Columbia University Press, 1997), pp. 62–5.

12. Quoted in R. W. B. Lewis, *The Jameses: A Family Narrative* (London: André Deutsch, 1991), p. 51. For James's account of this, see *Autobiography*, p. 340. The incident is discussed by Quentin Anderson in *The American Henry James* (New Brunswick: Rutgers University Press, 1957), pp. 84–7. See also Alfred Habegger's excellent biography, *The Father: A Life of Henry James Senior* (New York: Farrar, Straus and Giroux, 1994).

13. *A Small Boy and Others* (*Autobiography*), I, 196–9. See, for the problematic dating, Kaplan, pp. 32–3. James was first in the Louvre in 1885–6. Lewis's account of the Jameses supplements, but does not

replace, F. O. Matthiessen, *The James Family* (New York: Alfred A. Knopf, 1948). See also Carol Holly, *Intensely Family: The Inheritance of Shame and the Autobiographies of Henry James* (Madison: University of Wisconsin Press, 1995), pp. 86–90. James in his *Autobiography* (I, 196) sees the dream as linked with his access to art, the Louvre being for him 'the bridge over to Style'. An act of violence, on this basis, becomes necessary to take possession. Lionel Trilling reads the dream as 'having experienced art as "history and fame and power," his arrogation seemed a guilty one and represented itself as great fear which he overcame by an inspiration of straight aggression and dire intention and triumphed in the very place where he had had his imperious fantasy' ('*The Princess Casamassima*', in *The Liberal Imagination* (1951; London: Mercury Books, 1961), pp. 82–3). The important point here is that James alternates between fantasies of taking possession (cf. the Napoleonic identifications: see *Notebooks*, pp. 581–4) and the abject sense of the Medusa face of life: both of these states are seen as incomplete, though related, and both are suggestive of hysteria.

14. Kim Townsend, *Manhood at Harvard: William James and Others* (New York: W.W. Norton, 1996), pp. 43–4.

15. See Lewis, *The Jameses*, p. 200.

16. Quoted in ibid., p. 202. James goes on to say that it 'has made me sympathetic with the morbid feelings of others ever since'. The suggestiveness of this for the accounts of morbidity in *The Portrait of A Lady* and *The Bostonians* should be noted. See Chapter 3.

17. See Mark S. Micale, *Approaching Hysteria: Disease and Its Intepretations* (Princeton: Princeton University Press, 1995), p. 162, and p. 157, on Alice James. The Philadelphia-based neurologist Weir Mitchell (1829–1914), who defined hysteria in 1875 as 'the nosological limbo of all unnamed female maladies. It were as well called mysteria for all its name teaches us of the host of *morbid* states which are crowded within its hazy boundaries' (quoted by Micale, p. 109, my emphasis), is the doctor alluded to in Charlotte Perkins Gilman's *The Yellow Wallpaper* (1892), as a threat to the wife. The New York neurologist George Beard used the term 'neurasthenia' – lack of nerve strength. See Jean Strouse, *Alice James: A Biography* (New York: Houghton Mifflin, 1980), pp. 103–6.

18. Leon Edel, *Henry James: The Untried Years 1843–1870*, pp. 171–86; Kaplan, *Henry James: The Imagination of Genius*, pp. 54–6. See John Halperin, 'Henry James's Civil War', *HJR*, 17 (1996), 22–9, arguing that the 'obscure hurt' was psychic, a blow to masculinity.

19. See also the discussion by David McWhirter, *Desire and Love in Henry James*, pp. 166–9, and pp. 207–8. McWhirter refers to critics who have

speculated on James being impotent from this incident – Gelnway West-cott, Stephen Spender, F. O. Matthiessen, R. P. Blackmur and Lionel Trilling.

20. Elaine Showalter discusses the phenomenon of mutism amongst the soldiers diagnosed as hysterics in the First World War, so showing hysteria as male. See *The Female Malady: Women, Madness and English Culture, 1830–1980* (London: Virago, 1985), chapter 7, pp. 167–94 – her whole chapter is on First World War experiences. Showalter also discusses hysteria, including male hysteria (neurasthenia in America), in 'Hysteria, Feminism, Gender', in Sander L. Gilman (ed.), *Hysteria Beyond Freud* (Berkeley: University of California Press, 1993), pp. 286–344. For a comparison of Freud's treatment of hysteria with Dora, and 'The Turn of the Screw', see Paula Marantz Cohen, 'Freud's *Dora* and James's *Turn of the Screw*: Two Treatments of the Female "Case"', *Criticism*, 28 (1986), 73–87.

21. Sigmund Freud, *On Sexuality, The Penguin Freud*, vol. 7 (Harmonds-worth: Penguin, 1977), p. 311.

22. Roland Barthes, *Camera Lucida*, p. 65.

23. Walter Benjamin, *The Origin of German Tragic Drama*, trans. John Osborne (London: Verso, 1977), p. 166.

24. *The Diary of Alice James*, ed. Leon Edel (1964, Harmondsworth: Pen-guin, 1987), p. 230. On Alice James, see *The Death and Letters of Alice James*, ed. Ruth Bernard Yeazell (Berkeley: University of California Press 1981). Connections between Alice James and *The Turn of the Screw* are made by Oscar Cargill (reprinted in Kimbrough's Norton edition). Car-gill also suggests the influence of Freud and Breuer's *Studies on Hysteria*.

25. Lewis, *The Jameses*, p. 365, draws attention to Alice James's sister-in-law (William James's wife, also Alice James), saying of Alice James that 'she is not made as other women' – which Lewis takes as a reference to Alice James as lesbian – cf. her friendship with Katherine Loring. Wil-liam James's marriage, in 1878, blocking out Alice James, may have been a contributory factor to her breakdown that year.

26. *The Diary of Alice James*, pp. 148–9; see also Lewis, *The Jameses*, p. 197.

CHAPTER 6:   'WITHIN A MODERN SHADE': RACE, SEX AND CLASS IN *THE BOSTONIANS, WHAT MAISIE KNEW* AND *THE AWKWARD AGE*

1. On the history embodied here, see Ian F. A. Bell, *Washington Square: Styles of Money* (Boston: Twayne, 1993), pp. 42–52.

2. Compare James in December 1884, writing to Thomas Sergeant Perry, 'I have been all the morning at Millbank Prison (horrible place) collecting notes for a fiction scene. You see, I am quite the Naturalist' (*Letters*, III, 61). The novel was to be *The Princess Casmassima* (1886).

3. Quoted in Kim Townsend, *Manhood at Harvard: William James and Others* (New York: W.W. Norton, 1996), p. 23.

4. Beard in 1884, quoted in E. Anthony Rotendo, *American Manhood: Transformations in Masculinity from the Revolution to the Modern Era* (New York: Basic Books, 1993), p. 276.

5. Quotations from *Our Mutual Friend* are taken from the Oxford World Classics edition, ed. Michael Cotsell (1989).

6. Ruth Bernard Yeazell, 'Podsnappery, Sexuality and the English Novel', *Critical Inquiry*, 9 (1982), 339–57.

7. William Blake, 'Notes Written on the Pages of The Four Zoas', in *Complete Writings*, ed. Geoffrey Keynes (Oxford: Oxford University Press, 1966), p. 380.

8. Philip Magnus, *King Edward the Seventh* (London: John Murray, 1964), pp. 107–9. Further details about the madness of Harriet Moncrieffe – which the defence invested in as a plea – appear in Giles St Aubyn, *Edward VII: Prince and King* (New York: Atheneum, 1979), pp. 159–63.

9. Magnus, *King Edward the Seventh*, p. 108.

10. David Nicholls, *The Lost Prime Minister: A Life of Sir Charles Dilke* (London: Hambledon Press, 1995), p. 206. Further references are given in the text.

11. On the trial and links to James's *A London Life*, see Heath Moon, 'James's "A London Life" and the Campbell Divorce Proceedings', *American Literary Realism*, 13 (1980), 246–58.

12. Quoted in Moon, ibid., p. 250.

13. F. R. Leavis, *Anna Karenina and Other Essays* (London: Chatto and Windus, 1967), p. 83.

14. Karl Marx, *Surveys from Exile* (Harmondsworth: Penguin, 1973), p. 146.

15. *The Pupil* appears in the same New York edition as *What Maisie Knew* and with *In the Cage*, and I give references to this (volume 11). On the text, see John Griffith, 'James's "The Pupil" as Whodunnit: The Question of Moral Responsibility', *Studies in Short Fiction*, 9 (1972), 257–68; David Eggenschwiler, 'James's "The Pupil": A Moral Tale without a Moral', *Studies in Short Fiction*, 15 (1978), 435–44.

16. Criticism of *The Pupil* has tended, recently, to argue for a homosexual subtext to the tutor/pupil relationship, in which case Pemberton too would be blind to his own desire. See Helen Hoy, 'Homotextual Duplicity in Henry James's "The Pupil"', *HJR*, 14 (1993), 14–22. (A sceptical reading of the homosexual argument appears in Philip Horne, 'Henry James: The Master and the "Queer Affair" of "The Pupil"', *Critical Quarterly*, 37 (1996), 75–92.) However, if the subtext was accepted, it would be the case that thinking morally was Pemberton's way of blinding himself to his desire.

17. Pierre Walker makes an interesting point: 'These roles [Longdon and Vanderbank] are reversed by the end; Longdon has come to terms with the changing social norms of the awkward age in which the novel takes place, while Van has not. Longdon calls himself "Rip Van Winkle" . . . but in the end Van is the real Rip Van Winkle. This is the reason for his Dutch-sounding family name and the emphasis on the Dutch particule in the nickname given to him in the Brookenham set'. *Reading Henry James in French Cultural Contexts* (De Kalb: Northen Illinois University Press, 1995), p. 98.

18. Jonathan Freedman, *Professions of Taste: Henry James, British Aestheticism and Commodity Culture* (Stanford: Stanford University Press, 1990), p. 2. For James on Wilde, see Edel, vol. 4, pp. 4, 38–42, 114–21. See also Kaplan, pp. 300, 369–70, 403. Freedman, pp. 167–201, discusses James and Wilde, using *The Tragic Muse* and *The Ambassadors*.

19. See Paula V. Smith, 'A Wilde Subtext for *The Awkward Age*', *HJR*, 9 (1988), 199–208.

20. On the envelope, James added '*Quel dommage – mais quel bonheur – que J.A.S. ne soit plus de ce monde.*' J.A.S. is John Addington Symonds, whom James met in 1877 and who died in 1893. The author in *The Author of Beltraffio* (1884) is supposed to be based on Symonds. See James's letter of 9 June 1884 to Edmund Gosse. As Rayburn S. Moore traces it in his *Selected Letters of Henry James to Edmund Gosse: A Literary Friendship* (Baton Rouge: Louisiana State University Press, 1988), Symonds wrote two privately printed pamphlets on homosexuality, *A Problem of Greek Ethics* (1883) and *A Problem of Modern Ethics* (1891), the second of which Gosse loaned to James. James read the biography of Symonds by Horatio Brown in 1894, which indicates his interest. On Symonds, see the *The Memoirs of John Addington Symonds*, edited and introduced by Phyllis Grosskurth (London: Hutchinson, 1984). See also Joseph Bristow, *Effeminate England: Homoerotic Writing after 1885* (Buckingham: Open University Press, 1995), and, generally, Ed Cohen, *Talk on the Wilde Side* (London: Routledge, 1995).

21. Tzvetan Todorov, 'The Verbal Age', trans. Patricia Martin Gibby, *Critical Inquiry*, 4 (1977), 351–71 (p. 366).

22. Freedman, *Professions of Taste*, p. 173.

CHAPTER 7: HENRY JAMES'S 'AMERICAN GIRL': *THE WINGS OF THE DOVE*

1. For a setting out of the importance of this text to James in relation to *Roderick Hudson*, see R. D. McMaster, 'An Honourable Emulation of the Author of *The Newcomes*: James and Thackeray', *Nineteenth-Century Fiction*, 32 (1977), 399–419.

2. Quoted in Elisabeth Bronfen, *Over Her Dead Body: Death, Femininity and the Aesthetic* (Manchester: Manchester University Press, 1992), p. 59.

3. Frances B. Cogan, *All-American Girl: The Ideal of Real Womanhood in Mid-Nineteenth-Century America* (Athens: University of Georgia Press, 1989), p. 13. She quotes the research of the historian Thomas Cochran. On the differences between nineteenth-century English attitudes towards business – never wholly accepting it – and American, which endorsed it, see Pearl Chesler Solomon, *Dickens and Melville in their Time* (New York: Columbia University Press, 1975), pp. 24–31. James's attitudes, in this, seem aligned to the English.

4. W. D. Howells, 'Mr James's Later Work' (1903), in Edwin H. Cady (ed.), *W. D. Howells as Critic* (London: Routledge and Kegan Paul, 1973), p. 407.

5. Edel, *Letters*, III, 523–62, gives an account of the relationship and prints four letters from Constance Fenimore Woolson to James. See also Tony Tanner, *Venice Desired* (Oxford: Blackwell, 1992), pp. 195–209, for a consideration of Woolson in relation to *The Wings of the Dove*. Edel's account of the Woolson/James relationship is criticised by Cheryl B. Torsney, *Constance Fenimore Woolson: The Grief of Artistry* (Athens: University of Georgia Press, 1989), pp. 11–15, which sees it as patronising to Woolson.

6. On illness in *The Wings of the Dove*, see Diane Price Herndl, *Invalid Women: Figuring Feminine Illness in American Fiction and Culture, 1840–1940* (Chapel Hill: University of North Carolina Press, 1993).

7. Virginia C. Fowler, 'Milly Theale's Malady of Self', *Novel*, vol. 14, no. 1 (Fall 1980), 57–74 (p. 61), quoting Robert C. Mclean, '"Love by the Doctor's Direction": Disease and Death in *The Wings of the Dove*', *Papers on Language and Literature*, 8, supplement (Fall 1972),

128–48. I have not seen this article. Fowler's article is revised in her study *Henry James's American Girl: The Embroidery on the Canvas* (Madison: University of Wisconsin Press, 1984). Michael Moon, 'Sexuality and Visual Terrorism in *The Wings of the Dove*', *Criticism* (1986), 427–43, gives a reading of the text orientated by 'queer theory', on which see my Chaper 8; he draws attention to the reputation of Venice for sexual freedom.

8. Virginia Fowler, *Henry James's American Girl*, pp. 16–17.

9. Walter Pater, *The Renaissance* (1873; London: Cape, 1928), pp. 221, 222.

10. Jacques Lacan, *The Four Fundamental Concepts of Psychoanalysis*, trans. Alan Sheridan (Harmondsworth: Penguin, 1977), pp. 102–3.

11. Eve Kosofksy Sedgwick, 'Is the Rectum Straight? Identification and Identity in *The Wings of the Dove*', *Tendencies* (Durham, N.C.: Duke University Press, 1993), p. 77.

12. See Julie Olim-Ammentorp, 'A Circle of Petticoats: The Feminisation of Merton Densher', *HJR*, 15 (1994), 38–54.

CHAPTER 8: THE HAUNTED MAN: *THE BEAST IN THE JUNGLE*

1. *John Marcher* (the original title) was to go into a 'volume of miscellanies' (*AN*, 14, 246) called *The Better Sort*, the title implying and ironising notions of judiciousness and discretion. Like *The Wings of the Dove*, it was not to be put in a magazine. Re-naming it *The Beast in the Jungle*, James returned to it in October 1902 after working on *The Birthplace*. Both appeared in *The Better Sort* in 1903. *The Beast in the Jungle* was included in volume 17 of the New York edition. It has been frequently reprinted, but usually from the first edition: accordingly I cite chapter and page references from Christof Wegelin, *Tales of Henry James* (New York: Norton, 1984), which gives this.

2. Maurice Blanchot makes this an autobiographical tendency in James. 'James dreaded beginning' and his desire was 'to make the work present at every moment and to suggest, behind the structured determined work, different structures, the limitless, weightless space of the narrative as it might have been, as it was before all beginnings.' This aligns James to Borges. See 'The Turn of the Screw', in *The Sirens' Song: Selected Essays by Maurice Blanchot*, ed. Gabriel Jospivovici, trans. Sacha Rabinovitch (Bloomington: Indiana University Press, 1982), pp. 84, 85.

3. Eve Kosofsky Sedgwick, 'The Beast in the Closet: James and the Writing of Homosexual Panic' first appeared in Ruth Bernard Yeazell (ed.), *Sex, Politics and Science in the Nineteenth-Century Novel* (Baltimore: Johns Hopkins University Press, 1986), and was revised for *Epistemology of the Closet* (New York: Harvester, 1991), pp. 182–212, from which page references here are taken. Yeazell thinks so well of Sedgwick's essay that she also reprints it in her edition of *Henry James: A Collection of Critical Essays* (Englewood-Cliffs, N.J.: Prentice-Hall, 1994).

4. Eve Kosofsky Sedgwick, 'Shame and Performativity: Henry James's New York Prefaces', in David McWhirter (ed.), *Henry James's New York Edition: The Construction of Authorship* (Stanford: Stanford University Press, 1995), p. 236.

5. Sheldon M. Novick, *Henry James: The Young Master* (New York: Random House), pp. 109–10. See also Eric Savoy, '*In the Cage* and the Queer Effects of Gay History', *Novel* (Spring 1995), 284–307.

6. This is the argument of David Van Leer, 'The Beast of the Closet: Homosociality and the Pathology of Manhood', *Critical Inquiry*, 15 (Spring 1989), 587–644. Sedgwick replied in the following issue, pp. 745–57; Van Leer responded to her, pp. 758–63. Van Leer discusses her reading of James, and I am in debt to his reading. See also Ross Posnock, *The Trial of Curiosity: Henry James, William James and the Challenge of Modernity* (Oxford: Oxford University Press, 1991), p. 321. Posnock (p. 326) suggests that Marcher at the end approaches what he calls James's 'traumatophilia' (cf. p. 235), his desire for shocks. Perhaps Marcher also yearns for trauma.

7. This rests on a strong reading of Schreber's paranoia, as opposed to his schizophrenia, and may need revision: see Louis A. Sass, *Madness and Modernism* (New York: Basic Books, 1992), pp. 245, 504.

8. See, for example, Kaja Silverman, *Male Subjectivity at the Margins* (London: Routledge, 1992), pp. 157–81.

9. In contrast to this, Georges Poulet, *Studies in Human Time*, trans. Elliott Coleman (Baltimore: Johns Hopkins University Press, 1956), pp. 350–4, discusses James as unable to forget, the past acting for him as a perpetual present, the self therefore unchanged through time.

10. In a memorandum of 1905, drawing up the selection of texts for the New York edition, James said *The Tragic Muse* (1890) terminated his 'earlier period' (*Letters*, IV, 367)

11. Tzvetan Todorov, 'The Structural Analysis of Literature: The Tales of Henry James', in David Robey (ed.), *Structuralism: An Introduction* (Oxford: Clarendon Press 1972), p. 75. Further references in the text. For other accounts of the tale, see L. C. Knights, 'Henry James and the

Trapped Spectator', *Explorations* (Harmondsworth: Penguin, 1964); Kelly Cannon, *Henry James: The Man at the Margins* (London: Macmillan, 1994), pp. 58–62 (a reading in sympathy with Sedgwick); and James Gargano, in *Henry James: A Study of the Short Fiction* (Boston: Twayne, 1990), pp. 160–71.

12. On Todorov's reading as applied to *The Figure in the Carpet*, see J. Hillis Miller, 'The Figure in the Carpet', *Poetics Today*, 1,3 (1980), 107–18, and the response by Schlomith Rimmon-Kenan, in *Poetics Todc·'* 2, 1, 185–8. See also Ross Chambers, *Story and Situation: Narrative Seduction and the Power of Fiction* (Minneapolis: University of Minnesota Press, 1984), pp. 151–80.

13. Fredric Jameson, *The Political Unconscious: Narrative as a Socially Symbolic Act* (London: Methuen, 1981), p. 35.

14. Toni Morrison, *Playing in the Dark: Whiteness and the Literary Imagination* (Cambridge, Mass.: Harvard University Press, 1992), pp. 13–14. Morrison also draws attention to the black woman in *What Maisie Knew*.

15. W. E. B. Du Bois, *The Souls of Black Folk* (Harmondsworth: Penguin, 1996), p. 1.

CHAPTER 9: WHAT DOES THE AMERICAN WANT?
THE GOLDEN BOWL

1. Set in 1870, published in the *Cornhill*, 1878, then issued with *Daisy Miller* and *Four Meetings* in 1879. The wedding of Lord Randolph Churchill in April 1874 to the American Jennie Jerome, daughter of the 'robber baron' Leonard Jerome, suggests an important change in Anglo-American relationships.

2. Michel Foucault, *The History of Sexuality*, trans. Robert Hurley (Harmondsworth: Penguin, 1979), pp. 109–10 and 129–30 (for incest), 147–50 (for purity of blood, within the discourse of degeneration).

3. See V. G. Kiernan, *America: The New Imperialism: From White Settlement to World Hegemony* (London: Zed Books, 1980), pp. 61–135.

4. See Eric Haralson, 'James's *The American*: A (New)man is being Beaten', *American Literature*, 64 (1992), 475–95.

5. The 'source' for Touchett has been claimed to be Russell Sturgis, an American banker with Baring's in London, and with a house in Surrey which James visited in 1880. See Charles R. Anderson, *Person, Place and*

Thing in Henry James's Novels (Durham, N.C.: Duke University Press, 1977), pp. 92–3.

6. Thomas C. Cochran and William Miller, *The Age of Enterprise: A Social History of Industrial America* (1942; rev. edn, New York: Harper Torchbooks, 1961), p. 257.

7. Victor Burgin, 'Geometry and Abjection', *In/different Spaces* (Berkeley: University of California Press, 1996), pp. 39–56.

8. Compare with this Maggie's metaphorical space, Maggie Tulliver's more literal one, the 'Red Deeps', in *The Mill on the Floss*, Book 5, chapter 1.

9. I have discussed the absence of doors in 1900s American architecture on p. 149 and return to it with *The Jolly Corner*. Doors imply the uncanny; houses without the privacies implied by doors, the repression of the uncanny. Here James gives a third possibility which deconstructs that opposition.

10. Herman Melville, *Moby-Dick, or The Whale*, ch. 76, 'The Battering Ram' (Harmondsworth: Penguin, 1992), p. 368.

11. Gabriel Pearson, 'The Novel to End All Novels: *The Golden Bowl*', in *The Air of Reality, New Essays on Henry James*, ed. John Goode (London: Methuen, 1972), p. 343.

12. The phrase 'the other house' refers to the novel of that name, sketched as a play in 1894, and then written immediately after *The Spoils of Poynton* (at first called *The House Beautiful* – it will be seen how James's mind runs on houses). See on it, Priscilla L. Walton, 'The Tie of a Common Aversion: Sexual Tensions in Henry James's *The Other House*', *HJR*, 17 (1996), 11–26.

13. On collecting in the novel, see Beth Sharon Ash, 'Narcissism and the Gilded Image: A Psychoanalytic Reading of *The Golden Bowl*', *HJR*, 15 (1994), 55–90.

14. Poe's influence operates also from 'The Fall of the House of Usher' – the house's 'vacant eye-like windows' evoke the pagoda, and the 'fissure' running down the building makes it like the golden bowl. See *Selected Writings of Edgar Allan Poe*, edited by David Galloway (Harmondsworth: Penguin, 1967), pp. 138, 141.

15. Jonathan Freedman, *Professions of Taste*, p. 240.

16. Leo Bersani, *A Future for Astyanyax* (Boston and Toronto: Little, Brown, 1969), p. 128.

17. F. O. Matthiessen, *Henry James: The Major Phase* (Cambridge, Mass.: Harvard University Press, 1943), p. 85.

18. On this text and the detective novel, see Alexander Welsh, *Strong Representations: Narrative and Circumstantial Evidence* (Baltimore: Johns Hopkins University Press, 1992), pp. 236–56.

19. See Jonathan Crary, *Techniques of the Observer: On Vision and Modernity in the Nineteenth Century* (Cambridge, Mass.: MIT Press, 1990), p. 5.

20. Gilles Deleuze, *The Fold: Leibniz and the Baroque*, trans. Tom Conley (Minneapolis: University of Minnesota Press, 1993), p. 28.

CHAPTER 10: *THE JOLLY CORNER*: A TALE OF NEW YORK

1. *The Jolly Corner* appeared first in F. M. Ford's *English Review* in December 1908, and was subsequently reprinted in the New York edition in vol. 17, alongside *The Altar of the Dead*, *The Beast in the Jungle*, *The Birthplace*, *The Private Life*, *Owen Wingrave*, *The Friends of the Friends*, *Sir Edmund Orme* and *The Real, Right Thing*. Quotations are taken from the Norton Critical Edition, *Tales of Henry James*, ed. Christof Wegelin (New York, 1984), pp. 313–40. For a bibliography of earlier writings on the text, see Daniel Mark Fogel, 'A New Reading of James's "The Jolly Corner"', in James W. Gargano (ed.), *Critical Issues on Henry James: The Later Novels* (Boston, G. K. Hall, 1987), pp. 190–203; see also Deborah Esch, 'A Jamesian About-Face: Notes on "The Jolly Corner"', *English Literary History*, 50 (1983), 587–605.

2. For example, Leon Edel, in *Henry James: The Master, 1901–1916*, pp. 311–15. On James in New York, see Edel, pp. 288–94.

3. The implications of the house, or Brydon, as a Rip Van Winkle are evoked here, as Irving's tale also formed a context for *The Awkward Age*.

4. Jacques Derrida, *Dissemination*, trans. Barbara Johnson (Chicago: University of Chicago Press, 1981), p. 316.

5. *The Genteel Tradition in American Philosophy* appeared first as a lecture in 1911. I have quoted this passage from Robert Dawidoff, *The Genteel Tradition and the Sacred Rage: High Culture vs. Democracy in Adams, James and Santayana* (Chapel Hill: University of North Carolina Press, 1992), p. 172, who links it with *The American Scene*.

6. This account of the skyscraper in New York obviously leaves out Chicago's historical importance in pioneering these buildings. James visited Chicago in his American tour, but I take it that Chicago would be for

James an example of the modern only, not of discontinuous pasts and presents. On the specificity of the New York skyscraper, see the entry in Kenneth T. Jackson, *The Encyclopaedia of New York City* (New Haven: Yale University Press, 1995), and more generally, see Robert A. A. M. Stern, Gregory Gilmartin and John Massengale, *New York 1900* (New York: Rizzoli, 1983). See also Sarah Bradford Landau and Carl W. Condit, *Rise of the New York Skyscraper, 1865–1913* (New Haven: Yale University Press, 1996).

7. For Nietzsche on Napoleon, see, for instance, *Twilight of the Idols*, trans. Richard Polt (Indianopolis: Hackett Publishing, 1997), section 48, pp. 82–3. See also section 44, p. 79; section 45, p. 80; and section 49, p. 84. For James and Nietzsche, the standard study is by Stephen Donadio, *Nietzsche, Henry James and the Artistic Will* (Oxford: Oxford University Press, 1978); but see also Daniel T. O'Hara, 'Contagious Appearances: Nietzsche, Henry James and the Critique of Fiction', in Manfred Pütz, *Nietzsche in American Literature and Thought* (Columbia, S.C.: Camden House, 1995), pp. 79–86.

8. Rem Koolhaas, *S.M.L.XL* (New York: Monacelli Press, 1995), pp. 495–516. Koolhaas defines bigness as 'urbanism against architecture' – the defeat of architecture.

9. Quoted by Carol Willis, 'Form Follows Finance: The Empire State Building', in David Ward and Oliver Zunz (eds), *The Landscape of Modernity, Essays on New York City, 1900–1940* (New York: Russell Sage Foundation, 1992), p. 163.

10. Henry Adams, *The Education of Henry Adams* (New York: Modern Library, 1931), p. 499.

11. Sigmund Freud, 'The Uncanny', in *The Penguin Freud*, vol. 14 (Harmondsworth: Penguin, 1985), pp. 356–7.

12. In Lacan's mirror-stage, identity is related to a fear of the body in pieces: see Jacques Lacan, *Ecrits: A Selection*, trans. Alan Sheridan (London: Tavistock Publications, 1977), p. 4. I discuss Dickens's interest in the prosthetic (the other side of amputation) in my *Dickens, Violence and the Modern State* (London: Macmillan, 1995), pp. 1–6. See, for a meditation on the subject, David Wills, *Prosthesis* (Stanford: Stanford University Press, 1995).

Index

The index tries to be complete as regards names in the text, but names are not indexed when they are only referred to in the Notes, unless substantial information appears about them there.

245